Carole E Barrowman

The Popular Revolutions
of the Late Middle Ages

THE GREAT REVOLUTIONS SERIES No. 6

The Popular Revolutions of the Late Middle Ages

MICHEL MOLLAT
PHILIPPE WOLFF

TRANSLATED BY A. L. LYTTON-SELLS

LONDON · GEORGE ALLEN & UNWIN LTD
Ruskin House   Museum Street

ISBN 0 04 940040 1 hardback
   0 04 940041 X paper

Printed in Great Britain
in 11-point Baskerville Type
by The Aldine Press, Letchworth, Herts

Contents

Maps

Introduction

"POPULAR REVOLUTIONS": this expression has not been easy to select for the phenomenon we propose to study. Of the two words, "popular" is the less debatable. *Populares* is the word generally used in all countries to specify the class of people who take part in these risings. Other terms such as "the common people", "the lean folk" or "the mechanics" sometimes occur, while ill-disposed witnesses add that they are "base fellows of mean estate". In any case it is a question of a lower class of peasants and artisans, engaged in regular but not lucrative work, and also of vagabonds and of the destitute. We propose to examine the risings only in so far as the lower "classes"[1] as such take part in them and as they involve social disturbances —conflicts arising from economic and social causes. In some places we find workmen going on strike for higher pay; in others, conflicts among the rural nobility; in others again, risings for the purpose of imposing on the government a more just social policy in regard to taxation or in time of famine.

All this leads us to set aside political or religious disturbances, troubles in which the lower classes as such do not participate. Not that the dividing-line is always clear. The lower class

[1] In the sense of the poorer groups. The authors explain at the end of this book that class-consciousness hardly existed in the Middle Ages. (Translator.)

might be used, or more or less misused, as a main striking-force in conflicts that did not strictly concern it. Anti-Jewish pogroms throw light on the attitude of various classes in society and we shall be mistaken in not using the information they yield. The connection between popular agitation and the major heresies raises a thorny problem. Was not the Church an essential part of the established order? Was not an attack on the latter also an attack on the former? Was not a heretic also a revolutionary? What link was there between such major heresies as those of Wyclif and the Lollards, and of John Huss, and contemporary agitations? We shall be obliged, more than once, to overstep the border-line which a strict interpretation of "popular" risings would have imposed.

What of the word "Revolutions"? Were we to accept Littré's definition, that a revolution is "a sudden and violent change in the politics and government of a state", our harvest would be meagre indeed. How many mere riots which have quickly collapsed have left intact the conditions they appeared to threaten! But also how many less spectacular signs do we see of deep-seated dissatisfaction with certain institutions: lawsuits, controversies, attempts at reform due to social pressure. These signs have been largely neglected by historians, and so much of the documentary evidence has been lost that they run the risk of being ignored. We should, however, take some account of them if we are to appreciate the revolutionary character of the age.

The revolutionary movements of the fourteenth century have hitherto been studied only in a national or regional framework. The great Peasants' Revolt of 1381 in England; the revolutions in the Low Countries; the Jacquerie in the Ile-de-France; the "Tumult of the Ciompi" in Florence—to cite the most notable examples—have been the subject of numerous works, but these have been too often limited to the rebellions in question. Would it not be better to consider the phenomenon in general, to draw as it were a map which would reveal the main centres of disturbance and the secondary regions, to suggest possible connections in time and to examine the problems which these raise? Were there more or less simultaneous "waves of revolution" in Europe as a whole? And if so, can they be explained by contagion, or were they occasioned by similar causes? It seems important to compare these rebellions and try to discern their general, and their distinctive, features. Little has been accomplished hitherto. One may note Mendl's work in Czechoslovakia (1924); Aragoneses' rapid sketch (1949); and the symposium of Marxist historians at Wernigerode (1960). We have the impression of exploring an ill-marked road with no one to guide us.

However, we must limit our inquiry to central and western Europe. Eastern Europe and the Scandinavian countries are little known, and their social and economic development has followed ways too different from those of the West for us to include them in our picture, even if an isolated episode should now and again tempt us to do so.

The fourteenth century was clearly the age *par excellence* of "popular revolutions", and so, if we decide to take this age as the centre of our inquiry, we shall have to exclude the urban or middle-class revolutions, and the communal, which took place between the eleventh and the thirteenth centuries. These were certainly a social phenomenon, the emergence in the midst of a rural and feudal world of an urban class, and the efforts accomplished by this class to emancipate itself. The struggle was marked by spectacular episodes, which, however, do not fully explain its character. But it was closely connected with the economic expansion which, as most historians agree, was then greatly affecting our continent. The difference between the urban revolution and the "popular revolutions" of the fifteenth century is perfectly clear. Now, once the urban communities had won a recognized place in the feudal world, inequalities began to appear within these communities. They seem to have reached a kind of maturity in various parts of Europe towards the year 1280, and this marks the beginning of a new era.

But what of the country districts? As long as living conditions remained favourable, all seemed well there; and it was not until the early fourteenth century brought famines and a reversal of the trend in the price of wheat and other cereals, that the old manorial edifice was really shaken. There was, therefore, a time lag between developments in the towns and in the countryside, and a social lag (if one may so call it), the class challenged in one instance being the bourgeoisie, in the other the nobility. Meanwhile the connection between rural disturbances and urban agitation will continue to raise complex problems.

Our story will begin about 1280 and continue until 1435. The fifteenth century saw few "popular revolutions" comparable to those of the fourteenth, although some social unrest was to mark the first few decades. For some years past, historians have been trying to explain the social aspects of the Hussite War; hence we shall pursue our inquiry as far as the year 1435. During the century and a half which we are to examine, a good deal of new evidence has come to light, and to classify and analyse it will be a serious enough task. Should the reader ask whether the years following 1435 were to bring real social appeasement, it would be possible to discuss the question, but this will be better done elsewhere.

Our story, like those of our predecessors, will suffer from the nature of the sources available. First come the narratives, simplest of access and easiest to read; we also find help, in Italy for example, in public and private correspondence. Now, most of these sources are hostile to the *populares*. Some accuse them of things hard to credit; others are more subtle in their dislike, and such evidence is more likely to distort the picture. Rare indeed are those who really sympathize with the rebels and seek to trace their unrest to causes other than an inspiration of the devil. Of these one may mention the anonymous author of the *Annales de Gand*, or Jean de Venette who described the revolution in Paris and the Jacquerie; or again, for Florence, the author of the *Diario dello Squittinatore*—two Mendicant Friars, a fact significant in itself. Now the relative sameness of attitude towards social disturbances is of sufficient interest for us to dwell on it awhile. It is a mirror that reflects the social climate, but somewhat distorts the picture, and which we should distrust.

Judicial and administrative archives add further to our knowledge. Governmental decisions, communal discussions, proceedings of the law-courts, even the text of sentences—of such documents, particularly in England, there is no lack. The statements of property confiscated from rebels are extremely informative: this is the source of what we know for certain about the rebellion of 1323–8 in the Flanders coastal regions. In France a very large number of letters of remission have been inserted in the registers of the Royal Chancellery. The accused had obtained these from the King, or from his Lieutenant in Languedoc, in the course of judicial proceedings and therefore before sentence was pronounced, and generally in return for cash down. Drawn up in accordance with a petition presented by the accused, these letters reflect his point of view. If, however, he strove to paint his conduct in the most favourable colours, it was none the less to his interest to describe it completely enough to guarantee him against ulterior prosecution.

Our sources of information, whether more or less unfavourable to the rebels, never really come from them; nor do they reveal their hopes and aspirations. It could not be otherwise. The popular leaders, illiterate for the most part, could hardly leave us any traces of their thinking and they had indeed no opportunity to do so. One should distrust the supposed confessions complacently recorded by the chronicles. Thus we are witnessing a trial at which there is virtually no advocate for the defence and which never goes to the root of the question. One is tempted to act for the defence oneself, an impulse inevitable but very perilous. More than one historian has been reproached with having "read into the documents more than they really contain".

We ought nevertheless to make a real effort to understand; and at the same time indicate where the documentary evidence stops, say what we think of it, what problems it does not raise or solve; and where conjecture and interpretation begin. Nothing of value in this field can be achieved without the greatest care; and no narrative or analysis should be offered prior to a critical presentation of the documents that underlie them.

[Chapter One]

The Social Consequences of Economic Expansion

TOWARDS THE END of the thirteenth century western
and central Europe were experiencing a great economic expansion which had been lasting for at least 200 years—more
in some regions, less in others. We shall try to isolate the consequences of a movement which was already giving rise to social
conflicts and foreshadowing far more serious trouble.

In the first place, new forms of production had appeared,
manufacture had been concentrated in certain centres, and all
this inevitably provoked conflict. Flanders was the supreme
example of these great manufacturing areas which depended
mainly on the export trade. It was already engaged in that
"economic revolution" which England was to achieve only in
more recent times: namely, to increase industrial production—
of textiles in this case—to sell abroad, and to employ the
profits in importing foodstuffs. Flemish clothing materials
were, in fact, in universal demand; they were sold in regions
as far apart as Russia and Spain, England and the Near East.
This manufacture could expand only through the importation
of raw materials, English wool in particular which was the
best obtainable. Now between the English wool merchants and
the more or less distant buyers of woven cloth, middlemen
necessarily made their appearance: dealers in wool and cloth
whose desire for profit was the main reason for this growth in

trade. Over against them, the number of producers increased in proportion to the trade: spinners at work all day at their distaff or spinning-wheel; dyers whose nails had been turned blue by the liquid in which they plunged the thread or the cloth; and especially weavers and fullers. The latter, whose arduous task was to clean the dyed cloth by trampling it under foot in a bath of soapy water, then to stretch it to the regulation length and to prepare it, were more and more assisted by the fulling-mills. This made little difference; both fullers and weavers were strapping fellows. Their strength lay mainly in their numbers; at Ghent in the mid-fourteenth century there were some 4,000 weavers and 1,500 fullers.

The kind of conflict to which this industrial expansion gave rise is well illustrated by the episode of Sir Jehan Boinebroke, an affair that Georges Espinas brought to light some forty years ago. Boinebroke was a wealthy patrician of Douai, an important centre of French-speaking Flanders. Having bought the wool in England, mainly from Lincolnshire, Cumberland and Northumberland, he supplied it to the local artisans, from whom he bought back the finished product. In this way he grew extremely rich, as witness the buildings he acquired in Douai itself and even in fairly remote villages, and also the lands which constituted his patrimony. He lent money—at interest of course—and served as surety for debts contracted by the Count of Flanders. Jehan Boinebroke was not only a leading representative of commercial capitalism, he was also a symbol of the union between business and local politics, and we find him recorded as *échevin* (alderman) of Douai at least nine times between 1243 and 1280. He even founded a dynasty: of his four children, the sons, Jehan and Simon, pursued the same business, and Jehan was *échevin* on several occasions.

Sir Jehan Boinebroke seems to have died at some time between June 1285 and January 1286. The executors of his will recorded, as was usual, the declarations of all those who had claims against the estate of the deceased, and of those who considered they had been wrongly treated. After stating their grievances and the sums claimed, the plaintiffs often called witnesses who also gave evidence; in view of all this, the executors admitted or refused a claim, and fixed the amount of compensation. The details of this procedure have fortunately been preserved on a roll of parchment, five and a half yards long and composed of eleven pieces sewn end to end.

One must of course take account of the circumstances. Boinebroke was no longer there to defend himself. The executors usually granted the plaintiff less than the sum claimed. The picture is none the less extremely unfavourable to the deceased. He had practised most of the abuses which a study of fourteenth-century England has made famous. It was the "truck system", the payment in produce overvalued. Thus Sare des Lices, who served Boinebroke for twelve years, had to "accept produce at a higher rate than it was worth, for fear of losing the work which Sir Jehan gave her, and thus her livelihood". Her daughter estimated the loss at four *livres parisis* a year—an enormous sum at that time. In the same way Boinebroke furnished the raw wool at a higher price than it was worth. One witness complained that he "could not get paid unless he took the wool at a loss". Boinebroke even disputed the importance of the work and the time it took. Thus, after getting his cloth prepared in Pierre Houvastre's workshop, he refused to pay for more than two days' work. By complaining to the *eswardeurs* (wardens) of their craft, the workmen forced Houvastre to pay them for three days, and it was he who suffered the loss.

This affair informs us not only of the abuses committed by Boinebroke but also of the relations between commercial capital and the industrial producers. On one side we have the merchant who controls every stage in the chain of production from furnishing the raw wool to buying the finished cloth; on the other, the mass of artisans, little "masters" ruling their shops, workmen providing the labour, and all of them organized in "crafts", supervised by *eswardeurs*. The division of work into a large number of technical operations (from ten to fifteen) and consequently into numerous "crafts", still further weakened their members in face of the merchant who provided the work. The latter concentrated in his own hands the commercial side of textile production; but he also owned some industrial shops, those for example which stretched the cloth, and in which the workers, like old Sare des Lices, were paid employees. One can see clearly that Boinebroke gained by his political power; he could prevent people from openly complaining and making good their case. One also sees—for we must give a complete picture—how far the usages of Christian civilization corrected this inhuman situation. After the death of the exploiter, people began to complain and part of the wrongs he had inflicted were redressed—often too late for the victim to profit from it, if he himself had died in the interval.

We have insisted on the example unknowingly provided by Sir Jehan de Boinebroke. It has been a lucky, though exceptional, chance, and it throws a ray of light on conditions that must have been fairly general in this great industrial region. However, if the problem was singularly pressing in Flanders, it arose in all places where the new forms of economic life—industry and commerce—had grown up; where production exceeded local demand; or where its object was to supply markets more or less considerable abroad; in all places where the profit-motive existed. Everywhere, questions of wages, working-hours, prices and margins of profit, arose. In their most advanced centres, western and central Europe were experiencing an economic expansion productive of trouble and conflict.

Moreover this industrial growth had not been equally advantageous to everyone. As the economy expanded, deep social cleavages appeared and there was a keen sense of inequality.

Things were much the same in the countryside. The best general study we have is Georges Duby's *L'Economie rurale et la vie des campagnes dans l'occident médiéval* (1962), which insists on this point. "One can", he writes, " . . . regard the increasing disparity between personal fortunes as the most definite change that affected the structure of peasant society during the age of agricultural expansion, of which the last phase covers the thirteenth century." The documents hitherto studied—and they are few—reveal an average standard of living which seems fairly low: farms of limited extent, poor furniture—amounting to very little—and few savings in cash. Above and below this average, the differences due to good or bad luck, to the quality of work and skill, to what was owed in the service of the local lord, the cumulative effect of the best farming equipment available only to the relatively well-to-do, and the pitiless exploitation of the weak by the strong—all these factors impoverished large numbers and enriched others. On one side then we find those who, with a plot too scanty, farmed it badly, got into debt, tried to make ends meet by moving temporarily to the nearest town or to a district where labour was in demand for some big-scale work, and who, even so, lived miserably in poor hovels and scarcely had enough to eat—an underfed mass of peasants exposed to the onset of dearth or epidemic. On the other side we see a few individuals who have managed to round off their lands, to improve the yield by using better gear and to sell the surplus in the neighbouring city.

We already have a certain number of examples which speak for themselves; future research will doubtless multiply them. G. Duby writes:

"Here are two peasants, whose daughters were married, about the year 1330, in the same village of upper Provence. One man gave as dowry seventy-five pounds in cash, a tunic of Châlons cloth, a mantle of Ypres cloth lined with fur, a chest, and bedding for two beds. The other could offer only two sheets and a blanket, leaving his son-in-law to pay for the tunic and mantle which custom required a bride to wear. It appears that in the same village at that time certain rich peasants, who could give as dowry for their daughters some fifty gold florins, were practically on the economic level of the less well-to-do squires."

Duby writes elsewhere:

"Here, in an Alpine hamlet in Provence, are two brothers, rich peasants, who in 1334 purchased from a poor husbandman for twelve *livres*, the whole harvest that he would reap from his land in the space of fifteen years. In 1335 they lend four pounds and ten shillings to two of their neighbours: the sum was to be employed in ploughing and sowing two fields, the whole yield of which the creditors reserved for themselves."

We turn now to Picardy, one of the richest agricultural provinces of the west. Robert Fossier's research (1968) has revealed the great extent of social changes from the thirteenth century onwards. Technical progress, manifest in the increasing number of mills and ploughs, a greater variety in the crops grown and a more regular system of rotation, widened the gap between the peasants. Some were able to use up-to-date gear, increase the yield of their land, buy off, from the lord of the manor, the forced labour they would have had to provide, and devote themselves to the improvement of their own farms—others less fortunate were not. The line of cleavage was more and more clearly marked by the possession of gear and harness for ploughing, without which the labour was more painful, less rewarding and inevitably limited.

A good example of a well-to-do peasant was Jean Florent, a farmer of Inglevert near Saint-Omer, who died in 1301 and is known to us through the inventory of his estate. He owned more than ninety-nine acres of land and with the help of a dozen labourers exploited most of it himself. He disposed of a good deal of livestock, which he used to renew by a skilful policy of sales and purchases: thus in one year he had sold a sow and eight pigs, three cows and two calves; and he had just bought four heifers. His accounts reveal an income of 150 *livres*, while current expenses amounted to 130 at most.

Were such cases frequent? Robert Fossier has tried to calculate the relative distribution of wealth and poverty:

"One could draw the following picture of the peasants in Picardy at the end of the thirteenth century. 12 per cent are living on a bare margin of subsistence—beggars, vagabonds and impoverished folk who have built their shanties on the waste-lands and hire themselves out when possible for the grain- or grape-harvests. 33 per cent work on scanty plots of land and will escape destitution only by labour for the manor or for their neighbours. 36 per cent remain poor by modern standards; it is doubtful whether they own ploughing-gear; at the best they contrive to buy off the obligation of forced labour, to pay for grinding their corn and get what advantage they can from the expanding economy. The remainder are the well-to-do: of these 16 per cent own no more than 3 hectares [7·4 acres] but this is enough to free them from the heaviest burdens. An *élite* of 3 per cent, clerics or laymen, nobles or wealthy peasants, lord it over the others and, as far as they can, make them bear the expenses of their economic policy. At a rough estimate, one can say that of ten peasants, one is destitute, three are badly off, four are living modestly but with a certain security, and only two enjoy abundance."

It is not enough to distinguish between the nobles and the peasants, even though the former, more and more overwhelmed by military duties and the occupations of their class, tended to isolate themselves from the mass of the peasantry. The nobles also had to adapt themselves to the new techniques, to a society in which the management of the estate was increasingly expensive, in which the manorial system itself was being challenged, and in which the increase in population led to splitting up the estates and thus impoverished them. But not everyone could do this, and the result was the concentration of many lordships in the hands of a few.

"Roughly speaking, one can say that towards the year 1300, owing to the development of feudal habits, of a hundred lordships, representing three or four hundred villages, thirty or thirty-five are in the hands of the king or the apanagists, or belong to the Church; fifteen are in the hands of great families related to the counts; ten belong to some thirty groups of average importance. The remainder, namely 40 per cent, are divided among several hundred families."

Here, too, a growing inequality in the size of the estates explains certain of the attitudes which the nobles were to adopt in the fourteenth century.

The above examples are taken from far apart and different regions. Elsewhere—in England, in Italy and in the Empire—the manorial enquiries reveal the existence of a few big tenant farmers whose means were clearly above the average. These "cocks of the walk" often aim higher: to marry an heiress, sometimes a noble, or to worm themselves into the society of the near-by town. A certain Austrian peasant pretended to drink only wine, like a lord. In general however the social barriers prevented such men from rising out of their class. If the economic hierarchy was tending to acquire more importance than the old juridical structure—freeholders on one side, serfs or villains on the other—they by no means overlapped. In England, a country where serfdom had been fairly well maintained, a good number of prosperous peasants remained villains, and were more and more averse from enduring the disabilities of their class. This improvement in the lot of prosperous peasants did not give rise to dissension among the peasantry as a whole, but created a further challenge to the manorial system; and provided leaders for the attack it was to endure in the fourteenth century.

*   *   *

In the towns, changes due to expansion were not quite the same. Now as the contrasts between town-life and country-life were subject to very many gradations, we will consider only the conditions in great cities. In all these we find rich men who have benefited from the economic expansion, powerful dynasties of merchants, money-changers and financiers. The documents available scarcely enable us to analyse the whole urban population in such a way as to show, with exact figures, how far wealth was concentrated; we may however learn something about it from the oldest *registres d'estime*, which are lists of declarations of wealth made by heads of families in order to establish a basis for taxation; the taxes being proportioned to the "capacity" of each tax-payer. A study of this kind has been attempted for Toulouse, but it is far from complete. The only records we have are the "estimates"[1] for the borough which had grown up north of the old Roman

[1] *estimes.*—in practice these were more or less equivalent to assessments. (Translator.)

city; moreover these take no account of the citizens too poor for their property to be worth valuing. Even so, the results of our inquiry are suggestive. The *estimes* of 1335 enumerate 936 heads of families, whose properties are minutely described and valued. Now seventy of them, that is 7 per cent of the total number, possess 61 per cent of the total value of registered properties. If, on the other hand, we turn to the least well-to-do class, that of citizens assessed at from ten to ninety-nine *livres*, we find that this class comprises about half of all the taxpayers, 476 to be exact; but their combined property does not amount to more than 6 per cent of the total estimate. And we must not forget the multitude of day-labourers and poor folk of every description, who do not figure in our document. It is always possible to suspect the honesty of the declarations, although these were carefully verified. There is no reason, on the other hand, to suppose that fraud, even if it existed, operated at the expense of the well-to-do.

One must hope that the discovery of further documents will increase the number of such studies, for they offer the advantage of going beyond what might risk being no more than a subjective impression: that of a society in which inequality is steadily increasing and where only favourable economic development conceals the sharpness of the conflict between rich and poor.

It is unfortunately impossible at present to give examples of other cities as numerically exact as that of Toulouse. We shall therefore be obliged to use moral data, which at least afford the advantage of revealing men's consciousness of the inequality of their situations, and their respective attitudes to it. They also evoke the moral climate of the age, with its actual nuances.

No doubt the system of estimates, which had for long past been practised in Italian cities, has left records which are now being studied and which will permit an exact assessment of the disparity of wealth in the urban populations. The first application of this system has been established for the twelfth century, in Pisa, Genoa, Venice, Lucca and Siena; and for the beginning of the thirteenth in Florence. Each city gradually extended the system to its *contado*, and this will bring other contrasts to light, between the city and the surrounding countryside. In the thirteenth century no one questioned the principle of equality in regard to taxation, though it was far from being respected. The measures taken at Siena in 1257 are a proof that the principle was not always applied, and fiscal inequality was partly responsible for the difficulties from which Florence suffered in the last two decades of the century. An analysis of the situation in Florence has enabled historians to show how greatly fiscal inequalities explain social antagonisms. Of the social classes that constituted a population of some 80,000 in the thirteenth century, the *magnati* who were the least numerous and who were in traditional possession of political power, were vitally interested in escaping taxation. The rise in the cost of living weighed on them as on the others and in proportion even more so, owing to the high level of their way of life. Now property in land and houses which constituted a part of their capital, brought in scarcely more than 5 per cent, whereas about a third of these magnates could make at least 20 per cent in commerce and banking. They were therefore obliged, in order to survive, to oppose the interests of the *popolani* who wanted a decrease in rent and in prices of foodstuffs, and an increase in the taxation of the magnates. To act otherwise than the latter were acting would, it was affirmed, have prevented any accumulation of commercial capital and have thwarted an expansion of the economy.

The chronicles of the time echo the mutual scorn and hostility which broke out everywhere. In the eyes of the *magnati* the *popolani* were dogs, more stupid than donkeys and fit only to be thrown into noisome dungeons; as indeed befell an unlucky *popolano* who was captured by the *magnati* of Bologna in 1275. It is true that the *popolani* paid them back in their own coin. "Long live the people and death to the wolves!" was the cry raised at Viterbo in 1281. The *magnati* of Bologna were treated as "rapacious wolves" by those who regarded themselves as "gentle lambs". The standard adopted by Prato in 1292 bore pictures of a wolf and a lamb eating together under threat of a sword that represented the law. The dream of this ideal coexistence was expressed throughout the period by the word "justice". *Giustizia* was the rallying cry in all the civic commotions. It was on the "stone of justice" that covenants of reconciliation were engraved. "Companies of Justice" were commissioned to maintain public order. And lastly, in order to promote equity, "Statutes of Justice" were promulgated, at Florence for example in 1293, and the application of them was entrusted to a *gonfaloniere di Giustizia*.

There were, however, grades among the *popolani*. The term *popolo* did not designate a uniform class of people: the merchants who managed the principal crafts, or major "Arts" as they were called, formed a sort of well-to-do aristocracy; and it was their interests even more than ambition which led them to oppose the magnates. But in the eyes of the lower orders, all these people appeared as the wealthy class. It is true that the distance between the *popolani minuti* and the *popolani grassi* was not less than the distance between the *grassi* and the *magnati*. In this three-sided conflict, the *minuti* pretty soon found themselves in a position to arbitrate, and among them the butchers, who were the most active, sometimes played a decisive part. Now in their conflict with the *magnati*, it was not in the interest of the major "Arts", especially at the outset, to alienate the *minuti*; but they were scarcely anxious to share with the latter the advantages they had won in the struggle, and one should not regard the entry of the *popolo grasso* into the governing body of Florence, between 1250 and 1260, as creating a democratic system. It should not be forgotten, either, that the conflict between Guelphs and Ghibellines was superimposed on the economic and social cleavages, without coinciding with them.

Social disparities were no less clearly marked in the textile cities of the Netherlands. The majority of people, who were working for big contractors, were mistaken in supposing that dependence in the city was preferable to greater freedom in the countryside. A minority of merchants, not equally well-off, lorded it over a multitude of artisans, themselves as diverse as the professional classes. These Flemish merchant-drapers correspond almost exactly to the Italian *lanaioli* who were both manufacturers and merchants. It is difficult to estimate the exact numbers of this hereditary *élite*: perhaps a thirtieth or fortieth part of the population of Ghent, and in Arras between a tenth and a twentieth.

The language of the time exactly reflected the disparities in the social structure; and the elements of wealth, prestige, honour and power were often emphasized by the vocabulary applied to the privileged classes in general. A musty survival of the terms used of a hierarchical society, based on landed property, is preserved in the language, which gave a reassuring sound of stability, if not of probity, produced by the Manichaeism latent in social conflicts. It was only in later years that irony was to come into its own. These urban aristocrats shared ownership of the urban land; they were "hereditary men" (*viri hereditarii*). Possession of a small plot of land in the city made people authentic burghers, *poorters* as they were called. They were credited with probity and wisdom, and were the *ervachtighe lieden*; or, more simply, "the great" or "the rich". They were even accorded a title reserved of old to lords or prelates: "Sire" or "Sir" (*dominus*). They stood far above the common herd.

Housing as much as income marked the contrasts in social position. Inherited wealth, purchased property, and the effect of income from real estate, whether in the centre or the suburbs, enabled the rich to control the housing of the poor. It was through this housing—low dwellings which sometimes lodged several families—that the lower class was dependent on the upper, as tenants or as benefiting from a home provided by the employer. Splendid by contrast were the patrician mansions. In Metz one can still see the castle-like towers of the old burgher dynasties, and there were similar houses in Flanders and Artois. A Chronicle of Ghent, dating from the end of the twelfth century, tells of the patricians "powerful through their lineage and their towers". The rich drapers lived in stone houses (*steenen*) which were sometimes fortified. Moreover the location no less than the quality of the dwelling marked the rank of the occupant. Thus at Rouen and in Flanders artisans and workers occupied the outskirts, often outside the walls; this was the position at Ypres towards 1330.

Naturally, too, the way of life reflected the difference in fortune. Horny hands and blue nails on one side, white hands on the other. Rough working togs for some, elegant clothing worthy of lords for others. Queen Jeanne, wife of Philippe le Bel, visiting Bruges, was amazed at the luxury of the rich burgesses. "I thought", she allegedly observed, "that I was the only queen, but here I see six hundred." Their husbands wore swords and served in the urban militia; for them the jurists had invented the paradoxical title of "burgher-knights" (milites burgenses). They called themselves "Sir" or Damoiseau, and had their armorial bearings painted on the doors of their steenen. Why not? They were finding a place among the noble knights and regilding many an old coat-of-arms. The Hucque-dieu of Arras alone founded three hospitals. Baude Crespin, also of Arras, became valet de chambre to the King, who ennobled him; he married his children into old families, and was himself nobly interred in the Church of Saint-Vaast.

This urban aristocracy also enjoyed cultural privileges. In the north, as in southern France and in Italy, the merchants' children received in the city schools the kind of practical education needed for the conduct of business and municipal government; some rudiments of Latin no doubt, but especially accountancy and a knowledge of foreign languages. This was connected with the appearance of a middle-class literature in the vernacular, written by bourgeois for bourgeois. Beginning in Italy, it flowered in Arras with Adam de la Halle,[1] and its first representative in Flanders was Jacob van Maerlant. Some of their jeux no doubt amused the multitude; but the real substance[2] of this literature was accessible only to an élite.

On the religious plane however a certain moral conscience was developing among the poor, under the influence of the Mendicant orders and of various spiritual movements. The connection between the weavers and certain heresies has not

---

[1] His Jeu de la Feuillée (1262) and his Jeu de Robin et de Marion (1282) are about the only two non-religious comedies of the thirteenth century that have survived. (Translator.)

[2] "la substantifique moelle", an expression of Rabelais' to designate the inner meaning of his work.

yet been fully studied; in any case we find an assertion of scorn for the rich as a corollary to the eminent dignity of the poor. William Cornelius of Antwerp went as far as declaring that a rich man, even a virtuous one, was worth less than a prostitute.

The rich were also in control of municipal government.

"We observe that in several cities the poor and those of middle rank have no share in the administration, which is monopolized by the rich, for the common people fear them on account of their wealth or lineage. If it happens that a man has been mayor or *juré* (sworn magistrate) or tax-collector for a year, he contrives to be succeeded by his brother or nephew or other near relative, so that in ten or twelve years the rich will control the whole administration of important towns. Then when the commonalty demand a statement of accounts, the rich cover themselves by saying that they have accounted to each other."

This statement is by a good observer, Philippe de Beaumanoir, the Royal Bailiff of Clermont-en-Beauvaisis, who had been able to see what he was speaking of, and who was no demagogue. The system of appointing magistrates facilitated this kind of monopoly. In some places they were chosen by the great families: thus the six *paraiges* of Metz appointed the thirteen *jurés* who enforced public order. Elsewhere the method was one of co-opting. At Ghent in 1228 the system of the XXXIX, appointed for life, was adopted. They were divided into three groups of thirteen who occupied the posts of *échevins* (aldermen), councillors and so called *vagues*; if one of them died, his companions co-opted a successor. At Arras the method was even more complicated. Every four months the group of twelve municipal magistrates was renewed, four at a time, by co-opting. At Rouen an oligarchy of a "Hundred Peers" nominated every year three candidates for the office of mayor, and appointed the aldermen and councillors. For appointing a mayor of Provins, the retiring mayor submitted to the Count of Champagne or his representatives a list which he himself had established.

There was created in this way a patrician class, that is, a group of families which perpetuated its control of municipal government. This monopoly was more or less effective in Italy as well as in France. Government by the patricians was particularly marked in Venice from 1230 onwards, and a similar one appeared at Siena in 1277. In 1278 two artisans only were members of the Florentine councils. It was generally about the middle of the thirteenth century in Italy that the *popolo* launched an offensive to force a way into communal government, but again the *popolani grassi* were in no way desirous of sharing any benefits with the *minuti*.

Generally speaking the patricians applied the system of co-opting to the advantage of their own members. A limited number of electors transmitted power, year after year, to a handful of men belonging to a small number of families. At Liége between 1214 and 1312 nine families alone provided the thirty-one aldermen whom the Bishop appointed to administer the city: here the patrician class was composed of no more than thirty-seven families. At Lille it was composed of ten. The lists of aldermen and of mayors constantly mention the same names, from the time when surnames began to be fixed. At Ghent we find the names of Borluut, van der Meere or van den Pytte; at Lille, Warenghien, Hangowart, Destailleurs or Le Borgne; at Arras, along with Crespin and Fouchart, the significant names of Piédargent, Sacquespée and Hucquedieu. At Rouen the office of mayor seems to have been occupied continually by five families, the Du Donjon, Groignet, Des Essarts, Du Chastel and especially the Val Richer family whose name appears twenty times during the thirteenth century. The situation was similar at Provins where the mayoralty scarcely ever left the hands of the Reimon, Durtein and Acorre families. Many other examples, in many other regions, could be cited.

Abuse of power was easy; but was it general? The patricians were certainly not a closed caste; they sometimes admitted newly-rich artisans, through marriage. But those whom they refused were naturally the first to challenge the system. Certainly also, the monopoly of civic offices was not as strict everywhere. Thus at Lille the "Law of Friendship" (1235) admitted to the magistrature any bourgeois, whatever his family or fortune; it only stipulated that members of the same family could not exercise magisterial functions simultaneously; while similar arrangements regulated the appointment of assessors of taxes. This fairly exceptional liberalism perhaps explains why Lille did not suffer agitations similar to those which plagued the neighbouring cities at the end of the thirteenth century.

A rather similar situation obtained in the cities of the Empire, and the social differences were as clear cut. A relatively important part of the population of German cities was excluded from political life: this consisted of the non-burghers (*Mitwohner*) designated simply as inhabitants. In addition to clerics and Jews, this group comprised servants, "companions" in small workshops and day-workers, and might represent as much as a quarter of the population. To be a burgher one had to own freehold land and pay an admission fee. But among these burghers there appeared, from the outset, a group known as "the best men" or "the first men of the city"—merchants, landed proprietors and a few newly-rich artisans. They were the patricians.

They were strong not only by virtue of their wealth and mutual family connections. Not content with a monopoly of municipal government, they pretended to privileges akin to those of the nobles. Calling themselves *Herr*, they took the liberty of wearing fine clothes more luxurious than what the sumptuary laws permitted. At Ratisbon, at Bâle and elsewhere they crowned their mansions with towers, after the Italian fashion. They carried coats-of-arms, fought on horseback and wore silver spurs (golden ones being reserved for the nobility). And they recruited troops of clients, the *Muntmannen*, poor devils as a rule, and only too happy to render military or other service to an employer who paid them. These troops included criminals whose lack of scruple made them the more valuable. Such private armies were evidently a danger to the public peace and in many cities the custom was forbidden; whether effectively we do not know.

The patricians also formed associations which helped to perpetuate their primacy. Such a group might be the guild-merchants as in north Germany. In some fifteen cities of the

Rhineland and the upper Danube it was the association of minters (*hausgenossen*) who controlled foreign exchange and monopolized the trade in precious metals. Elsewhere it was the clubs, like the *Richerzeche* of Cologne which has been recorded in 1180 and which lasted for two centuries. All these groups had a meeting-hall (*Stube*) where they could drink, dine and discuss public and private business.

This class of German patricians was still largely open to the newly-rich; although Cologne, metropolis of the Rhineland, where the patricians maintained their primacy until the end of the fourteenth century, was an exception. To the eighty-four families recorded in the twelfth century, only about thirty-five were added in the thirteenth. These families continued to dominate municipal government during periods often very long: over 500 years (seventeen generations) for the Judes and Lyskirchens, and more than 250 (eight to eleven generations) for eighteen others. In general the great patrician families appear in the front of the stage only for four or five generations, so that these families were largely renewed or replaced. Prior to 1250 Strasbourg is known to have had seventy-four patrician families; in the next half-century there appeared not less than sixty-seven. At Ratisbon the corresponding figures are sixty before 1250, and seventy in the following century. The rise of the newly-rich is still more clearly marked in the northern cities which had grown prosperous mainly in the thirteenth century. By admitting the ambitious to its ranks the patrician class safeguarded its predominance over a long period.

Towards the year 1300 the city council (*Stadtrat*) was the usual form of municipal government; its existence is recorded in about 400 cities. It usually numbered twelve members, frequently twenty-four, sometimes an intermediate number. The councillors were normally appointed for a year; collectively they managed the government, defence and finance of the city; while the law-courts were dependent on them. Little by little the council acquired the right to represent the city in its juridical capacity, to the exclusion of the local lord. Beside the council we often find a burgomaster, sometimes several, with varying duties.

It was not exceptional at the outset for these officials to be elected by the burghers as a whole: this was the system at Strasbourg (according to the constitution of 1214) and at Cologne. In 1245 Ratisbon, in 1246 Bremen, and other cities acquired the right of proceeding to annual elections. But this system of relatively democratic election usually gave place, more or less quickly, to appointments by a minority. This co-optation by the retiring councillors was adopted at Strasbourg in 1263, then at Augsburg and Vienna. At Hamburg fourteen of the sixteen retiring councillors would meet to announce their successors, of whom six were to be those who had just retired. At Cologne each of the fifteen councillors had the right to choose his successor from his own family, and this helped to perpetuate the power of the same families in control of the city. And in any case these elections by small groups of men maintained the primacy of the patricians; while the new families they admitted to their ranks hastened to contract marriages with the old families, led the same kind of life and were soon indistinguishable from them.

Until the latter part of the thirteenth century, however, this primacy of the patricians seems to have been generally accepted; although there were a few insurrections, such as that of the "pestilential multitude" at Mainz in 1160. But patricians and plebeians made common cause against the nobles in their struggle to establish urban autonomy. It was in vain that the Archbishop of Cologne in 1259, and the Bishop of Strasbourg in 1261, sought to divide opinion in order to recover a part of their earlier power.

The general development of the economy, the organization of labour and lastly the financial question contributed to produce a new situation. From as early as the twelfth century associations of artisans had appeared under different names, of which *Zunft* and *Innung* (union) became the most usual; and though sometimes prohibited or dissolved, they continued to multiply. In this way the artisans (*Handwerker*) grew stronger and more united, and were able to challenge the crushing supremacy of the patricians. The general political situation added fuel to the flames. Since it was evident in the thirteenth century that the Emperor could no longer assert effective power, the cities were obliged to use their own resources to maintain or re-establish some kind of order in the country. The league of the Rhenish cities in 1254 provides an example. But this external commitment involved great expense: ambassadors had frequently to be sent out, and mercenaries paid. It was this increase in urban expenditure that, most of all, explains the discontent of the craftsmen.

It was much the same everywhere. There were abuses in the administration of justice. At Ghent, according to Pirenne, the pranks of well-to-do youths were treated with a leniency that would not have been extended to others, but it was less this kind of thing than the size of the funds handled by the magistrates that brought out the disadvantages of oligarchical government. Again, the more a city grew in size, the heavier became the burden of taxation. Bureaucrats had to be paid, the city-walls to be maintained or extended, and public works to be financed. On the other hand the cities, which were the sources of wealth, constituted the basis of the state budget—when indeed they were not obliged, as in Germany, to assume its responsibilities. States were already coming into being and their budgets were growing heavy. Sometimes it was a national state, such as France. Here the rise in the power of the Crown was accompanied by an increase in its financial burden such that Philippe le Bel was obliged to fall back on expedients. Elsewhere it was a feudal state. The Count of Flanders derived his resources from the great cities of his domain; these cities were therefore obliged to levy taxes more and more frequently, and more and more heavily. Now this increase in financial burdens, itself an outcome of economic expansion, brought social discontent more into the open. What kind of taxes should be levied; how should the burden be distributed; and how should the money be expended, in a useful way and so as to avoid abuse and wastefulness? Such problems appeared everywhere and their outcome explains the passions that were aroused.

That municipalities did not, for the most part, know how to solve these problems is fully proved by experience. The irregularities and peculation with which the patricians were reproached were not the only source of trouble. Incompetent management led some cities to have recourse to a "rector" who was a stranger to city life because he had acquired his reputation elsewhere; this happened at Bayonne, La Rochelle, Compiègne, Senlis and Rouen. Many of the great French cities found themselves in debt. A bad distribution of the taxes levied for the upkeep, in the first instance, of monuments, markets and city-walls, aggravated the disquiet which, by the middle of the thirteenth century, was felt at Rouen, Noyon and Beauvais. The control instituted by Louis IX in 1262, in the form of an annual check on urban budgets by the royal accountants, did not restore a situation already burdened by debt. There thus ripened, little by little, at the expense of the bourgeois aristocracies, the bitter fruits of a fiscal system often unjust, subject to abuse and also inadequate. The debts already incurred naturally affected regions outside the cities as well; while the weight of taxation by which the cities strove to subsist also aggravated the indebtedness of individuals.

There was a last cause of tension which deserves to be noted. The general burden of debt which weighed on country districts as well as cities was often a sign of impoverishment. This particularly affected the peasants who had raised loans from Jewish money-lenders, loans which have been studied by G. Nahon, thanks to the minutes of inquiries ordered by Louis IX for the north and west of France, although they also affected the townsmen of Laon and Saint-Quentin. In the same way, of the 1321 Jewish bills of credit which R. W. Emery discovered among the notaries' registers of Perpignan between 1261 and 1286, 862, that is two-thirds of the total, concerned the peasants of the region. In many instances the latter were borrowing in order to overcome temporary difficulties or to improve their equipment. In any case these loans were made without security, which means that the Jews were fairly confident that their debtors could repay them. Payment of an annuity was the usual formula adopted in return for a loan. The borrower appeared as seller of an annuity; in return for a sum which he received at once, he undertook to pay the buyer an annuity in theory perpetual. The relation between the annuity and the money borrowed might vary, but it was often 10 per cent. By means of this money the debtor could purchase a profitable piece of land, or buy better equipment or otherwise improve the yield; and the profit thus obtained was only partly absorbed by the annuity. Debtor and creditor shared it. If, however, circumstances proved unfavourable, the increase in income could fall below the amount of the annuity. The burden of the latter, not hard to bear at the outset, became more and more painful. In the case of an annuity representing 10 per cent of the purchase price, the loan was repaid in ten years; a few more years could represent the reasonably accepted amount of interest. In the long run, the profit realized by the creditor appeared out of proportion to the risk he had incurred, and the debtor bore the burden of repayment with increasing aversion. In all regions where the economy had markedly expanded, owing to a great effort to improve equipment, a large number of people—the middle classes in general—laboured under the burden of these annual payments or annuities, a burden which the least decline in business might render unendurable.

In so far as widening social disparities were a consequence of economic growth, the development of credits to the consumer could be regarded as indirectly caused by it. We come here to the question of loans raised for the purpose of expenditure—in order to live, to buy food, to pay taxes—loans which people had great difficulty in repaying. Even if the Jews had had only this string to their bow, even if—which was by no means the case—they had been the only lenders or "usurers", one may suppose that the increasing dislike of which they were the object was not unconnected with the growing burden of debts, and, before long, the increasing difficulty in paying them off.

Such, in brief, were a few of the social consequences of an expanding economy; or, if you prefer, the "contradictions" of this economy. New forms of production appear and give rise to inevitable conflicts. The contrast between the very rich and the very poor becomes more real, more keenly felt and more charged with consequences. The debts incurred weigh more and more heavily on the shoulders of the middle and lower classes.

*   *   *

Thus even before the end of the twelfth century the social structure showed signs of cracking. It would be impossible no doubt, and even useless, to draw upon an exhaustive list; we shall limit ourselves to a few significant examples.

It is not surprising if these began in Italy, the country *par excellence* of urban development. In many cities the magnates opposed the progress of the people. As early as 1218 coexistence had become very difficult at Piacenza, and the social atmosphere had grown stormy enough to justify the great effort of pacification undertaken by the Mendicant orders in 1233, an effort to which Salembene gave the name of "Alleluia". Under the influence of religious like Giovanni da Vicenza, the reform of the communal statutes of Parma, Bologna, Vicenza, Verona, Milan, Monza and Vercelli, tended to appease antagonisms which were sometimes very violent.

This effort had the merit of tackling some of the old systems, but it was incomplete and ephemeral. The causes of conflict were too deeply rooted and circumstances were constantly renewing them. The most frequent problems arose out of taxation and food supply. Conflicts were not lacking during the decades 1250–60, and 1260–70; and the political events of the time were not such as to favour appeasement. In July 1250 the people of Piacenza revolted because of the high cost of food; in September the Florentines rebelled because of the incompetence of the magnates: on this occasion, as all the Arts had made common cause, the people seized control of the government. Disturbances took place at Parma in 1255, at Bologna in 1256, at Milan in 1258, at Siena in 1262, and again at Florence in 1266; as also, in the interval, at Pistoia, Perugia and Chieri. Almost everywhere the rioters attacked the incompetent administration of the patricians, protesting against those who speculated on food-shortages and demanding the prohibition of exports. The rich men in power were held to be responsible. To understand the nature of this constant agitation, a study of the language used in the documents is most informative. Popular movements are treated as plots, conspiracies, confederations or leagues. The old title of "Defender of the People" or "Defender of the Arts" is used of a new body of magistrates which appeared at Milan in 1240, at Florence in 1282; but 1282 belongs to a characteristic phase of Florentine social politics.

In northern France and the old Netherlands industrial and commercial expansion had not yielded its final fruits before resentment broke out against the rich, supported at times by former members of the governing class who had changed sides from motives of jealousy, ambition or idealism; but also by the associations, not yet fully organized, of artisans and professional workers. The poorest folk entertained the illusion that to destroy the patrician class would reverse the situation.

In 1225 a rumour began to spread in Flanders that Count Baudouin, the Latin Emperor of Constantinople, had returned from the East; whereas he was really dead. The rancour and hatred of the "poor folk, cloth-makers and fullers" were concentrated on the person of this "bogus Baudouin". Philippe Mousket's *Chronicle* has recorded this commotion which overthrew the patricians of Valenciennes and imperilled the life of the Countess. Such events engraved themselves in the popular imagination. In 1245 *takehans* (strikes) took place at Douai; and the same word was applied at Rouen to the agitation of the weavers which broke out in the square where the workmen's market was usually held; they were then refused the use of it. At Arras *gueudes* (guilds) were prohibited in 1253, under suspicion of being hotbeds of unrest. The frequent prohibition of strikes and coalitions is significant.

In the mid-thirteenth century the disturbances spread to Brabant and the territory of Liége. At Léau in Brabant people plotted to overthrow the magistrates; while an attempt was made to unite all the movements of discontent by means of a promise of reciprocal extradition of all enemies of the popular cause. This tendency spread to Flanders, and the men of Ghent

signed an agreement of the sort in 1274. But it was in the
territory of Liége, noted for its "ardour", that rebellion
acquired its most egalitarian colouring. Saint-Trond was the
scene of agitation in 1253, while in Liége itself there were
demonstrations claiming that the poor should have equal rights
with the rich. Three years earlier the magistrates had been
faced with "the clamours of the poor". In 1254 these clamours
gave place to violence. Henri de Dinant, brother of a merchant
of Liége, led an insurrection, became dictator, and levied a tax
on rich men's incomes. This affair, which soon ended, left
with the patricians the memory of a demagogue, with the
others that of a hero. Henri's example was followed in 1255
at Huy, where the people assaulted the magistrates. The fire
was to smoulder for thirty years in the Liége country and in all
the old Netherlands. Thus early symptoms of crises that were
to afflict the fourteenth century reduce the duration of the
"brilliant 1200s", so far as social and economic conditions were
concerned.

Agitation broke out late in the Empire, and it was only at
the end of the thirteenth century that the first municipal
reforms were imposed. Sometimes representatives of the major
crafts were admitted in small numbers to the patrician councils;
this happened at Ulm, Esslingen and Freiburg-im-Breisgau; at
Magdeburg in 1281 delegates of the five major crafts—tailors,
mercers, furriers, linen-weavers and tanners—entered the
municipal assembly. Elsewhere these crafts formed a single
body which the council consulted on occasion, as with "the
masters of the crafts" in 1289 at Halberstadt, and with "the
Sixteen" at Worms in 1298. Yet the predominance of the
patricians was not really threatened as yet.

Social agitation also appeared in Languedoc about the
year 1200, though this was not a region of great economic
activity, but rather of an ancient civic tradition. By studying the
lists of consuls of Toulouse, J. H. Mundy discerned a tendency
towards monopoly by a small number of old families. In 1202
some new names appear in the consulate—business men and
perhaps artisans representing a kind of "popular-party".
During the years that followed, however, the reappearance in

force of the traditional names discloses an aristocratic reaction. Now these struggles—which can be described as partly social—for access to the consular body were accompanied by conflicts between heretics and orthodox believers; heretics being mostly found among the "new men". These were also the most ardent partisans of a sort of Toulousan "imperialism", which aimed at bringing under the control of the city, with the help of the urban militia, the whole of the surrounding region, with its nobles and smaller towns—a real *contado* as the Italians would have called it. The Albigensian Crusade was to nullify this effort and also to arrest the progress of heresy. One wonders if by this means the old families recovered their power.

However that may be, Toulouse was definitely divided towards 1250, the supremacy of the patricians, composed of nobles and bourgeois, being challenged from below. In 1248, the last "native" Count of Toulouse, Raimon VII, died, having just ordained that the twenty-four consuls should be selected, half from among the "great", half from among the "middle" ranks. Alphonse de Poitiers, the brother of Louis IX, who succeeded him, at once set about reducing the autonomy and traditional privileges of the city. In opposition to the consuls who naturally defended them, he welcomed the complaints brought by the attorneys of the urban community (1268), who asked for the taxes to be raised *à sol et livre*, that is in proportion to people's estates, and who also required that the consuls should produce annual accounts before an assembly of forty-eight *prud'hommes*, and so on. So we see how social enmities were added to the old struggle for the freeing of the cities, a struggle on which circumstances were conferring a new importance.

This combination was more clearly manifest at Cahors than elsewhere. Like the natives of Quercy in general, the merchants of Cahors had, in the twelfth century, acted as important middlemen between England and the Mediterranean lands. Those who had grown rich on this trade invested their capital; and the name of "Cahorsins" (to be distinguished from the usual "Cadurciens"), synonymous with usurers, which made them famous, refers to this phase of their activity; but at the outset they had been simply merchants. We are therefore led to suppose that the social evolution of Cahors had been singularly precocious. As so often in the Massif Central and adjoining regions, the cities were lordships of the bishop, and the bishops were particularly "difficult", finicky and conservative. In spite of the traditional lordship, we learn from a document of 1207 that the city had consuls. After this the bishop and the consuls were almost always at loggerheads, one or other appealing to the King or the Pope. The bishop, being impecunious, was compelled to borrow and therefore to make concessions: he granted the consuls the right to mint money. At times, however, he sought to react; thus in 1238 he entered into a defensive and offensive alliance with a part of the population; an alliance from which the *grands bourgeois* were of course excluded. This league was directed by a council which raised taxes, and compensated those of its members who might suffer harm in the course of a struggle which was regarded as inevitable. One of the league's objects was the suppression of heresy, but the magnates reacted vigorously, compelling the lower orders to abjure the oath they had taken with the bishop.

But the struggle was to continue without him. In 1268, following complaints by day-labourers, cobblers, weavers, carpenters and others, who declared they were too heavily taxed, the consuls agreed that in future the taxes should be assessed *à sol et livre*. But they soon asserted that the concession had been wrung from them by violence, and had it annulled by the *Parlement*. The result was an insurrection of the *populaires*. The King's official took refuge in flight, and one of the richest bourgeois was burned alive in his house with his wife and children. Now of course the King sent troops and order was restored. Some fifty of the lower class were hanged and several hundreds banished (1270).

The example of Cahors is interesting because it combined two kinds of conflict, the old struggle between the city and its lord, and the new one between the lower and upper classes; only, at Cahors, the turmoil was particularly spectacular. Similar troubles occurred in several other places; but before the end of the thirteenth century important results were achieved both as regards the recruitment of consuls and the assessing of taxes.

To guarantee for the principal social classes a seat in the consulate was the object of a certain number of urban "constitutions". In lower Languedoc a system of "scales" became widespread. A decree pronounced at Nîmes in November 1272 by a royal commissioner, who had been invited to arbitrate, established a council of twenty-seven, chosen by the retiring consuls but in accordance with the following rules: apart from the six councillors representing "the castle of the arena" (the Roman arena had been turned into a fortress where the knights of the city lived), there were to be twelve from the city as a whole, but also nine selected to represent each of the nine "scales" or categories among which the merchants, artisans and others were divided. These were the groups in question:

1 Money-changers, apothecaries, grocers, and everyone who sold goods by weight.
2 Merchant-drapers, furriers and tailors.
3 Weavers, curriers and tanners.
4 Herdsmen and butchers.
5 *Pelhiers* (second-hand dealers in clothes) and carvers.
6 Blacksmiths and all who work with a hammer.
7 Carpenters and stone-cutters.
8 Labourers and *brassiers* (that is, who had only their arms to work with).
9 Jurists, physicians and notaries.

Next, in joint session, the eight retiring consuls and the twenty-seven councillors were to elect the eight new consuls, four being knights from the arena, and four bourgeois of the city. In spite of the concession represented by the above formula, it is clear that the predominance of the wealthier class was practically untouched, as was the traditional over-representation of the knights. The system did not work smoothly and in 1283 it was agreed that of the four city-consuls, two had to be representatives of the special categories called "scales"; which was no great satisfaction for the lower and middle classes.

This system of categories had been established also at Montpellier in 1252; ten were represented in a group of sixty persons from among whom the twelve consuls were chosen by lot. The system was extended to Alès in 1294, to Lodève in 1301 and to Béziers before 1322: here the seven retiring consuls appointed their successors by selecting one out of each of the seven categories. There were many variations; but one can hardly go into raptures over the "democratic" nature of the system.

In other cities the population was divided into official categories corresponding to their wealth or income. In 1262, at Perpignan, the King of Aragon decided that the seven *prud'-hommes* who assessed the taxes should be elected by the people at large, three being chosen from among the magnates, two from the middle class and two from the lower. And a similar organization was to be found in the fourteenth century in several cities of Languedoc.

Whatever one may think of these formulae, it is certain that they did not always temper the arbitrary nature of many elections. In 1283 the electoral system was fixed at Toulouse for centuries. The twelve retiring consuls or *capitouls* put forward eighty-four names—two for each quarter of the city—and from these the *viguier* (provost), representing the king, selected the twelve new *capitouls*. In this way the Crown assured its control of the city government; it then abandoned its alliance with the middle and lower classes whose support it had previously welcomed.

More important were the results achieved in the matter of apportioning taxation. From as early as Alphonse de Poitiers' regime the rules were fixed very clearly for the county of Toulouse. Alphonse seems on the whole to have sided with the lower classes against the arrogant consuls who were trying, in opposition to him, to secure civic autonomy. In 1263 he ordered his agents to draw up, in every township, an estimate of the movable estate and real estate of heads of families in order to provide a solid basis for the assessing of tax. One cannot be sure that his instructions were carried out everywhere; but they were effective in a number of cases, as at Toulouse. In 1270 while Alphonse was on the crusade, his governing council decreed that in all big cities, general expenses higher than forty *livres tournois* should be covered by taxes graded in proportion to estates; and the limit was lowered to twenty *livres* for medium-sized towns and ten for small ones. Similar decisions outside the county of Toulouse insured a minimum of fiscal justice. But where similar measures were not taken, the dispute was to continue, not without disturbances, throughout the fourteenth century.

Nevertheless—and this is why we have insisted on conditions in Languedoc—the essential of what was to be achieved, was achieved there as soon as the thirteenth century. Elsewhere it was not the same; and we still have to show that in about 1280 signs of discontent were increasing, heralds so to speak of the tumultuous fourteenth century.

*   *   *

In the area of industrial and commercial expansion between the Seine and the Rhine, the agitation, hitherto sporadic, degenerated into simultaneous and, sometimes, concerted outbreaks of violence. The first symptoms, towards 1275, seem to have been caused by disturbances in the cloth-trade. Imports of English wool were interrupted between 1270 and 1274, and this resulted in temporary unemployment; moreover, the levy in England of a tax on wool-exports involved for Flanders a rise in the price of the finished product which could only be checked by a reduction in the cost of labour and a stricter regulation of the work as a whole. All these circumstances aggravated an already latent tension.

We find a revealing sign of this in 1274 when Ghent and several cities of Brabant signed a mutual agreement to refuse asylum to rebels who had fled or been banished, and to expel them. Was this a Holy Alliance of the patricians? In any event protests against them became more general and more intense, in the first instance at Ghent and Arras.

At Arras, satire was undisguised. Adam de la Halle and his fellows were no revolutionaries but they frankly named the men they were attacking. The *Jeu de la Feuillée*, allegorical though it is, brings on the stage a succession of men and events, as well as a warning. We see the "wheel of fortune" worked by a figure "mute, deaf and blind". On the top of the wheel are two characters who "seem" to be great men, "at present" masters of the city; they are misers; their children, who will want to reign after them, follow them step by step. Who then are they? Two bourgeois with well-lined pockets—Ermenfroi Crespin and Jacquemon Louchard. And this other character who is turning a somersault—has he already emptied the till? This is Thomas de Bourriane, who was speculating on prices and getting the city to pay his debts. "Fortune" has brought him low and is turning him upside down. Now at Arras in 1275 an enquiry was demanded into the way the magistrates were managing the city's affairs. In 1280 events forced this to be made, and the testimony collected in 1289 shows that the satirist had not been lying. Here are some of the heads of accusation. At Arras as at Saint-Quentin, Amiens and Douai, an attempt had been made to apportion the taxes by a system similar to the southern estimates (*estimes*). Once a year everyone, parish by parish, declared what money he had of his own, either orally, at Amiens and Douai, or in a written statement, at Arras. Now this was an occasion of scandalous fraud. A man who possessed "such great wealth that everyone marvelled at it" had declared fifty *livres* income. Another had admitted to 500 instead of 7,000. In addition to false declarations, tax-allowances were granted consequent on the transfer of income to relatives and friends; whereas the main burden fell on those least able to support it. A singular reversal indeed of the principles then held dear! The "wheel of fortune" had turned the wrong way up, and it was the weak who had to carry the strong.

The patrician governments were challenged in the other cities too, and for similar reasons. The people began by calling the Count to their aid, and so in 1275 the men of Ghent forced the "Council of the thirty-nine" to accept a complete reform of its membership; while at Douai in 1276 they secured a cancellation of the magistrates' sentences which were particularly unfavourable to artisans.

From 1279 and 1280 onwards events were rapidly to take a more serious turn. This time the whole system, administrative, financial, economic and social was challenged, and the people, not content to count only on the support of their feudal lord, began to settle their grievances by violence. In 1279, at Ghent, Douai, Ypres, Bruges and Arras, the people were still only making demands; though the weavers of Tournai were already conspiring against the magistrates. In 1290 however insurrections broke out everywhere, almost simultaneously. "At this time", wrote the chronicler Jean de Thilrode, "the commons in nearly every part of Flanders rose in rebellion against the Count, against the magistrates and the wealthy burghers."

In spite of their different objects, however, the Count of Flanders and the commons of the cities were drawn together by hostility to a single enemy. If the common people were revolting against the great merchants, it was a matter of necessity for the Count to quell the insubordination of the communes, that is, the municipalities governed by the same merchant-oligarchies. The political aspect of the question should not, on the other hand, conceal the social—which appears in the neighbouring regions, between the Meuse and the Seine. At Ghent, meanwhile, the people were demanding a whole programme of reforms: membership in the council for the artisans, abolition of hereditary succession to the office of alderman, control over the magistracy, and suppression of the monopoly in the imports of raw wool, hitherto reserved for members of the London Hanse (i.e. a guild of Flemish merchants). In the hope of support from the Count, the men of Ghent abstained at first from any excesses, but it was not the same at Bruges, Ypres and Douai, where the insurrections exceeded the limits of the support which the Count thought he could get from the people. In the summer of 1280 the textile workers revolted at Ypres; in September at Bruges, in October at Douai. At Bruges, disturbances again occurred in the May and September following. On each occasion the weavers and fullers formed the spearhead of attack; at Ypres they were supported by the weavers of neighbouring villages who were, like them, under the thumb of the merchant-drapers. The levy of a heavy tax at Douai provoked a strike, followed by an insurrection. At Ypres and Bruges the craftsmen demanded publication of the accounts, and a share in the magistrature. Personal rancour added fuel to the flames, and violence degenerated into pillage, murder and the desecration of churches. Eleven of the sixteen magistrates of Douai were assassinated. The rebels as usual went for the archives, which recorded the titles to positions of control, and the famous belfry of Bruges was set on fire.

In the end it was the craftsmen who paid for all this. The repression was particularly severe at Douai where men were hanged, beheaded or banished. In other cities the Count's agents took the matter in hand, seizing this excellent opportunity of reducing the power of the magistrates, at Ypres and Bruges, but if the Count imputed the responsibility for these troubles to the magistrates, he punished the commoners no less severely, and with heavy collective fines. He profited from all this, but rancour remained, and with it the memory of the "Kokerulle" of Ypres and the two "Moorlemaye" of Bruges. It could hardly be otherwise. The problem, deep-seated as it was, was not peculiar to Flanders. At Liége the younger generation had not forgotten Henri de Dinant; and the determined opposition of the "mechanics" to a *maltôte*, i.e. an extortionate tax on consumption, resulted in 1287 in a withdrawal of the tax and a reform of the judicial system thanks to which, we are told, "the poor could live beside the rich, and the rich beside the poor". For how long?

There had been no bloodshed at Arras in 1280, although new magistrates had been appointed only after heated argument. But in 1285 the harangue delivered by a certain Jean Cabos, a popular leader like the one who had inspired the Kokerulle of Ypres, incited the crowd which had collected in the Petite Place for the Whit Sunday procession, and led it to pillage the houses of the rich. The most violent of the rioters were hanged, and Cabos imprisoned; but the Count ordered an inquiry to be made into the doings of the patricians.

The Rhineland was not exempt from popular agitation, even in the cities where the formation of a merchant oligarchy had not gone as far as in the Netherlands. Owing to his conflict with the magistrates of Koblenz the Bishop was obliged in 1282–3 to leave the city which was in a state of turmoil. Four years later the Bishop of Andernach managed to forestall a similar rebellion by granting a council of twelve elected members to the new class of magnates.

Were these troubles contagious, or simultaneous reactions to a situation the same everywhere? Provins, which had prospered through its fairs, was now suffering from their decline. It had an unpopular mayor, named Guillaume Pentecôte; and the proposal to increase taxes aroused the opposition of all the drapers, both masters and workmen. The mayor thought to divide their forces by adding an hour to the length of the working-day. The reaction of thousands of workers was immediate. The mayor was killed and his house pillaged; as were the homes of several magistrates and bourgeois (January 1281). A few days later the mayor of Rouen was no more fortunate. Some unknown circumstance put a spark to the long-smouldering discontent against the magistrature and the fiscal system. The winter of 1280–1 had been severe, with heavy rains, floods, and frosts. At the fair held at Candlemas, the crowd rioted and lynched the mayor. Punishment was severe, as usual, and the fine which the city had to pay aggravated the inequalities in the fiscal burden. The social climate naturally remained unpleasant. It was in vain, in 1289, to prohibit any assemblage of weavers because, in 1292, in a more serious riot, the crowd pillaged the house of the King's Collector of Taxes and laid siege to the *Vieux Château*. Here, as elsewhere, the fiscal system gave a political turn to the problem; but the problem remained social, fundamentally, and for this reason was connected with all the disturbances which were beginning to shake the structure of society.

That the northern districts of France were not the only scene of tumults, we find evidence in the *Coutumes de Beauvaisis*, which were written between 1280 and 1283 by Philippe de Beaumanoir:

"There is an alliance against the common good when a certain kind of people swear, or guarantee, or agree that they will no longer work at as low a wage as before, but raise the rate of pay they demand on their own authority, agree not to work for less and establish penalties or utter threats against those workers who do not observe the alliance. The person who tolerated this would be acting against common law, and never would good contracts be concluded, because the members of all the crafts would demand wages higher than is reasonable, and to permit men not to work is contrary to the common good. For this reason, as soon as such alliances come to the knowledge of the sovereign or of other lords, they should lay hands on all the men who have made the agreement and hold them closely imprisoned for a long period; after which one can make each of them pay sixty *sous* of fine."

One does not know which part to admire in this declaration—its clearness, its perfect frankness or its "modernness". It bears witness to certain facts: in the Paris Basin artisans had been forming unions and agreeing to take strike action, on occasion, with sanctions on "blacklegs". The reason is the demand for higher wages, provoked no doubt by the general rise in prices. The *Coutumes de Beauvaisis* imply that certain employers were yielding to the pressure, and it was severe on those who would "tolerate" it. Beaumanoir opposed all this in the name of the "common good". He thought that if certain wage-rises were granted, a whole series of other demands would follow, that it would prove impossible to conclude agreements at rates of pay so high, and that in the end work would cease altogether. Beaumanoir therefore advised the Lords who were faced by such conditions to imprison those responsible, and to free them only on payment of the traditional fine for a violation of public order.

Elsewhere he denounces the monopoly of municipal offices by the magnates and the abuses of every kind which were a consequence. One is tempted to compare these reflections with the statements of Stefani, an Italian chronicler:

"The merchants and artisans were badly treated by the arrogant magnates. Those citizens who were appointed "priors" sought not to observe the laws but to corrupt them. If one of their friends or relatives ought to have been fined, they took care, with the help of the "Signoria" and the officials, to conceal their infractions of law and prevent them from being punished. By failing to safeguard the Communal Treasury, they found means of stealing from it. In this way they drew a great deal of money from the funds belonging to the commune on the pretext of remunerating the persons who administered it. The weak were not assisted, the magnates did them wrong and the rich[1] citizens who occupied public office and were related to the magnates acted in the same way. Many guilty men were escaping the sanctions which they had incurred. For all these reasons the good citizens among the people were discontented and were criticizing the priors because the Guelph magnates were in power."

This is a partisan statement because Stefani was a Ghibelline; but the reasons advanced for the reforms which were decreed in September 1289 confirm his criticism of administrative disorders: denial of justice, useless expenditure and embezzlement, at the expense of the most elementary good of the community.

During 1289, in Florence, as elsewhere in Italy and in Europe for some years past, a very definite state of unrest is revealed by agitation and other kinds of disturbance. The development of the city both in extent and population raised every sort of problem. The importance in social life which the minor Arts had now acquired was manifest in the demands they made, and it was to the interest of the *popolo grasso*, who were again in power, to take account of them, in order finally to supplant the preponderance of the magnates. The *grassi* or "rich men" thus contrived to spare Florence any serious disturbance. A popular commotion, accompanied by a cry for "justice" had been the reaction to an attempt made by a few magnates to prevent the capital punishment of one of their number. In 1289–90 the Minor Arts were preparing, by the "Ordinances of Justice", for the reign of the *popolo* which was established three years later.

[1] *i grassi*—"the fat", that is the well-to-do merchants and manufacturers who were not *magnati*. (Translator.)

In other cities people had not been content with merely demonstrating and clamouring. In 1281 Viterbo had known some critical moments; but it was Bologna, it seems, which had set the example for serious disturbances, whereas Florence had taken the path of reform. At Bologna the lower classes had risen in support of the former *podestà*, Antonio Plisigara, and this was a new phenomenon. At Florence a few years later, and in Flanders, and then throughout the fourteenth century, the people were to find men able to lead them either among their fellows or among the patricians themselves.

Another such episode took place at Barcelona, which had developed very notably in the thirteenth century. In 1285, led by a certain Berenguer Oller, the lower classes were agitating until, on Easter day itself, King Pedro III arrived in haste and suppressed the conspiracy. This affair has been regarded from a political angle. A few weeks later Philippe III of France, surnamed "the Bold", launched a crusade against the King of Aragon. Now it was easy to regard the agitation in Barcelona as due to French intrigues designed to weaken the adversary, that is, King Pedro. But there is no proof of collusion, and the social nature of the revolt seems to be very clear.

Our principal witness is the Catalan chronicler, Bernat Desclot; he was most hostile to the rebels and was seeking to extol King Pedro's qualities. For this reason we should read his narrative with caution; and, besides, he is far from providing the exact details which one desires. Here is what he says:

"There was at that time, in the city of Barcelona, a man named Berenguer Oller. He was of base condition, but had won the support of many of his peers; he had induced nearly all the lower classes of Barcelona to swear, willingly or perforce, to obey his will. Under pretext of doing good he had wrought great evil in the place, to the prejudice of the King and of the city's *prud'hommes*: thus he had pronounced sentences, and, on his own authority, had stripped the Church, the Bishop and a great number of the burghers of their *rendes* and *sensals*. And he would not desist, whatever letters or messages the King or his officers sent him. When anyone opposed him, rightly or wrongly, he would always attack him with the support of the people, of whom he had made himself Captain or Governor, so that on many occasions he brought the said city to the brink of ruin.

"Now among the many evils he had wrought or planned, he had ordered that, on the coming Easter day, with the people who had not been warned in advance, an attack should be made on the clergy, the Jews and all the rich men of the city who were not willing to recognize him, that they should all be killed, and that their houses with all they contained should be confiscated for the benefit of his followers, who would then hand over the city to the King of France so that the King of Aragon could never make them pay for their misdeeds."

Let us draw from these lines all the information they can yield:

1 Desclot, who knew on occasion how to portray a character, has not troubled to leave us a portrait of Oller; he simply notes that he was of humble birth. At the end of the thirteenth century, when the use of hereditary family names was already widespread, it would be risky to suppose Oller to have been an oil-merchant, but one of his ancestors doubtless was. Further on, Desclot states that he "was a very glib speaker": the gift of the gab has nearly always been recorded of the popular leaders in the Middle Ages.

2 The organization of Oller's movement is indicated by little touches. With the title of "Captain and Governor" (supposing Desclot to record the title accurately, which his habits make likely enough), he appears clearly as the head of the movement. He was, however, surrounded by a council which pronounced sentences. The movement—composed of the lower classes whom the text several times opposes to the *prud'hommes*, emphasizing the social difference—derived its strength from the oath sworn to the Captain. It was possible to mobilize the members in case of need, in order to overcome by intimidation any attempt at resistance.

3 Desclot's text, brief as it is, contains valuable indications of the objects of Oller's movement. He is accused of having—

by means no doubt of judgements pronounced by his council—
stripped the Church, the Bishop and a great number of
burghers of their *rendes* and their *sensals*—terms which describe
the rent annuities the use of which had become very general
in Barcelona. That this practice had, by 1285, provoked discontent keen enough to constitute at least one of the sources of
social friction, is interesting. One may see in it a result of the
economic expansion of Barcelona. Many small artisans and
little merchants or shopkeepers had doubtless, in order to
establish themselves or extend their businesses, been led to
borrow capital. We may therefore suppose that Berenguer
Oller's partisans were not a crowd of impoverished wretches,
but a lower middle class which, by means of borrowing and of
hard work, had managed to find a place in the sun, and wanted
to depend no longer on the furnishers of capital, namely the
Church and the magnates.

4 The passage suggests that the revolutionary situation lasted
for some time, say a few months. Oller and his followers were
coexisting with the legal authorities, which had been rendered
practically impotent. Several times the King and his officials,
by means of missives and orders, strove to restore the previous
situation. The final project of Oller and his followers was
denounced, but it was represented as so monstrous that we
are not obliged to believe Desclot's account of it. Besides, the
choice of Easter Sunday for such a massacre sounds like a
useless piece of bravado.

Although concise up to this point, Desclot dilates at much
greater length on the measures taken to suppress the insurrection, because they testified to qualities of decision on the
King's part, qualities which our author extols. From Lerida,
Pedro III arrived at a gallop with a small escort, and entered
the city without warning. In the early morning of Easter
Saturday (24 March) there was rumour of the King's
presence, to the joy of the *prud'hommes* and the disquiet of Oller
and his friends who were unable to "prepare" the King. After
daybreak the latter rode through the city. Oller met him and
tried to kiss his hand, but the King ironically prevented it,
observing that "it was neither the custom nor usage of kings

that one should kiss the other's hand". Oller protested his loyalty as a subject and asked for a conversation. The King made as if to agree and took him to the palace where he ordered the gates to be closed; they were to be opened only to admit Oller's companions. Seven of them got caught in this mouse-trap.

The next day, being Easter Sunday, Pedro promised to "regale" Oller and to "extract him honourably from the palace, dragged at the tail of a mule, and followed by seven of his companions, with ropes round their necks"; he completed the grotesque ceremony by having all eight of them hanged. Whereupon he attended Mass and feasted, as was right and proper on this great day. Before nightfall some 600 men of Barcelona more or less compromised, left the city, but the King had 200 of them arrested.

Orders issued by the Royal Chancellery assure us that these details are not mere exaggerations of Desclot's. They also give us the names of a score of "guilty men" whose arrest was particularly desired; among them, several artisans and a notary. But a foreign war was shortly to break out, and the affair of Barcelona had no aftermath.

All the same, it completes our picture of the situation at the end of the thirteenth century. But even before the recession of the fourteenth, even before the great revolutionary troubles, cracks were beginning to appear very distinctly in the old social and political structure, and not simply in those regions which were economically most advanced.

[Chapter Two]

The Middle "Class" Versus the Magnates[1]

SOCIAL FERMENT had naturally begun where economic expansion had been most precocious, that is, in the urban centres of the textile industry. In country districts one discerns only the slow rise to fortune of a few families favoured by luck. In both cases, however, certain individuals had grown rich and had been able to rise a few degrees in the hierarchy of wealth; hence those who were most advanced wanted to make their voices heard. A kind of middle class had been formed in this way among the craftsmen and large-scale farmers. Towards 1280 the former had been knocking, noisily at times, on the doors of the magistrature and the consulates; a few had infiltrated them. In the background one might have heard a still vague grumbling, the confused and intermittent anger of the craftsmen in one region, the minor arts in another, who were protesting against their exploitation by the magnates and taxation by the prince. These humbler folk had served their more advanced fellows as a main striking-force, and they did not cease to play this part for some time to come.

Remarkably varied were the episodes in the struggle of the middle "class" to force the magnates to yield it the place it aspired to; and the various circumstances of time and place

---

[1] *Les Moyens contre les Grands*. The word "class" is not to be taken in our sense. (Translator.)

54]

lent to these struggles a colour sometimes social, sometimes political, professional, or economic. They all, however, had certain features in common. Their objects were similar: access of the artisan class to municipal office. Their methods and procedure were similar: a professional association, sometimes in the form of a confraternity, with a view to institutional changes; fiery rhetoric above all, for popular speechifying proved extraordinarily successful in the fourteenth century; and lastly, leadership of the popular movements by a dynamic personality, a man of the people or even, often enough, a patrician who had changed sides.

It was logical that the most typical episodes should occur in districts where a certain middle class had begun to take account of its interest, that is, in the Netherlands, northern France, then the Rhineland, southern France, Italy and the Mediterranean shores of Spain. In all these places, during the first half of the fourteenth century, the pressure became so evident that we can call it, in the words of Pirenne, the *Révolution des Métiers*. But the movement did not advance everywhere at the same rate. If at the outset we hear of tardy episodes of the communal movement in western France, we must on the other hand note that access of the craftsmen to a place in municipal government was achieved only in the second half of the fourteenth century in certain cities of the Empire. In country districts the differences were strongly marked. At the beginning of the fourteenth century in northern Italy the peasant insurrection, with which the name of Dolcino is still associated, represented an heretical challenge to the organization of the Church; while the insurrection in maritime Flanders, between 1323 and 1328, was inspired by fairly prosperous farmers, very different from the famished and disorderly rebels whose sporadic risings were a prelude to the Jacquerie.

There is no reason to dwell on the disturbances at Saint-Malo in 1308. They were only a late episode of the communal movement, though they illustrate in their own way the time-lag between the precociously industrialized Netherlands and western France, which was basically rural. One should recall, however, that the sedition at Saint-Malo followed a traditional

pattern: conspiracy, disorders, election of a mayor and magistrates, assemblies in a communal building. More important
was the pretension, revolutionary in its way, of the men of
Saint-Malo to free themselves from feudal tutelage, by disposing as they liked of their loyalty to the Bishop, to the Duke
of Brittany, or to the King of France. It was also the sign of
an independent mood among the men of Saint-Malo, a mood
shared in general by the coastal populations.

In 1298 the men of Calais had already given vent to their
feelings. The exact cause of the rebellion is unknown. It seems
that they took advantage of a change in the person of the
bailiff, agent of the court, and a temporary reduction in the
size of the garrison to demonstrate against a fiscal surcharge,
onerous for a budget already out of balance. As in many other
cities an oligarchy of wealthy shipowners controlled the
business of a majority of small tradesmen, fishermen, sailors and
artisans. The city, encumbered with debts owed to the financiers
of Arras, had seen the amount of its debt doubled in twenty
years. The outcome of the revolt was little better than the evil
which provoked it. Heavily taxed by the Count of Artois, the
city lost all its privileges for a time.

The region covering the old Netherlands and the district of
Liége furnishes the classical example of the Craftsmen's Revolution: a revolution slow and incomplete, marked by retreats and
associated with strictly political circumstances. The repression
carried out in 1280 had settled nothing and the bearing of the
problem remained unaltered. The craftsmen of Flanders were
lucky because they identified their lot with a national cause.

The social tension persisted, giving rise to trouble at Douai
several times between 1296 and 1306. As elsewhere, the
commoners complained bitterly of the patrician regime, of the
indebtedness of the city over-burdened by long-term annuities,
and, to crown all, a supplementary tax of 2 per cent on incomes.
In September 1296 the two sides met face to face in the Church
of the Friar Preachers, and a few months later the lower middle
class wrested the election of aldermen from the patricians.
And now for ten years power passed alternately between the
people and the patricians, with no result but the subjection of

the city to the control of the King's officials and a series of
mutual repressions. If things were to continue at this rate, the
situation looked disquieting. In 1304 and 1305 several riots
had been led, not by nobodies but by a collusion between about
ten clerics and two butchers, whose trade was always at the
spearhead of the fight. They were reproached with having
"cried alarm and stirred up the city", with having gone to find
"various craftsmen" in order to "seek strength and help to
maintain the cause of their [own] trade". One of them, in the
market, had insulted and threatened the aldermen, asserting
that a certain number of one of the councils "would get his
head turned red". A number of men were excluded from their
trades, and some of them banished.

Events took a graver turn in the other Flemish cities. What
had encouraged the artisans of Douai was the support of Gui de
Dampierre, Count of Flanders, against the patricians who were
partisans of Philippe le Bel: *clauwaerts* versus *leliaerts*. This volte-
face on the part of the Count, to save his crown, was a piece of
luck for the craftsmen; while the clumsiness of the King's
representative and of Jacques de Châtillon, particularly at
Bruges, did the rest. Thus the Anglo-Franco-Flemish war was
the occasion which caused the seeds sown at Bruges and Ypres
in 1280 to bear fruit. They in fact came up just where they had
been sown.

It was not certain that Gui de Dampierre would be able to
benefit from the somewhat demagogic support which he had
given the craftsmen. Gui had restored to Bruges, as to Douai,
the liberties which, under pressure of the insurrection, had been
conceded in 1280. At Ghent he had condemned the abuses
committed by the patrician government. Now in 1300 the
King intervened to chastise his vassal. He outbid him by granting the craftsmen of Ghent half the seats in the magistrature.
Why had Châtillon to sacrifice the advantages which his
sovereign had won in this way? By serving the cause of the most
wealthy, he alienated the great crowd of weavers, fullers,
croppers of cloth and dyers. An unpopular tax, followed by a
severe repression of the opposition it provoked, blotted out the
memory of what the King had intended.

After an interval of twenty years the events of 1280 had their replica; but this time with an amplitude, a cohesion and a unity of direction significant of the strength gained by the commoners. The insurrection at Bruges was original in that it was headed by a real leader and not a mere agitator. The *Annales de Gand* and the *Chronique Artésienne* paint from life a portrait of the man whom his name, Pierre de Coninc (i.e. Peter the King), seemed to destine for command. The people recognized in him one of themselves. The *Chronicle* stated:

"Now it happened that there was then at Bruges a man named Pierron Le Roy, who was small of body, and poor of lineage. He was a weaver, and had made a living in that trade and had never had ten *livres* at his disposal, any more than others of his family, when the war began. [His powers of resolution and gift of oratory made him the revolutionary idol of the multitude.] He had so many words and could speak so well that it was a marvel indeed. And for these reasons the weavers, fullers and croppers believed him and loved him so dearly that he could not say or command a thing without their doing it."

The *Annales de Gand* complete the portrait. Pierre de Coninc inspired a lively fear in the authorities by opposing them with an authority of his own, founded on popular feeling and demagogic appeal. "Pierre Coninc", they said, "had such influence with the weavers, fullers and other commoners—he won them over by the sweet and skilful words that he uttered so easily—that the royal *bailiff*, the magistrates and the magnates of Bruges dared attack neither him nor his partisans."

But Pierre de Coninc also had real political sense and breadth of vision. He was thus able to impart to the movement he had initiated a wider bearing. "He sent word", the *Chronicle* tells us, "to the commons of Ghent, who were in great fear because he had worked against the King, that if they were in need of 4,000 or 5,000 men, he was in a position to help them."

After the failure of a first insurrection, repressed by the troops of Philippe le Bel, Coninc had been freed from prison by the crowd and had driven the royal bailiff from Bruges. It was then that his great capacity revealed itself. He took in hand the government of the city and at the same time won over the men of Ghent and the Count to his side; extending to the whole of Flanders the movement which had been successful at Bruges. With Gui de Dampierre, Coninc shares the merit of having fused into a single cause, popular and national, the interests of the Count and of the commons. The patricians of Bruges had borne the brunt of the pillaging in 1301, and those of Ghent fared no better. Besieged in the castle by the craftsmen, some were burned alive, while others endured the humiliation of emerging between two ranks of their armed enemies. The survivors were banished.

The commoners' insurrection against the French contingent of Jacques de Châtillon, who was detested for the severity of the repression, turned into a national insurrection led by Coninc and Guillaume de Juliers, the Count's grandson. At daybreak on 17 May 1302 Châtillon's soldiers were surprised in their sleep—victims of the *Matines Brugeoises*—and the city fell once more into the hands of the commoners. This event lit the flames of rebellion at Ypres and indeed from the sea as far as Courtrai; and it was here that the popular rising, victorious in street fighting, triumphed over a royal army in the open country on 11 July 1302. Few such revolutions triumphed in the Middle Ages. With more rage than glory, and giving no quarter to their foes, a mob of commoners on foot had vanquished the most knightly army of the most powerful prince of the age. The reason for this defeat was social. It was because they despised the common mob which faced them, that the brilliant French knights charged it without taking the least precaution. Seven hundred golden spurs were collected after the battle and hung up in the Church of Notre-Dame de Courtrai; hence men often spoke of this affair as the "battle of the golden spurs". It was not only the King of France but the patricians who were vanquished. The commoners triumphed, at least for some years, even in cities like Ypres and Lille where no excesses had been committed.

It would however be a mistake to regard the events in Flanders as local or merely contingent. They were a manifestation both of a weakening in the structure of society and of

difficult circumstances. As between 1280 and 1290 corresponding events took place in the neighbouring principalities, and
these were not merely due to contagion. Jean Lejeune has
shown that the territory of Liége was rarely backward in
ebullience. At Huy in 1298 the mob had attacked the *maïeur
qui opprime les nôtres* (the mayor who oppresses our people);
it pillaged houses and drove the aldermen into exile. Agitation
spread to the countryside where the peasants of Fosses had
rioted to defend their customary rights in the forests. At Liége
itself, a year after Courtrai, the craftsmen with the secret
backing of the Bishop had only to show themselves "drawn up
and armed" to win a first victory: the suppression of an
unpopular tax, and representation in the city council. But this
was not the end. The agitation continued for nearly ten years,
and the trouble ended with an attempted *coup* on the night of
3 August 1312. Under cover of darkness a force of knights and
patricians from Huy, which had gained entry into the city
through the treachery of a plebeian leader and had reached the
market-place, set fire to the Butchers' Market-Hall. From every
side the workers swarmed in to the defence. The patricians
slowly retreated but found the gates closed against them. They
sought refuge in the Church of Saint-Martin where they were
burned to death. The bodies of 134 patricians, including ten of
the fourteen aldermen, were found among the ruins. This was
called *le mal Saint-Martin*. In the end the "Peace" of Angleur
(1313) formally registered the gains of the commoners. Henceforth no tax could be imposed at Liége, without the consent of
"all magnates, middle class and lower class, assembled for this
purpose". The power of hereditary castes was abolished and
entry to the magistrature was open to everyone.

Like causes producing like effects, Brabant had not been
spared, although hereditary offices were less closed than in
Flanders and replaced more easily from below. Even so there
was pillaging and assassination at Brussels in 1302; agitation
also at Louvain and Tirlemont. A regular battle took place at
Vilvorde where the victorious patricians buried the prisoners
alive. In Brabant therefore the commoners had still to await the
day of victory.

Even in Flanders, and after Courtrai, the craftsmen's victory was neither complete nor decisive. This can be explained by several circumstances: the patricians' and the prince's ability to react; the failure of the artisans to understand that their interests required collective co-operation; the internal rivalries between the crafts—between city- and country-weavers, between weavers, fullers and dyers; and successive crises affecting the drapers. In short, we must note some prolonged signs of social and professional disagreements. Common to the whole of the fourteenth century society was the crystallization of social groups. After the success of their revolt the crafts almost everywhere agreed to limit their numbers according to their special functions. Now, even if the list included the crafts which were most looked down on, this was to imprison men in definite categories, to limit their chances of promotion, and also to fix, if not to freeze, the modes of access to municipal office. At the same time the regularization of work became narrower and more rigorous in every profession; and the possibilities of rising to a mastership remained very slim for those who were not sons of a master. Thus, to the inevitable reaction of patricians anxious to recover lost privileges and to defend those that remained, were added the most varied grounds of misunderstanding between the artisans.

This was the situation at Ghent. Each craft seems to have worked only in its own interest. The reaction which took place there from 1319 to 1337, just before the Hundred Years War, benefited the newly rich *poorters* only because they were assisted by the little drapery crafts, especially the fullers; the latter being glad of a chance to humiliate, and get their own back on, the weavers. The weavers had the advantage of numbers, and the nature of their activities enabled them to control the work and wages of the fullers.

Although raised to power by an insurrection, Jacques van Artevelde was the opposite of a people's man. In taking the affairs of Ghent in hand, he no doubt intended to preserve the interests of the whole cloth industry from the effects of the Anglo-French war, because the fullers depended on that trade just as the great merchants did. The kind of "sacred union" formed in 1338 was to be an ephemeral affair, although Artevelde had associated the deans of the fullers and of the weavers with himself in the government of the city, but at bottom he despised workmen. The favour which he at first granted the weavers provoked the wrath of the fullers. On 3 May 1345, in the "Friday Market-Place", which was the centre of civic life, the members of the two crafts came into conflict. The weavers had the better of it, and won a pre-ponderant influence; but when Artevelde tried to free himself from the grasp of the "great craft", he signed his death-warrant. He was assassinated in a riot fomented by the weavers, towards 22 July 1345. This is how Froissart, following Jean le Bel, related the affair with his usual vivacity;

"Jacques d'Artevelde came to a window which looked out on the street where all the people were assembled. He asked them: 'Good people, what do you lack? Why are you so agitated?' They answered: 'We want to speak with you, so come down.' Then answered Jacques: 'And if I were there, what would you wish to say to me?'—'We wish thee to render account of the great treasure of Flanders which thou hast had, and raised, at thy will, for the past seven years; and to tell us what thou hast done with it and where put it.' Jacques d'Artevelde who saw that matters were not going as usual, thought to appease them with gentle words. He said: 'Good people, withdraw each of you to his house and in three days' time I will summon you and shall be able to render you such good account that you will be satisfied.' They answered with one voice: 'We will not wait so long. Come out of thy house and render account.' Jacques d'Artevelde considered that the affair was going ill, and that he was in danger of death: 'My lords', said he, 'stay there; I will come anon and speak with you.'

"It was then that Thomas Denis, the dean of the weavers, was the first to smite him on the head with an axe, and so struck him down."

The weavers did not enjoy their triumph for very long. The fullers were awaiting their hour. It struck on 13 January 1349. A little before this, the weavers of Ypres and Bruges had already been excluded by the members of the other crafts. But at Ghent, on "Good Tuesday", there was a horrible massacre of weavers, 6,000 victims according to a contemporary, Gilles Li Muisit, Abbot of Saint-Martin de Tournai.

The "wheel of fortune" however had not completed its turn. For a moment it had raised the weavers to the level of the *poorters*. This time their craft was struck off the roll of the three "members" of the bourgeoisie of Ghent; while at Bruges they were subjected to strict supervision. A certain number went into exile, endowing English industry with the addition of experienced craftsmanship. The power of the minor crafts was not to last, however. Vengeance fell on them ten years later and on the same spot. In 1350, in the "Friday Market-Place" of Ghent, the weavers massacred the fullers. For two years Flanders was a scene of bloodshed, which brought desolation to Ypres and Bruges, as it had to Ghent. The reaction was total. The fullers, reduced to the position of second-class citizens, lost the right to elect their dean; while ten years later they were practically excluded from the governmental reorganization of the crafts of Ghent. The "revolution of the crafts" had not benefited everyone. It had been thought to put an end to all these vengeances; but the future of social peace had been compromised.

It is none the less true that the transformation of municipal government at Ghent, as in the other cities, is a sign of the advantages which the craftsmen had won. The organization of the councils and the magistratures, as fixed in 1369, reflected the relative powers of the principal social groups. Thus, on the bench of the *Parchons*, a tribunal of first instance, representatives of the weavers sat in equal numbers (five) to those of the secondary crafts; while in face of the ten delegates of the crafts the *poorters* occupied only three seats. In the same way, for the appointment of the twenty-six aldermen, the influence of the deans of the two categories of crafts was preponderant; and they, on the expiration of their mandates, were habitually appointed as magistrates. Lastly, in the *Collace* or great council, the fifty-three crafts would have been assured of a majority, if the fear of demagogy had not restrained the new government from calling a meeting more often.

The constitution of Ghent is a significant example; very similar principles obtained in the other cities between Seine and Rhine, and even beyond. What varies from place to place is the number of crafts, the number of councils and magistrates, and the names they bear. Amiens had eighty "banners"; Lille twelve aldermen; Liége thirty-two crafts. Where the professional framework of the crafts was not as rigid as in the industrial centres of the north, the parochial divisions served as a base for the commoners' struggle to gain access to the city councils. Rouen offers a mixed example. Towards 1315–20 the grievances of the "lower class against the wealthy bourgeois" were associated with disagreements between the craftsmen, fullers and weavers against drapers. These quarrels had been embittered in 1316, when insults and even blows were exchanged during an interview with the Mayor, Vincent du Chastel, whose family had for long figured at the head of the government. Finally, the dispute which had been referred to the Exchequer, was entrusted to the royal commissioners. The records show us what grievances were aired and what solutions adopted in the Charter of 1321. The commoners complained of being kept out of the council. The commissioners admitted them, by deciding that the thirty-six "peers" should be chosen from among all the bourgeois, without exception by quarters and parishes, one third elected at a time and for a term of three years only. To break the solidarity of the patricians, it was forbidden for two near relatives to sit together on the council. The commoners obtained the assurance of an annual and public statement of the accounts, too often eluded up to that time, or made secretly between friends and relatives. Thus the old patrician government was broken, at least to the advantage of the lower middle-class. Rouen retained this system until the *Harelle* in 1383; though not without some jolts, because in 1345, and even more in 1358, the commoners accused the wealthiest bourgeois of not fairly applying the Charter.

In the south, the struggle, without changing its object which was access to the consulates, seems to have grown more bitter. In the thirteenth century, it had been mainly, apart from

Cahors, a conflict of influences. With the multiplication of subsidies, and various taxes and levies, it grew harsher. Cahors of course continued to draw attention. The rising of January 1336 was directed against the royal officials, and we cannot affirm that it had social causes. But in 1338 the "popular party" appointed procurators who reproached the consuls with remaining in charge too long, with making no statement of accounts, with assessing the salt-tax unfairly. . . . Tension remained great in 1339, and the elections of 1340 were difficult. At last at the beginning of 1341 an arbitrator gave judgement that, of the twelve consuls, five would have to be artisans, and two merchants. Even so the conflict went on.

It was about this time that in other cities too, the pressure of the *populares* led to definite arrangements, at least on paper. In 1328 Philippe VI ruled that the ten new consuls at Montauban should be co-opted every year by the retiring consuls, but that five should be *populares* and five bourgeois. At Foix, magnates, middle class and lower class formed three groups which appointed procurators; but in 1320 these groups came into conflict owing to the levy of a subsidy for the war in Flanders. It was then decided by arbitration that in future taxes should be assessed *à sol et livre*, and that a general survey of personal wealth should be drawn up—a task that should be assigned to sixteen of the inhabitants, eight of whom would be elected by citizens possessing less than 100 *livres*. In 1322 the men of Foix agreed that there should henceforth be six consuls and twenty-four councillors, one third of them from each of the three classes. The agreement was not well applied and in 1355 the number of consuls was reduced to four, one for the magnates, one for the lower class, and two for the middle class. It was also about 1330, no doubt, that a system was established at Castres, by virtue of which the rich, the middle class and the poor should be equally represented by a consul and six councillors. However, rumours of agitation, discontent and disturbance at elections came from towns as diverse as Sarlat and Pamiers.

*　　*　　*

In the Empire a series of conflicts arose at the beginning of the fourteenth century, and continued for over 100 years, between the patricians and the craftsmen. Mainly in dispute was access to the city councils. A first wave of insurrections, usually described by the word *Auflauf*, can be discerned from 1301 onwards, doubtless more or less influenced by events in the Netherlands. The craftsmen revolted, unsuccessfully as a rule, at Magdeburg in 1301, at Augsburg and Trier in 1303, at Speyer in 1304, at Strasbourg and Bremen in 1308, at Erfurt in 1310. From 1327 onward, a new series of urban "revolutions" took place. These often gave the craftsmen, at least for a time, some share in municipal government. This happened at Ulm in 1327, at Speyer and Ratisbon in 1330, at Mainz and Strasbourg in 1332, at Breslau in 1333, and after about 1350 disturbances became endemic.

Yet this chronological outline gives no complete picture of the various changes or of the factors which led to them. It would probably be best to select a few examples. What knowledge we have of them derives in general from a comparison between two groups of sources: firstly mention in the annals, often too sparse and distorted by partisanship; secondly, the *Schwörbriefe*, or charters of sworn agreement, descriptions of the civic constitutions established in settlement of the disputes.

At Strasbourg the patricians were far from being as homogeneous as might be suggested by the very general description we offered above. Nobles and burghers lived side by side and were jealous of each other, for in addition to the descendants of some seigneurial agents of the Bishop (*ministeriales*) and some rural nobles who had come to live in the city, there were a good number of new nobles. Following the disturbances of the great Interregnum, Rudolf of Hapsburg, elected King of the Romans in 1273, had ennobled a very large number of people in order to win personal adherents. Now he held possessions in Alsace, and was united by strong ties of friendship with the men of Strasbourg who profited greatly from his favour. The majority of these noble families were therefore of bourgeois origin. Their opposition to these rivals was therefore all the greater.

The nobles rich enough to have themselves equipped, namely the knights, wore golden spurs and enjoyed a prestige which they strove to maintain by an exceptional way of living. The squires (*Edelknechte*) being less well-off were less clearly to be distinguished from the bourgeois, but both groups were content to invest their capital in business concerns, without engaging in them as did the bourgeois. Philippe Dollinger has admirably described the spirit of this feudal aristocracy, and clarified the divergences between bourgeois and nobles. The wars in which they engaged, and the tournaments, obliged the nobles to absent themselves for periods more or less prolonged, and this inevitably weakened the sense of common interests with the city and its inhabitants which they had originally felt, and strengthened the more and more numerous bonds which attached them to their feudal superiors and to the rural nobles to whom they were related. Their chivalric ideal manifest in, among other habits, the custom of banqueting at a round table, a custom imported from France,[1] led them not only to despise activities which they considered unworthy of their rank, but also to set above all other considerations the honour of their lineage, even at the cost of their own interests. Their pride made it hard for them to endure patiently the necessary vexations of city life, such as the interdiction of bearing arms and the military and fiscal burdens. They were persuaded that their noble birth placed them above regulations and conferred on them the right to privileges, to dignities, to positions of command, even to feminine favour, which partly explains the number of rapes recorded by the chroniclers and so exasperating to the bourgeois. These nobles, in short, were growing conscious of the incompatibility of city life with the life of chivalry.

A small place only in the conduct of public business was conceded by the nobles to the burghers; and it was by co-optation that the former had perpetuated their power. "Every year twenty-one councillors, including four burgomasters, were appointed, and no other burgher, however worthy or deserving,

---

[1] The round table mentioned in the legend of King Arthur.

could enter the council, unless he was nominated by the holder of a seat in it." So writes the chronicler, Closener. In 1319 all the councillors were knights; in 1330, out of twenty-four councillors, five were burghers; in 1331, four.

It was however dissensions among the nobles which brought about the fall of this patrician class, a fall obviously desired by most of the population. A series of quarrels, leading often to bloodshed, divided the two noble families, the Zorans and the Müllenheims which dominated the city (noble though of burgher origin) so much so that thereafter they were called "the Montagues and Capulets of Strasbourg". In the course of a round table banquet in 1332 a brawl among the diners became so violent as to disturb public order. Burghers and artisans at once came to an agreement to take over the government. Together they adopted measures for security and organized armed patrols. The council was now "shared" between twenty-five representatives of the artisans and twenty-five elected "patricians"—the latter all burghers. For three years the nobles were excluded. When readmitted, they had a right to eight seats as against fourteen for the burghers. But the power of the burghers derived still more from the positions they occupied: those of burgomaster (four, then two appointed for life) and especially that of *ameister*. Hitherto the representative of the crafts, in a more or less honorary capacity, he now became their effective leader, with a place on the council. It was to him in the first instance that the people took an oath. This veritable "Head of the City" (P. Dollinger) was elected for life by the burgher and artisan members of the council; and he was regularly a burgher. Thus the alliance between burghers and artisans against the nobles had brought appreciable advantages for the artisans, though it was mainly the burghers who had profited from it.

Their preponderance did not last. The nobles resented it and the artisans were discontented. The appointment of magistrates for life, first planned as a means of excluding the nobles, created a new monopoly which provoked increasing jealousies. In 1346 the Swarber family alone held the offices of burgomaster and *ameister*, and a chronicler points to Peter Swarber, the *ameister* as having, "by his power become odious to the nobles and the plebeians". This bourgeois regime was challenged at the first opportunity, in 1349. The council having pronounced against the massacre of the Jews in the city, which had just taken place, the opposition accused it of venality. It was Jewish gold, people said, which had corrupted the councillors. Armed gatherings of artisans led by nobles summoned the burgomasters and the *ameister* to resign, which they did without a struggle. The council was dissolved, Peter Swarber exiled and his property confiscated.

The new charter registered the new equilibrium. The council contained eleven nobles, seventeen burghers and twenty-eight artisans. The satisfaction received by the nobles was rather illusory. They could again share in the election of burgomasters. But the latter, who were to be four in number, were renewable annually, nor could they counterbalance the power of the *ameister* who was henceforward elected only by the artisans. The latter appointed a butcher. They were to remain in power until 1789.

Their preponderance increased in the years that followed. The *ameister* reduced the burgomasters to merely honorary functions—to being "lackeys", it was murmured. The Council reduced the judicial attributes of the old burgher law-courts. In particular the artisans separated themselves more clearly from the burghers. Not only were wealthy crafts, hitherto mingled with the patricians, now established as self-governing corporations, for example, the boatmen, the corn-merchants and the goldsmiths; but a measure adopted in 1362 ordained that "every individual, sprung from an artisan family, however rich and powerful he might grow, and even if he had married the daughter of a knight, should remain, he and his descendants, among the artisans". This was to dry up at source the recruitment of a bourgeois patrician class. Deprived in this way of its most active elements the latter made common cause with the nobles in a "fellowship of defeat". When some sixty nobles left the city in 1419 in order to disorganize the government and dictate their terms for coming back, they were followed by the thirty most highly respected burghers. But after two years of skirmishing, they had to submit or go into exile; and thereafter the council contained no more than fourteen patricians (nobles and burghers) as against twenty-eight artisans. The victory of the latter was final.

The main interest of the Strasbourg experience is that it offers us an example of the interplay of three forces—nobles, bourgeois and artisans—and so foreshadows certain revolutions of the eighteenth and nineteenth centuries.

*　　　*　　　*

Events at Zürich were clearly influenced by the Strasbourg "revolution", and they also reveal the part played by the nobility. But here the predominance of one man was so marked that one wonders if Zürich was imitating the Italian system of *podestàs*. One observes at the same time the intervention of the Hapsburgs.

Excellently situated as it was on the routes leading from Italy across the Splügen and Saint-Gothard to the Rhine valley, the city had in the thirteenth century become an important centre of commerce. It had once been the seat of a royal palace, and in the eleventh century emperors and dukes of Suabia had lived there. It also sheltered a notable aristocracy. The latter had at first dominated the council, but in 1291 they had had to accept a position in which they were outnumbered by the burghers by two to one. But the burgher patricians soon closed their ranks to new members: five only entered the council between 1300 and 1312, and none after that. One can well understand the coalition of malcontents which led to the explosion of 1336.

This rising is known to us from a brief mention in the city *Chronicle*: "In the year of our Lord 1336 occurred the insurrection of Zürich on the seventh day of June. Rudolf Brun became first burgomaster, and the new council and corporations were established. The former councillors were unseated and driven from the city." The sworn constitution which was promulgated in July liquidated the old regime. There was no longer to be a "small council of four knights and eight of the greater burghers". Former councillors and their sons were excluded from the new council and corporations. The many abuses of which they had been guilty were held, officially, to justify these measures: "They had shamefully and severely treated the poor folk whom necessity had obliged to appeal to them. The money of the burghers and the patrimony of the city were dilapidated, but they rendered no account of it to anyone."

The new council was very much larger. On the one hand it numbered thirteen patricians, of whom six were nobles and seven burghers (which shows that the nobles had almost regained equality of representation); and on the other, representatives of the thirteen corporations, each provided with a banner. The crafts, far more numerous here, were grouped in very complex and skilful patterns. Thus the mercers formed a group by themselves; the tradesmen who dealt with food and drink were divided into four groups: innkeepers and wine-tasters associated with painters and harness-makers; bakers and millers; butchers; gardeners, oil-merchants and pedlars. Five corporations only were formed of real artisans: weavers and fullers of wool; weavers and fullers of linen; smiths, makers of swords and breastplates; pewterers and barbers; cobblers. The carpenters, masons, timber-merchants, coopers and vine-growers were grouped into a single corporation. One should not be too much impressed by the enlargement of the electoral body, because the real artisans were rather swamped by the other trades.

Far more important was the exorbitant authority conferred on the man who had led the insurrection. Rudolf Brun was descended from an old noble family—agents, no doubt, of the former overlords—as attested at the first meetings of the council. The office of burgomaster was created for him; he was appointed for life and the constitution even designated the four men from among whom, on his death, his successor was to be chosen. He governed with the assistance of the council; but as its membership was renewed every six months, it could scarcely obstruct him. It was moreover Brun who, assisted this time by six electors delegated by the retiring council, chose the thirteen new patrician councillors. The corporations appointed

their own thirteen representatives, but in the event of disagreement regarding the election of the head of a corporation, the
burgomaster was to intervene. It was to the burgomaster that
the burghers of Zürich were to take the oath, and promise
"to be subject to him and obedient as long as he lived". On the
other hand he himself swore "faithfully to guard corporations
and burghers, and preserve their bodies and property, and to
judge them, poor and rich, with equal justice". Behind a
deliberately democratic exterior, this was the dictatorship of one
man—a representative of the old nobility—which was assured.

In fact, the revolution of 1336 was followed by a long period
of disturbances. A number of those who had emigrated, or
been banished, were received by Count Rudolf of Hapsburg
at Rapperswil, a lake-side town less than twenty miles from
Zürich; while others settled in the little towns and castles round
the city. And now a minor war was waged for several years.
Finally most of the exiles were permitted to return. Several of
them, however, plotted with some of the malcontents whom the
new regime had alienated. Their conspiracy was broken up in
1350, when seventeen of the rebels were killed. Of the prisoners
eighteen were broken on the wheel and nineteen others
beheaded. The more fortunate of the conspirators managed to
flee, but the city confiscated their property. There followed a
war with the Hapsburgs, and Zürich was besieged three times.
Peace was at last made in 1355, but negotiations with the
exiles continued until 1368. These troubles greatly hampered
the city's trade, and further damaged the economic situation
which was already deteriorating; so much so that Brun's
"revolution" is regarded as a turning-point in the history of
Zürich.

The example of Nuremberg reveals the confusion between
social and political factors. The city had received many favours
from King Ludwig of Bavaria. He had even agreed that on the
decease of the sovereign, the castle should be handed over to the
burghers on condition that they restored it to the successor
whom they recognized. In fact when Ludwig died, the city
recognized Charles IV of Luxembourg, who now (2 November
1347) confirmed its privileges and even made a short stay

there on his way to Bohemia (1348). On 4 June, however, the *populares* rose in rebellion and accepted his rival, the Margrave Ludwig of Brandenburg. That the conflict was of a social kind is certain; the principal rebels were the smiths, led by a certain Rudel Geisbart: Nuremberg was after all one of the main centres of the metallurgical industry. The conspirators took an oath of union and called upon the burghers to swear fidelity to the new council and its two burgomasters who were changed every four months. Some of the burghers agreed, but very many fled and the rebels arrested those clerics who tried to follow their example. Thanks to the insurrection the crafts were now organized.

But a struggle was inevitable. Charles IV authorized the burgher exiles to form a league. Inside the city, the financial situation quickly deteriorated, and the new regime attempted to meet this by seizing the property of the Jews. However, the harmony between the various crafts was far from perfect; we can presume that the butchers defected on account of advantages which they subsequently obtained. The game now became political. On 26 May 1349 Ludwig of Brandenburg recognized Charles IV as King, on obtaining a promise of amnesty for the rebels. Repression now went ahead. Five men elected by the exiled burghers formed a league of opposition, and in September re-entered the city together with the King. The latter pardoned the rebels on certain conditions, but insisted that the property of the exiles should be restored. He dissolved the council, cancelled its enactments and had a new council elected exclusively by the burgher families. This was practically a return to the *status quo*. It is true that in 1370 eight representatives of the crafts were admitted to the council, but in a consultative capacity only, and it was the King who chose them. "The people attends to its business; in public affairs it is not too much concerned": such is the melancholy conclusion of a chronicler. Nuremberg was to continue to be governed by patricians.

These few examples are enough to suggest how varied were the situations and the outcome. To generalize beyond these particular cases requires great prudence; though one must insist on the widespread character of the conflicts, which moreover continued in the fifteenth century. Virtually no town, whether great or small, was not affected on widely varying occasions. There was no lack of violence. We have mentioned some examples, and could continue. At Magdeburg in 1301 ten heads of the crafts were burned alive; at Cologne in 1371 thirty-three weavers were executed and several hundreds banished. Dollinger concludes:

"On the whole the conflicts[1] were less bitter and the repressions less bloody than in the Flemish and Italian cities where one can say that massacre was an element of daily life at the end of the Middle Ages. This moderation is partly explained by the intervention of the kings who very often imposed arbitration and reconciled the opposing parties; still more no doubt by the fact that social disparities were less strongly marked in Germany than in Flanders or Italy. It is of interest to note that the corporations did not, at least at the outset, attempt a brutal elimination of the patrician body, but sought only to obtain a share in municipal government. Their victory did not generally involve massive expulsions; and for this reason hatreds were less inexpiable."

Beyond the variety of situations and the impression of confusion arising from this, it is still possible to discern three groups among the German cities. Some of them, especially the Hanseatic towns of the north, retained a patrician regime. Despite ephemeral successes, the crafts failed to win any durable influence in politics. This can be explained by the commercial activity which maintained a prosperous patrician class constantly renewing itself. The same cause also operated in several cities of the centre and south, like Breslau, Leipzig, Ratisbon and Nuremberg—where there existed however an advanced artisan class, engaged in the metallurgical industry. But commercial activity was not enough to preserve most of the Rhineland cities from more or less notable changes. Among the patrician cities one may also mention those with less external

[1] i.e. in the cities of the Empire.

trade and in which the rural economy exerted a great influence, like Metz.

In contrast to the "patrician" north, the south-west may well appear "democratic". It was in the cities of Suabia, Alsace and Switzerland that the crafts were most definitely successful, even if their victory often came in stages. We have seen how this happened at Strasbourg; in the same way the patricians at Freiburg-im-Breisgau, at Worms and at Bâle retained a more or less notable representation on the council. The crafts were more radical in other places, where the councils represented them exclusively. At Ravensburg towards 1346 and at Speyer in 1349 the patricians were reduced to forming a corporation of their own, with no more rights than any of the others. At Magdeburg after 1300 and at Cologne in 1396 the patricians were obliged to register individually in the various corporations. Cologne deserves special attention here. The patricians dominated the place until very late, despite the support given to the crafts on some occasions by the Archbishop. The importance of Rhineland commerce, the strength of family bonds among the patricians and the cohesion of their ranks owing to the club of the *Richerzeche*—these factors explain the long maintenance of the *status quo*. It was only in 1396 after a series of violent conflicts that the crafts won a complete victory. The *Richerzeche* was abolished, and all the burghers, whether belonging to crafts or not, were divided into twenty-two corporations (*Gaffeln*). These elected thirty-six councillors who increased their numbers by co-optation, to a total of fifty-one. This system of election which has been described by H. Planitz as "truly democratic", was to be imitated by various cities, like Mulhouse and Mainz, in the fifteenth century.

In a few cities the patricians and the crafts shared power between them, each group having the same number of seats on the council. This was the situation at Haguenau in 1331, at Constance in 1370 and at Vienna in 1396. But the equilibrium was transitory, one side or the other gaining the upper hand.

Therefore, in most of the German cities, with the exception of the Hanseatic, the political "revolution" had ended by giving the crafts towards 1400 a more or less complete share in

political power. But was this really a revolution? We must ask
the question for the moment, but we shall return to it when
we try to draw up the balance-sheet for Europe as a whole
during this troubled period.

*   *   *

In the Italian cities the existence of an old aristocracy, the
magnati, gives a peculiar character to the movement which
brought the business aristocracy of the *grassi* into power. The
grassi were really the upper layer of the *popolo*; but between them
and the *popolani minuti* the distance was considerable. "Rabble",
is what Pagnozzo degli Strozzi said of the *minuti*; while another
patrician, Caffo degli Agli, was to use even less academic
language: "*Questi arteficiali! de la merda!*" At the beginning of
the fourteenth century therefore the promotion of the *minuti*
was not at hand. However the support they lent the *grassi*
in their gains from the *magnati* allowed them some hopes for the
future. Discontent among them, if not rebellion, was however
smouldering and came into the open on occasion when the
oligarchy was shaken by a domestic crisis or a risky war.

In 1310 the Venetian Republic had lost a war which she had
undertaken to subjugate Ferrara, Pope Clement V having
formed against her a league which had all the air of a crusade.
The *Serenissima* was therefore obliged to abandon her ambitions,
and for the Doge Pietro Gradenigo who had conducted the
war, and for the patrician government which he represented,
the loss of prestige was serious. Since 1297 the "closing" of the
Maggior Consiglio to any new member had definitely established
an oligarchical regime. During the thirteenth century the
Popular Assembly had been gradually deprived of its attributes
to the advantage of the hundred members of the Great Council;
and the latter had thus become the fount of all activity, political,
administrative and economic. From it everything issued; to it
everything returned. The Signoria, which governed by means
of the Doge and a Small Council of six members, emanated
from the Great Council. It was also the latter which delegated
their powers to the court of the *Quaranzia*, to the senate and to

all the officials entrusted with administration, justice and the various sectors of the economy. To belong to the Great Council was therefore to share in supreme power. Now there had been a constant effort and tendency to reserve this dignity to the members of commercial families established prior to 1250. Co-optation was organized by a complicated system whereby some were elected, and others chosen by lot. Finally Gradenigo obtained the adoption of a rule, provisional at first (1297), then declared perpetual (1299). The renewal of the Great Council was only a fiction, since all the retiring members of the past four years re-entered it as of right, also since to them were added the members of the Small Council, of the *Quaranzia* (Council of Forty Wise Men), and of the senate, and since the new councillors were co-opted by the old. In spite of its total membership of 2,500, the Great Council represented no more than 200 old and wealthy families.

In 1299 however a popular movement was formed with the purpose of overthrowing Doge Gradenigo, who was detested; but this failed. Later in 1310 a new and different conspiracy planned a suprise attack on the Doge's palace. This also failed; and its only result was an aggravation of the oligarchic system, matched by the addition of the famous *Consiglio dei dieci* (Council of the Ten). The failure of the plot was due to the fact that the existing regime enjoyed the tacit complicity of the people at large, because the latter benefited in various degrees from the commercial prosperity of the Republic, which was competently maintained by the men in power. Moreover the leaders of the conspiracy were far from being men of the people. Marco Querini and Baiamonte Tiepolo were patricians, and Tiepolo's name figures on the list of former Doges. Rather than a democratic movement, this conspiracy simply expressed the rancour of men excluded from the council by those who were monopolizing access to it.

One must also regard as a settlement of accounts between patricians the failure of Marino Faliero's conspiracy, forty-five years later. It is hard to conceive of a Doge of eighty taking such risks in order to retain power to the end of his days. He seems to have plotted like a young man, since the plan was to destroy a number of senators in what would have been a blood-bath—liquidating a good part of the patrician class. The secret leaked out because too many people were in it. The many accomplices were hanged and the old man himself was beheaded.

This drama inspired a play by Byron; but the story is informative in two ways. It exemplifies the patricians' fear of seeing a personal power established through an alliance between the Doge and the populace, and it reveals the impossibility of transforming the State without the support of the men in power, and of course, of changing it against them. In order to see the development of democratic movements, and to witness really "popular" revolutions, it is to other cities that we must turn.

It is true that the merchant aristocracy was, as a rule, quite strongly installed in power. At Siena, for example, the patrician regime stood firm until 1355, though not without difficulty. Back in 1280 it had not been easy to establish a stable government. The members of the council which ruled the city might be named "governors and defenders", or "priors and defenders" or simply "priors"; they might number fifteen, nine, six, eighteen and again nine. This made little difference. The principle was adopted and then fixed by statute in 1309–10, that they had to be "merchants of the city of Siena or members of the middle class", and must not be "either knights or judges or notaries or doctors". The system operated therefore through the agency of middle-class men, and co-opting remained the rule: all of which, obviously, was not to the taste of the nobles or of the minor Arts. Every modification of the names and numbers of the councillors corresponded to a period of disturbance, sometimes violent and always complex. The lower class, which often bore the brunt of the riots, was often allied with one or other family of the merchant aristocracy which was seeking support against commercial rivals or against another faction. This, for example, was how the Tolomei proceeded against the Salimbeni in 1315, when there was street-fighting. Three years later the *Signoria* was assailed by the people to the cry of "Death to the Nine". But it was not easy to dislodge the middle class from the seat of government.

At Genoa, competition between the Guelph families (the Fieschi and Grimaldi) and the Ghibellines (Doria and Spinola) for occupancy of the two offices of "Captains of the Republic" (1270–1308) made the political regime singularly fragile. The *popolo* actually constituted a single body, the "Society of the Holy Apostles Simon and Jude", which was headed by an "abbot" assisted by a council. This made it logical for the *popolani* to be led to arbitrate between the rivals by lending their support to one faction or another. Such an interplay of forces and influences risked leading to a one-man dictatorial *Signoria*. This nearly happened in 1309, when Opizzino Capitano was proclaimed perpetual rector of the people. After this, a new mixed system was tried, in which power was shared between six nobles and six *popolani*, who formed a council of twelve governors, similar to the College of Priors in Florence. In reality the Emperor and the House of Anjou proved to be factors of greater weight than social antagonisms. The latter however occasioned the events of 1339. The silk-workers and the seamen—a turbulent folk—expelled the Guelph nobles from all their offices and conferred power on Simone Boccanegra, a member of a Ghibelline family which had governed Genoa in the thirteenth century. This affair had begun with a mutiny of the sailors against the galley-masters. The rioting multitude saluted Simone with the usual name of "Abbot of the People". As he refused it, they cried out: *"Signore, Signore, Doga, Doga."* By conferring on Simone the ducal dignity for life, Genoa preceded Florence by a few years in the experience of a personal *Signoria*. At the same time the nobles were excluded, and the power of the middle class, assisted by the lower classes, was so to speak consecrated.

At a date earlier than other cities Florence had recognized the regime of the *popolo*, although the actual institutions were extremely complex. Already in 1284 the Communal Council had laid down the principle that every decision should be debated in the presence of the *magnati*, the *popolani* and the artisans. Nine years later, the Decrees of Justice aroused many hopes by codifying decisions previously taken in favour of the accession to power of the *popolani* and by eliminating the nobles. The latter, that is those of whom a relative had reached the status of knighthood for twenty years or more, or even those who lived nobly, were excluded from any public office and regarded as second-class citizens. The minor Arts had recognized a benefactor in the promoter of these laws, a noble of ancient stock, who however belonged to the craft of the *Calimala* and had gone over to the people's side. This was Giano della Bella, who governed Florence for two years (1293–5). Giovanni Villani has described him as "the most loyal of men, seeking to promote the public weal"; and he calls him *caporale del popolo minuto*. Giano however met with the usual fate of those popular leaders who find themselves unable to keep all their promises. On a day of riots, some of the crafts deserted him. He was prosecuted, and went into exile to Paris.

The eviction of Giano benefited only the upper stratum of the *popolo*, namely the *grassi*, who were interested in preventing the lower class, or *magri*, from attaining equality with them. At this moment when the regime of the "second *popolo*" is beginning to take shape, it may be useful to pause a moment in order to distinguish its main features. The *popolo* was first of all, the ensemble of the organized crafts: the seven major Arts (judges and notaries, doctors, money-changers, furriers, drapers, the Art of silk or *Por Santa Maria*, the Art of wool or *Calimala*) constituting the *popolo grasso*, that is the *grassi*. The five middle Arts (butchers, cobblers, smiths, carpenters and dealers in second-hand clothes) were the *magri*. Finally, the nine Arts established since 1289 (wholesale wine-merchants, innkeepers, dealers in salt, oils and cheese, tanners, *lormiers*, lock-smiths, curriers, joiners and cabinet-makers, bakers) received the name of minor Arts. Inside the various Arts, all did not enjoy equal rights. At the bottom of the hierarchy were the *sottoposti* (subordinates), that is, the workmen.

The Arts constituted the basis of the municipal structures, for the reality of power belonged henceforth to the *popolo*. The *Signoria*, that is the priors and the gonfalonier of justice, derived from it. The priors (six, later eight) were renewed very frequently (every two months after 1328) by a mixed system in which selection by drawing lots was combined with election by an electoral college composed of "prud'hommes" and of the consuls, or priors, of the twelve major and middle Arts. The priors thus chosen were always *grassi*. The gonfalonier of justice was also selected from among the *grassi* by the gonfaloniers of the major Arts. A council of nineteen assisted the the *Signoria*. The Captain of the People was also assisted by councils, one of which contained the consuls of the twenty-one Arts; the captain was always a noble. Hence the ancient commune now retained little more than the functions of police and administration, which had devolved upon the *Podestà*, on his council and on the communal council.

In 1309 the predominance of the *grassi* was still further reinforced by the establishment of the *Ufficio della Mercanzia* (Office of Merchandise), invested with supreme competence in, and jurisdiction over, commercial affairs and controlled by the five principal major Arts (*Calimala, Por Santa Maria,* wool, foreign exchange, grocery).

A truly parallel power was in fact exercised by the Guelph party. Endowed with a solid structure, with councils and captains composed of influential businessmen, without excluding the nobles, this party not only exercised control over the direction of policy; it was also, prior to the *Tumulto dei Ciompi*, a decisive instrument for the maintenance of the influence of the richest men over the government.

The Florentine Constitution seems then to have been a very empirical affair. It was elaborated little by little, at irregular moments, under the pressure of circumstances and movements of opinion. Hence, it was in perpetual mutation, almost in a state of permanent revolution. When the situation required it, the assembly of the people could appoint an exceptional commission invested with *balìa*, that is, it was entrusted with all powers of legislation and execution, the powers of the priors being suspended. On the other hand the institutions were so devised that the *grassi* could reserve to themselves the real direction of public business. Political problems and social problems were closely interwoven, and the woof of political life was woven by an effort of the "middle" group of citizens, and then of the *magri*, to secure a voice in the conduct of public business, an effort opposed as strenuously by the *grassi* to keep them out of it.

Even greater was the effort to prevent the lowest class from being able to use their only effective weapon, namely union among themselves. About 1292 some merchants asked the priors to punish the artisans' insolence, while strict laws were passed to prevent their raising their heads. In 1335 *Por Santa Maria* (the Art of Silk) forbade any coalitions, using arguments they found in St Paul. The Art of Wool, on its side, increased the difficulty of access to the offices of consul, which for that matter the *sottoposti* had no chance of reaching in 1338. The dyers, who were the most numerous and restive workers in this branch of the textile trade, were subjected to special supervision, because the quality of the fabrics which made this Art so famous depended on their work. This supervision was exercised by a special official, a foreigner (*forestiere*) like the *podestà* and, on that ground, impartial, at least in theory, but docile to the councils of the craft.

The constant anxiety of the major Arts was to keep the system of the crafts closed, for the benefit of their members. The system in fact was in danger of being shaken loose by any crisis, internal or external. We saw this in Venice at the time of the war with Ferrara. It was also the case at Florence, at the beginning of the fourteenth century when the two factions of the Guelph party came into collision, the "Whites" and the "Blacks", representing respectively the radical and the moderate tendencies. We know that Dante was exiled because he was a "White". The merchant patricians feared lest a man of ambition might take advantage of faction rivalries to seize power for himself, with the help of the *magri*: that is why, in 1304, they thwarted Corso Donati, the head of the "Black" faction. The struggle between Blacks and Whites involved social interference, indirectly, through the opposition of social groups and owing to the government's policy towards Pisa and Lucca.

It is in this connection that one should regard the short

period of the dictatorship of Gautier de Brienne, Duke of Athens (1342–3), as a second stage in the "revolution of the crafts". Gautier had been appointed as an arbitrator by King Robert of Naples, at the request of the Signoria; but he was just as much the man of the minor Arts. Stefani's chronicle represents the dyers and the carders as his "favourites". He created two new Arts for them, and, to give effect to their complaints, he tried to limit the arbitrary procedure of the weavers in the matter of wages, and to promote a more even-handed justice. He fell owing to a new insurrection provoked by the *grassi*, who were still very powerful. But for the major Arts, the alarm had been terrible. More than 230 great palaces had been set on fire; Stefani calls the affair a *cosa orribilissima*. The problem had been postponed, not solved. But the victory of the "middle" group over the *grassi* inevitably invited a revolt of the "lower" against the "middle" who had now come into power. The quarrel was to smoulder for a generation and burst into flames thirty-five years later in the *Tumulto dei Ciompi*.

*   *   *

The rural community has always been slower than the town to become conscious of its situation and its grievances. This consciousness, growing silently and secretly, was more violent in the end. France had witnessed in the very age of Saint Louis the agitation of the shepherds (*pastoureaux*), due to poverty. One must in fact distinguish between outbreaks of fury on the part of the unfortunate—outbreaks sudden, incoherent and suppressed without further consequence—and, on the other hand, deeper and calculated movements which leave lasting memories, once the flames they kindle have been extinguished.

From the beginning of the thirteenth century in England the peasants were in a state of unrest. Both the royal and the manorial records are exceptionally abundant, enabling us to observe definite facts, which may indeed have occurred in other countries where the records have been lost. England was at that time producing wheat and other cereals in abundance, and the lords were seeking to increase the yield from their lands; encouraged by the rise in prices, they exported the surplus. With this in view they did not hestitate to exact further service from their tenants. From the "villains" or serfs they could do so legally. The "villains" had to pay special dues (*merchet* for permission to marry the serf of another lord; and *leyrwite* for extra-marital association); they could not dispose of their land or stock, except by cession in the manorial court. They could not move from the village except by the lord's permission. Their goods and their persons were the lord's property. Above all, their services were not fixed, as were those of the free tenant. One could repeat the no doubt exaggerated formula of a jurist by saying that the "villain" did not know one day what his lord might ask of him on the morrow.

Of this status of "villainage", which remained widespread in England, the lords found it to their interest to make the maximum use, and even to extend it to free peasants. Here they encountered a resistance all the more obstinate as the free tenants had acquired a modest affluence by raising crops of their own and selling the grain. These well-to-do peasants regarded the lord's pretensions as unendurable; they made common cause with the poor peasants, who were defending their "vital minimum", and put their knowledge and resources into the struggle. It was this union among the peasants which explains the intensity of the struggle, and the very abundance of the records preserved.

The tenants had recourse to the royal courts to establish their status as free men and to condemn the pretensions of the lords. This was done in 1224 by a certain William FitzAndrew, whose lawsuit was carefully noted by Henry de Bracton, the contemporary jurist, thanks to whom we know about it. But the Abbot of Battle, who wanted to double the services due from William, forced him to recognize that all the other tenants were villains, and that he had a cousin who was one; so the court ruled in favour of the Abbot. These individual lawsuits had the less chance of success as the courts were, on the whole, more favourable to the lords.

So collective action soon began to appear. The manors which had belonged to the royal demesne, and which the King had diverted, for example to bestow them elsewhere, benefited from a recognized right. The new lord could not increase the amount of service which before the alienation had been required by the King. To prove the soundness of their case, the peasants could have it established that their manor belonged to the demesne at the time of *Domesday Book*, the great inquiry to which William the Conqueror had proceeded in 1086. Now in 1278 the villains of the Prior of Harmondsworth in Middlesex, without denying their status, claimed this protection; but their manor did not figure in the *Domesday Book*, and the court declared that the Prior could exact what dues and services he liked.

More simply, the peasants could get their free status recognized. The manor of Mears Ashby, near Northampton, had been acquired by a lord who, for seven years, had proceeded according to custom; then he had tried to raise the tax, but the tenants had forced him, we do not know how, to abandon the attempt, a little before his death. His widow renewed the attempt, and the case was referred to the royal court at Northampton in 1261. Such appeals to the courts must have been fairly common. In 1278 a jury declared that the tenants of the manor of Stoughton, in Leicestershire, were descended from villains, and condemned them. We know about this case, not only from the court records but from a curious poem, written no doubt by a canon of Leicester, to amuse himself at the expense of the plaintiffs and to celebrate the success of the Abbot. He depicts the peasants as "singing and laughing aloud" when setting out, and in tears on their return. Yet a "clear-sighted advocate" had warned them:

"Peasant William, tell me your case, I pray.
I think you were mad to bring it to court.
You don't see clearly; to despise one's lord is to be guilty.
I don't counsel you to plead against your lord:
You will be vanquished, peasant, you who wish to vanquish
   your lord.

You must bear what the custom of the land requires of
you.
Twice six bearded jury men, summoned as guarantors of
justice,
And ready to take oath,
Will declare against you that you were a serf. . . ."

This is an allusion to the jury system at work in the royal
courts; but was not the jury sensitive to pressure from the lord?
In any event, the canon concludes severely: "What can the
serf do, and his son after him, except serve?" More than once
the lord must have intimidated the jury. We can presume that
he did, when we hear of peasants abandoning their case, which
however they had brought before a royal court.

The daily contest between lords and peasants appears even
more prominently in the archives of the manorial courts. The
latter punished refusal of service, and service badly rendered.
Between 1279 and 1311 the court of Ramsey Abbey gave no
fewer than 146 judgements in this sense. Sometimes the
peasants proceeded to acts of violence, as in the trouble at the
Manor of Harmondsworth, mentioned above. The tenants
invaded the Mayor's house, made away with the charters and
threatened to burn everything. Sometimes, too, the resistance
lasted for a long time. Between 1309 and 1327 the tenants
of the various manors which the Norman Abbey of Le Bec
owned in England, revolted in succession, appealed to the King,
and refused work.

It is true that the peasants did not always encounter a
"combative lord". Towards 1330 the Prior of Christ Church in
Canterbury, when appealed to by his tenants at Bocking Hall in
Essex, formally and in writing disavowed his steward who had
committed various abuses, for example by demanding services
in excess of those which were customary. But one wonders
whether the many promises given on this occasion proved
useful. At the beginning of the fourteenth century the peasants
had recourse more and more to "conspiracies", and established
a common fund to assist them in the struggle. Certain agitators
encouraged the villains to refuse a particular piece of work.

Some tenants who had been imprisoned were freed by main force. And so the storm-clouds were gathering on the horizon, a distant prelude to the tempest of 1381.

Of quite another kind were the disturbances that took place between 1304 and 1307 in the Val Sesia in northern Italy. Historians are still arguing about their exact nature and bearing. Fra Dolcino, the outstanding figure in this agitation, belonged to the region, and it was in these Alpine valleys that he and his companions had taken refuge against the Inquisition. More than fourteen hundred partisans lived on the country and were joined by sympathizers, attracted by a preacher who announced the abolition of oppressive hierarchies and the return to an evangelical society, herald of a new golden age; but first of all it was necessary to eliminate the rich and overcome Antichrist. Dolcino belonged to the sect of the Apostolic friars who were then proliferating all over Italy. Some historians think that the movement may have arisen from great economic and social tension between the landowners and a multitude of peasants too numerous for the soil to maintain. Other writers think that there was no particular tension in that region which would make it receptive to such sermons. In any case, the Piedmontese valleys became permanent places of refuge for heretics: it was in them that the "apostolic" current found its first centres and its last refuges. But its features were not specifically rural. Recruited among the lower middle-class townsfolk and the fairly well-to-do peasants, as also among the poorest, it was presumably a religious movement, with some social connection, rather than a really social uprising. Whatever possible parallels may be found between the ephemeral and tragic drama of Dolcino and the Chiliasts' movement in 1420 in Bohemia, this episode was evidently a limited one, inspired by Utopian dreams.

It was a different matter with the insurrection on the coastal plain of Flanders twenty years later. From 1323 to 1328 a cruel civil war devastated the country round Bruges and Ypres, without spreading north to the Waes district or south towards Ghent, whose rivalry with Bruges led it into the opposite camp.

The insurrection, mainly of peasants, had begun with gatherings in villages and attacks on the country gentry and the Count's officials. It then spread to the cities, Bruges taking the lead and Ypres remaining one of the last centres of rebellion. News of the war resounded far and wide, even in Italy, where Giovanni Villani, in his *Istorie Fiorentine*, compared it with the agitations in Florence. To estimate its social significance and true importance, we also dispose of judicial documents, notably lists of properties confiscated when the rebellion was suppressed. It was in response to the Count's appeal that the King of France intervened and, on the battle-field of Cassel, on 23 August 1328, overcame the insurgents who had thought to repeat their fathers' success at Courtrai. Documents which have been discovered since Henri Pirenne analysed these events (1900), enable us to describe more clearly the outstanding features of the affair.

It is evident that the movement could not have been so vast and important if it had not affected the mass of the population. Its causes are a proof of this. It was not a prolongation of the effects of the great famine of 1315–17. It seems, however, according to the writer who continued Guillaume de Nangis' *Chronicle*, that the rebellion had been preceded by a series of natural calamities for two years running: very dry summers interspersed with storms and followed by months of rain and a severe winter. Poverty was so widespread early in the July of 1324, that the Count had to instruct the religious of the abbeys in Ghent to distribute the whole of their tithes to the indigent. The exchanges were in disorder and unemployment was threatening, the Count of Flanders' *Chronicle* tells us. This was not a good moment for increasing the taxes which were already heavy. The trouble began with a refusal to pay the Count's tax and also the tithes. In the countryside the moderately prosperous peasants (*mediocres*) unanimously responded to the summons of the church-bells. In Bruges and Ypres the fullers and weavers, whom Villani regards as corresponding to the *popolo minuto* of his city, provided the men for the insurrection, as they usually did.

The seriousness of the movement did not escape contemporaries. The Count of Flanders' *Chronicle* tells us that it was "a tumult so great and so dangerous that the like of it had not been seen for centuries". Most witnesses had no words strong enough to describe it or to say what they though of the rebels. It was a rebellion, a conspiracy, an impudence, a crime. Its leaders were malefactors, transgressors of public order, perjurors, shameless, presumptuous and arrogant men. The last words well express what, in the eyes of men attached to the established order, was the major crime: a rebellion against the social hierarchy and, what was worse, a rebellion of rustics. Thus the hatred which had provoked the rebels against their masters and against the rich, was repaid with scorn. A song, the *Kerelslied*, contemporary with these events, expresses this horrible scorn for the poor:

The Karls are the subject of our song; evil-minded men, they wish to subjugate the knights. They all have long beards and wear torn garments. Their hoods are all askew on their heads, and their boots are in rags. Curdled milk, bread and cheese—that is what the Karl eats all day, and more than is needed to dull his wits.

A big hunk of rye-bread is enough for him. He holds it in his hand as he goes to his plough, followed by his wife in tatters, her mouth half full of tow. She works with her distaff until it is time to prepare the meal in a porringer. Curdled milk, *etc.*

He turns up at the Kermesse, proud as a lord and ready to knock everyone down with his club. He drinks deep of wine, and soon intoxicated, dreams that the whole world, cities, towns and estates, belongs to him. Curdled milk, *etc.*

See the Karls walking by, giving you a glimpse of the Zealand knives in their pockets. . . . Ah! may Heaven curse them! Curdled milk, *etc.*

We shall know how to punish the Karls; we shall gallop our horses across their fields. They nourish only evil designs. We shall drag them to execution, we shall hang them. They must again submit to the yoke. Curdled milk, *etc.*

The civil war left perhaps more than 3,000 dead on both sides. The population, it was averred, wanted to get rid of the nobility for good. It attacked everything that represented authority, the Count's officers, the magistrates, the tax-collectors. Cases of murder, arson and pillage seem to have been common. Some Franciscans who tried to intervene had their trouble for nothing; although, at the very end, in 1328, the priest of Saint-Michel of Ypres was encouraging the rebels. After this the repression was severe; some men were executed. A certain number of the victims whose goods were confiscated possessed very little: a poor house, a little land, and the meagre remains of inherited property. A study of the documents unknown to Pirenne shows that this was the condition of 95 individuals out of 143. They owned, on an average, about five and a half acres, not enough for serious farming. Seventeen others owned nothing. These data concern fifty-three places in the Castellany of Bruges.

On the whole, however, Pirenne's interpretation remains sound. The rising was led by men of moderate and sometimes considerable importance. It was not a Jacquerie. There was no incoherence in what the leaders decided, and their objects seem to have been definite. The insurrection spread rapidly to the population of Bruges. The action of the rebels, encouraged by popular orators acting perhaps by order, was co-ordinated; for example between the weavers and fullers of Ypres and the peasants of the surrounding plains. There was no anarchy. The rebel leaders, acting with a sense of responsibility, substituted a kind of administration parallel to the Count's; for the insurrection had real leaders, big landowners for the most part. Among them was even the lord of Sijsele, who was general of the popular army; also Guillaume de Deken, burgomaster of Bruges, who had the honour of being prosecuted in the *Parlement*; but also fairly well-off peasants like Nicolas Zannekin or Jacques Peyte, the most radical of them, who attacked every kind of hierarchy and declared that he would like to hang the last priest with his own hands. The object of the movement was a complete subversion of the existing order. It was an insurrection of free and independent-minded men. The common people were directed by a sort of peasant middle class. Its leaders knew at least how to die with dignity.

[Chapter Three]
Revolts Against Poverty

A REVOLUTION is something planned and prepared: it has a programme. A revolt is a spontaneous reaction, a reflex of anger or self-defence, sometimes of both. The Revolution of the Crafts was the result of tenacious action, directed by men of a middle status who were jealous of the profits, powers and dignities of the heads of the trade and anxious to share them. They aimed at improving an intermediate, though tolerable, condition. The "humble" class, that is the poor, dependent on precarious employment and therefore at the mercy of unemployment and natural calamities, had been able to discount the improvement of their lot thanks to the agitation of the intermediate class. They served the latter as a main striking force, for the cause pursued by one class was not the others' cause, and indifference or exploitation rebounded from one social level to another.

Does this mean that the opposition of the middle group (whom, for convenience, we may call a "middle class") to the powerful group provided the lower class with an example and a precedent? Perhaps. Yet extreme poverty was enough to cause protest, unless it was so severe that it neutralized any immediate reaction. This is not the place to discuss the various crises and the economic depression of the fourteenth century. For the moment we will consider only the facts, numerous because of the rapid increase in poverty.

It is not certain that the sociologist will find the pattern familiar to him in the fourteenth century. He will find a record of natural calamities, famines, high mortality, a high cost of living, speculation, rumours and panic, varying in degree and not always present; any more than revolts always occurred when conditions were at their worst.

In any case the frequency of occasions for revolt in town and country, their widespread and increasing seriousness, the culminating point towards 1350, the series of recurrent troubles thus produced, combined to create "rising perils", a prelude to the great tumults of the 1380s.

Every famine does not provoke rebellion. There was none, for example, in the days of the great calamity of 1315–17. In all the countries on the Atlantic seaboard a succession of bad seasons had destroyed the crops and raised the price of corn. The poor died of hunger in thousands. The example of Flanders is particularly striking. The accounts for the burial of corpses at the expense of the cities show that the mortality affected the paid workers of the cloth industry at Ypres more severely than elsewhere. Wheat was not completely lacking, according to the chroniclers, but was carted to neighbouring districts which were in even shorter supply, owing to flooding, because the price was higher. In all the Netherlands the price of grain rose to levels eleven, twelve and even twenty-four times above the normal rate. Monopolizers and speculators profited from this, and only the wealthiest people who had reserves of food or money could really face the situation. The number of the indigent increased, but of rebellion there is no word in the chronicles. The unfortunate "let themselves die in the streets". One needs some strength if one is to rebel.

One cannot however generalize either as to regions or to all the crises. We should need to know why, in August 1316, a workers' rebellion broke out at Provins—rather than in Flanders—"on the occasion of the public famine and the high cost of bread". It seems probable that the town's economic difficulties, due to a crisis in the cloth trade and the decline in the fairs, added to the tragic food shortage a problem of wages and unemployment absent at that time from Flanders, at least to the same degree. A proof of this is furnished by a renewal of difficulties at Provins in 1330 and 1348. In the same way Douai, which was struggling against the competition of the rural cloth industry, suffered in 1322 from dearth and rioting at the same time.

It seems then that a rebellion breaks out spontaneously when a calamity has not become a total scourge and men are still able to become aware of their misfortune and are still strong enough to express themselves. Famine was not the only cause of trouble; very often also there was oppressive taxation, there were currency variations, a rise in the cost of food and lodging, and exploitation.

Among all the causes of rebellion, the instability of the monetary system and the disparity between prices and wages, acted deeply but often in a way which contemporaries failed to perceive. The play of such circumstances showed itself in France before the misfortunes of the Hundred Years' War. During the very first years of the fourteenth century, the monetary "disturbances" provoked strong emotions in Paris. Philippe le Bel had the excuse that he was innovating in currency matters, and that he could not benefit from the many subsequent experiences. In 1306 he had the imprudence or simplicity to announce in advance a devaluation of the currency of about 39 per cent. The result was automatic. Prices shot up, and creditors demanded payment at the higher rate. The operation had the effect of tripling debts and house-rents. Now at that moment the capital was growing rapidly, and without going into the controversies to which this has given rise, one can admit that the population was not far off 200,000. Lodging was probably not cheap. In 1306 the tenants protested vigorously against the rise due to the devaluation. Some of them damaged the buildings, the owners then appealed to the King's officers, and when these arrived, they were soundly thrashed by the occupants.

In January 1307 things went from bad to worse. Isolated incidents gave place to collective action; then, instead of attacking a few individuals or the King's officers who were

unable to cope with the situation, the revolt first found a scape-
goat and then ascribed responsibility to the King himself.
The rioters were artisans and their enemy was a representative
of the business and administrative bourgeoisie, Etienne Barbette, a former Provost of the Merchants who had been made
Master of the Mint. He was held to have instigated the devaluation. The mob began by sacking his country house near
Paris, then came back into the city to empty his wine-cellar,
throw his furniture out of the windows and pillage his chests.
From the King's counsellor to the King himself, from the
Hotel Barbette to the royal residence, was a natural step. The
rioters besieged the King in the Temple, where he had taken
refuge. This affair went on all day, and, words not sufficing,
it was force that compelled the demonstrators to return home.
As those responsible for the insurrection could not be traced,
it was resolved to make an example: twenty-eight masters,
one from each of the main crafts, were hanged.

Those who were subdued could only wait or have recourse to
raillery, as in a song of the time which is itself a document.
In 1313 when the trouble in Flanders made a fresh demand on
the treasury, taxpayers went on strike. Meanwhile the succession of currency fluctuations provoked angry satire on these
monetary jugglings:

> It seems that the King has us under a spell.
> First he turned twenty into sixty,
> Then twenty into four; and ten into thirty.
> . . . Gold and silver: all is lost
> And none will be restored
> To the destitute, not a penny to bless himself with.
> The money turned into one grain of corn,
> And so they juggled, all over the kingdom,
> As a man juggles under a felt hat.
> Of the wheat, we got only the stubble,
> The wheat was for the King, the straw for us.

Taxation and currency difficulties continued to provoke
commotion. The age is full of it, and only a few examples need
be noted. The experience of one generation rarely helps those

that follow. Thus at Rouen the sons of the men who had experienced repression at the end of the thirteenth century rebelled in their turn against the tax-collectors at Martinmas, 11 November 1348; and most of the Norman cities were the scenes of similar incidents. Three years later other riots broke out, and twenty-three workers in the cloth industry were hanged. In 1349 Provins against experienced unrest.

As regard conflicts provoked by the exploitation of labour, it would be confusing to associate them all with rivalries between crafts; thus, we should be underestimating the importance of conflicts among members of the cloth industry at Ghent, if we regarded them as simply a competition to gain admittance to the councils, or membership of the urban magistrature, and so to acquire influence. For the fullers and the artisans in more modest branches of the trade, it was their subsistence that was at stake. The situation of the little watermen in relation to the privileges of the *Francs Bateliers* in the same city of Ghent offered similar contrasts.

Amiens provides others, which are fairly typical of what happened elsewhere. In 1339 the weavers supported by the finishers, shearers and others embarked on a long dispute with the aldermen. To put an end to the demonstrations and agitation a decree had to be issued in 1346; and only in 1357 was the trouble settled by the *Parlement*. It was not only the crafts which were involved in conflicts: in 1331 the furriers were on the brink of rebellion. Normandy, especially Rouen, was agitated by similar troubles: here, discontent with wages and conditions of work smouldered both among the curriers in 1340 and the tow-makers in 1309, 1329, 1338 and 1345, and to these must be added the interminable conflicts among members of the cloth industry. City life was poisoned by dissension between the weavers on one side and the drapers, the fullers and others on the other, the more so as the weavers were at odds with the Mayor. Trade quarrels were associated, rather obscurely for us, with strictly municipal conflicts. In 1320 the problems were referred to the Exchequer of Normandy, which conducted a long and minute enquiry before it could reach a solution—of which we know little. Tension was as severe at Louviers. In 1325 the statutes of the cloth industry required the weavers to respect the decrees, referred to the agitation of the dyers and forbade all the crafts to form confraternities ... "in order to remove all grounds for assemblages ... and conspiracies".

The problems being so widespread correspond quite evidently with economic as well as social trouble. In 1321 the masterfullers of Saint-Denis complained that their workmen were agreeing together not to begin work. In Paris at the same time the workmen in the same trade reproached the masters with employing more apprentices than the number provided for in the regulations; while the masters, on their side, accused the men of beginning work late, of interrupting it, and of refusing to work in the evenings. In short, long before the difficulties that accumulated towards 1350, there prevailed in France a tension severe enough for these limited and sporadic conflicts to be succeeded by a really serious situation. And it was the same almost everywhere.

The aggravation of social hatred owing to famine is clearly illustrated in a series of letters that relate to Barcelona. In the Catalan metropolis 1334 was the *any mal* (bad year), the year which heralded difficulties. The harvest of 1333 had been notoriously inadequate, not only in the immediate vicinity but in the areas which normally provided grain. As early as Christmas, prices were markedly rising, and with prices, anxiety. On 4 January 1334 the councillors of Barcelona wrote to the Prior of the Carmelites of the province of Spain to complain of Friar Bernat Puig, Reader to the House of Barcelona ... that in the cathedral on Christmas day,

"at a time when very high prices prevailed in this city and when he ought to have urged the people to endure them as well as possible and to implore divine help, the said friar added evil to evil by inciting the people against the councillors and rulers of the city; he said—saving your Reverence, and contrary to truth—that it was the councillors and rulers who were the cause of these high prices, because they held the wheat hidden and would not distribute it to the people, and that it was very just that God should send tribulations and dearths on the city, by reason of its bad government."

The councillors asked the Prior to have this "sower of discord" punished, and to expel him from the province, "so that his punishment may inspire terror in the others"—a sign no doubt that he was not an isolated case. They added that they had been able to pacify the city, thanks probably to the arrival of a convoy of grain.

The troubles did not always end as easily, as we learn from a letter which the same councillors sent, this time to Alfonso III, King of Aragon, on 16 April. "At the Devil's instigation and consequent on the action of unjust and malevolent persons, great excitement and uproar took place yesterday, Friday 15 April, against the councillors of the city of Barcelona, because the corn which has recently arrived here was not sold at the price which people desired." The councillors, in peril of their lives, went into hiding; while the royal Provost (*viguier*) who wished to protect them had to flee. The houses of a councillor and a wealthy citizen were invaded, and the rioters vented their rage on the furniture which they removed and broke up; on the horses, one of which was killed; and on the wine-casks which were emptied. This was an example of spontaneous insurrection, a simple explosion of fury among people exasperated by privations. According to the same councillors, nightfall was enough to disperse the malcontents. Nevertheless the councillors begged the King to intervene, and the *populares* were severely repressed.

Several royal letters acquaint us with the third act of the drama. The King's son, who was his Procurator-General in Catalonia, dispatched to the scene of action Noble Guilhem de Cervelló, who had recourse to the strong hand. According to a royal letter, "he subjected several of the prisoners to the rack or to other tortures, without previous inquiry, without a regular trial and in the absence of the notables and defenders, and without observing any legal rule. He then had ten of the prisoners hanged out of hand, simply by pronouncing sentence and without having made any public inquiry or granted any defenders." The sense of legality was highly developed in Catalonia. The councillors themselves, interested as they were in the repression, protested against the proceedings, and the King granted them a letter of non-prejudice—affirming that these doings could not create a legal precedent. This did not restore life to the poor devils who had been executed, mainly no doubt as a warning.

The situation was no less tense in some of the great Italian cities. Venice lived through one of the most tragic periods of her history between 1343 and 1354. She experienced "almost continuously", writes Sanudo, "war, pestilence and famine". Everything went wrong. Apart from the epidemic, there was a tempest and an earthquake in 1347, while monetary inflation affected the smaller silver coinage in a ratio of 1 to 42; and finally there was a crisis in prices. The famine of 1347 which took place just before the outbreak of plague, aggravated the whole situation. The general state of distress very gravely affected the poor and, poverty giving rise to insecurity, crime and disorder prevailed.

In 1347 Cola di Rienzo's adventure in Rome was above all no doubt a political affair, though its social aspect was far from negligible. During the Pope's absence the situation in Rome was being constantly disturbed by faction fights among the nobles and by economic trouble which was endemic. Rienzi (as we usually call him) was the son of an innkeeper and a laundress. Born in 1313, he had early been left an orphan and had lived among orphans until he was twenty. He had married the daughter of a notary and had entered his father-in-law's profession, one of the few to which a *popolano* had access. He thus acquired a good knowledge of Latin, which led him to study the history of ancient Rome and to collect inscriptions relating to it. This brought him the friendship of Petrarch. Having reached only a minor position, he did not think of denying his lowly birth. He had suffered from the haughtiness and violence of the Roman nobility: his brother had been murdered and he never had obtained justice. In 1343 he took part in a Roman embassage to Avignon, which enabled him to speak as advocate of the *popolo*. Now, prior to this, a popular movement of opposition to the nobility had profited from the absence of pontifical representatives in Rome to establish an insurrectional government of thirteen *boni viri*. Rienzi delivered a fiery but visionary oration in its defence: this turned the *Curia* against him and failed to persuade Clement VI to recognize the new institutions. On the other hand he had been commended by Cardinal Giovanni Colonna to the Pope and the latter displayed some sympathy for the generous-hearted plebeian.

There was in fact in Rienzi, as in many adventurers, a mixture of sincerity with a spirit of intrigue, of violence and persuasiveness, of idealism and pragmatism, of boorishness and culture. It was on behalf of the people that he, a man of the people, wished to restore the institutions of Republican Rome. On the other hand he shared with the Franciscan groups of "spiritual" tendency the messianic and egalitarian dreams inspired by the "Eternal Gospel" of Joachim de Flore, a Calabrian monk of the twelfth century. But these forward-looking views were associated with the nostalgia of an austere democracy such as Cato had represented.

Rienzi counted not only on his personal charm and eloquence: he contrived to win over, not only the *popolo*, but the middle class composed of the smaller aristocracy and tradesmen, known as the *gentilezza*, all united in aversion for the great landed nobility. A plot was formed and, taking advantage of the absence of the troops who were then protecting a convoy of wheat from Corneto, Rienzi was invested with supreme power by the Roman people. The nobles, believing that the only object of the great assembly which he had convened, was to listen once again to a nostalgic discourse on the past greatness of the Republic, had taken no precautions. This took place on Whit Sunday 1347. Rienzi had spent the previous night praying in the Church of Sant' Angelo in Peschiera, the titular church of his protector Cardinal Colonna. The episode is described by Giovanni Villani as follows:

"On 20 May 1347, being the day of Pentecost, a certain Cola di Rienzo had just returned to Rome from a mission on behalf of the Roman people to the court of the Pope, to beg him to come and live, with his court, in the see of St Peter, as he should do. The fair words he had obtained proved vain. There was then held in Rome a great assembly before which he rendered account of his embassage in flowery and elegant terms, a rhetoric of which he was master. ... By public acclamation he was elected Tribune of the People and invested on the Capitol with the lordship. ... Certain of the Orsini and the Colonna, as well as other nobles, fled from the city to their lands and castles to escape the fury of the tribune and the people."

So that is how, in the cities of fourteenth-century Italy, they appointed a popular dictator. On 20 June Rienzi mounted to the Capitol, preceded by a procession, surrounded by armed guards and accompanied by the Bishop who represented the Pope as his spiritual vicar in Rome. On the 24th he received the ancient title of Tribune, with "power" to effect reforms and to preserve the city and the Roman province in a state of peace. This power was unlimited, and three months later the people renewed it for life.

In the social domain the programme which Rienzi inaugurated justified the fears of the nobility. In pursuit of "purifying justice", he spared no one. Without regard to privilege, he had criminals pursued on the lands where the nobles had enjoyed traditional immunity; he sought out and pitilessly punished those officials of the former government who had been guilty of peculation; he did not fear to cause a member of the old family of the Stefaneschi to be executed in front of the Capitol. The Tribune of the People undertook to bring the nobility to heel. Their castles were to be placed at the disposal of the community and occupied by the militia. To compel the nobles to return to the city and to humiliate them, he demanded that they should come in person to the Capitol and swear fidelity to him. Lastly, he imposed a special tax on them, and—to the joy of the populace—deprived them of the revenue from the tolls which had weighed heavily on food prices. All these decrees were marked with the seal of democratic purity, while blasphemy, gambling and corruption were suppressed.

Rienzi knew how to join the magic of symbolism to the prestige of oratory. He handled the weapon of social provocation with the consummate art of the actor and the demagogue. The choice of Whit Sunday for the assumption of power had already symbolized the advent of the reign of the Spirit, so long awaited by the "Spirituals". But the peculiar ceremonies of 1, 2 and 15 August 1347 were intended to have an historical and political bearing as much as to flatter the people. Villani writes:

"On the day of San Pietro-in-Vincoli, that is 1 August, the Tribune was dubbed Knight by the Syndic—that is the Captain—of the Roman people in front of the altar of Saint Peter. He then was perfumed with rosewater and bathed in the bath of the baptistery, where the Emperor Constantine had bathed. Clad in white silk with gold brocade, he held solemn court and in a great harangue declared that he wished to bring back the whole of Italy into obedience to Rome, as in ancient times."

The *Chronicle* of Siena also describes the event. "It was a great marvel. The Tribune called himself: Knight, candidate of the Holy Ghost, severe yet merciful, liberator of the city, zealous for Italy, friend of the universe, and august Tribune. It was thus that he signed his decrees." On emerging from the bath—judged a profanation—in the porphyry basin of the baptistery of San Giovanni in Laterano, Rienzi now a knight, sprang on to his horse and rode successively in three directions with raised sword, crying out: "This is mine." All this was the behaviour of a visionary; but of one who also meant to humiliate the nobility by arrogating to himself, a son of the people, its honours and titles.

On 2 August a festival of fraternity was celebrated, a sort of medieval festival of federation. Representatives of the Italian cities attended, with their banners. To each Rienzi gave a golden ring as a pledge of union. But the strangest ceremony of all was the coronation of the Tribune, in Santa

Maria Maggiore, on the day of the assumption of the Virgin, 15 August: "a fantastic caricature of an imperial coronation", writes the Italian historian, Dupré-Theseider. According to the *Chronicle* of Siena, "the Tribune received five crowns, one of oak-leaves, one of lilac, one of myrtle, one of laurel, and one of wild olive". These crowns were offered him by the priors of the Roman Basilicas, with a formula to explain the symbolism:

"Receive this crown of lilac", said the Prior of St Peter's, "because thou lovest religion."

"Receive this crown of myrtle," said the Prior of San Paolo fuori-le-Mura, "because thou hast honoured duty and knowledge, and hated avarice."

"Receive this crown of laurel", said the Abbot of San Lorenzo fuori-le-Mura, "because thou hast fulfilled thy duties and hated avarice."

"Receive this crown of olive-leaves, O modest man", said the Prior of Santa Maria Maggiore, "because thou hast vanquished pride by humility."

A sixth crown, this time of silver, was bestowed on him by the Prior of the Santo Spirito, with the words: "Illustrious Tribune, receive the gifts of the Holy Ghost, with the crown of the Holy Church." And finally he was given a globe of gold, symbol of universal lordship.

All this was a curious mixture of curious honours. It was probably recalled that on Easter day 1341, a different sort of man, namely Petrarch—a friend of Rienzi—had received a simple crown of laurel. But the crowning of Rienzi was more than an academic ceremony. The rites performed were full of political significance, implying as they did a usurpation at the expense of the Pope and the Emperor. Following on his assumption of power at Whitsuntide, Rienzi's crowning amounted to a revolution; and he was not slow to perceive that he had gone too far.

Yet his power lasted for a few months more. It was in the social domain that he had to struggle. The nobles had boycotted the festivities in August. A plot to overthrow the Tribune was unmasked, and Rienzi then tried both to intimidate and to placate, by inviting the barons who were in Rome to a

great banquet in the Capitol on 14 September. They dared
not refuse, and when present were arrested. They rather
expected the worst, but Rienzi set them at liberty after exacting
a new oath of loyalty. Yet this only deferred the reckoning.
An armed conspiracy was now formed, and on 20 November
a bloody battle took place at the Porta San Lorenzo, a struggle
in which eighty of the nobles were killed.

Rienzi had not only treated the nobles with violence, he had
provoked the supreme authority in Christendom. His revolution, if it were to triumph, could not afford to relax. Now, on
the morrow of his victory, the Tribune laid down his sceptre
on the altar of the Church of Ara Coeli. Was this a sign of
thanksgiving, or an act of resignation? It seems that he had
felt discouraged and had suffered an attack of "nervous
depression"; for in fact he was no longer assured of the support
of the *popolo* and the *gentilezza*. The former had been won
over by his anti-aristocratic policy and fascinated by the
splendid shows which he had put on, but in the long run the
multitude grew tired of the Tribune's mania for discoursing on
ancient history. The gaudy ceremonies had also to be paid for.
Finally, people began to complain because the food-supply,
intercepted by the rural nobles who had not come over to the
new regime, was sometimes scanty and expensive. All this,
when the demagogue had promised an advent of felicity! The
gentilezza, for its part, was disquieted by the demagogue's
speechifying and, not without reason, foresaw a conflict with the
Holy See; some of them began to negotiate with the nobles.

After another month the *popolo* had forgotten the acclama-
tions of May and August and, moreover, the Papal Legate
had excommunicated Rienzi. On 15 December the insurrection broke out, to cries of: "People! rise up! Death to the Tribune!" The bell ringing on the Capitol rallied no one to his
side; deserted by his followers, Rienzi took refuge in the
castle of St Angelo, while in response to the conspirators, the
crowd acclaimed a new leader, Giovanni Cerroni, a man of the
people like Rienzi, but really a straw-man of the nobility. The
Pope appointed him Senator and Captain of Rome.

Was this the end of Rienzi's career? He had taken refuge in

the Apennines, among the *Fraticelli* who were once again
supporting him, and he was planning a return to Rome. With
this in view, he went to Prague with the intention of obtaining
from the Emperor, Charles IV, the title of Imperial Vicar;
but the Emperor dismissed him. He next intrigued with Cardinal Albornoz, who was engaged in recovering the patrimony
of the Church; and then, relying on the title of Senator which
the Papal Legate had granted him, he tried his luck. Fra
Moriale, a condottiere, helped him to recruit 500 German
soldiers and with this escort he re-entered Rome. Once again,
this time on 1 August 1354, the crowd acclaimed him, but he
abused his power, and had great numbers arrested or executed.
On 8 October the *popolo*, being now tired of him, invaded
the Capitol and set it on fire. Rienzi tried to escape, disguised
as a peasant, but on the great stairway of the Capitol he
was recognized. Someone stabbed him in the belly, another
man split his skull, and his body was lynched by the mob.
Albornoz was now able to restore the papal government.

Peace no more prevailed in the Patrimony of St Peter than in
Rome itself. Most of the cities behaved as places independent
of the administration by papal rectors, and experienced an
alternation of communal rebellions and aristocratic reactions.
The history of Orvieto may serve as an example. A degree of
political equilibrium had been reached towards the end of the
thirteenth century, after the triumph of the *popolo*. Beginning in
1252 the people had gradually wrested from the nobility the
principal organs of government; seven consuls representing
the Arts formed the executive branch, while the Council of the
People exercised legislative power. A renewal of rivalry
between Guelphs and Ghibellines, at the time of Henry VII's
descent into Italy in 1313, had been accompanied by a violent
conflict between two great families, the Monaldeschi who were
Guelphs, and the Filippeschi who were Ghibellines. Following
an oscillation between aristocratic and popular regimes,
Orvieto had become subject to the tyranny (1334–7) of
Ermanno Monaldeschi; after which there had been a growing
instability, further complicated by numerous wars within the

papal states. But behind the changing fortunes of rivalry
between neighbouring cities, social tension can clearly be
detected. "Nobles, upper class, artisans, lower class and
peasants—each group has its own history and interests"
observes Elisabeth Carpentier in a recent work. The share
of the craftsmen in the city councils was now constantly
dwindling; after 1346 two of the five consular seats were lost
by the Arts, while at the head of the Council of Seven was a
gonfalonier, chosen from among the seven gonfaloniers who
had assured the defence of the city during the last war. It was
the *popolo* who suffered most from the famine and from the
increased cost of food, and indeed the provisioning of the city,
which in 1345, 1346 and 1347 was a major care of the government, was such as to cause serious complaint and, by March
1347, tension. The rich were suspected of speculating on the
shortage; many poor debtors had no means of freeing themselves. Which feeling predominated: hatred of the rich, or
fear of the poor? To preclude worse trouble the consuls imposed
a special tax on sixty of the richest men in the city, requiring
them to pay 1200 florins for the purchase of corn; they also
decreed a moratorium on debts, and abolished imprison-
ment for debts below 50 *livres*. It remains clear that social
tranquillity was at the mercy of a defeat in war, or of a famine,
or a business crisis; and the year before the outbreak of plague
was one of the most troubled.

This increase in social tension was common to the cities of
central Italy in the mid-fourteenth century. Famine had been
general in 1347. At Bologna the peasants had made a mass
assault on the city, but the situation was even more serious in
Florence and Siena. In Florence it was the culmination of a
series of crises. Gautier de Brienne's "tyranny", short-lived
though it was, had left the city in a precarious condition. As
early as September and November 1343 the streets had
resounded, says Villani, with cries of "Long live the *minuti*!
Down with the taxes!" The rioters stoned the palace of the
priors, presumably in order to overthrow the established
order; though they had in fact been the pawns of demagogues
like Andrea Strozzi; they afterwards confessed that they had

taken his word that "from being poor they would become rich". Both Strozzi and Francesco di Lapo were condemned for having tried to provoke an insurrection in the quarter of San Lorenzo.

After the fall of the Duke of Athens everything had indeed conspired to maintain the *minuti* in a mood of rebellion. The hope inspired by the benefits he had conferred, ephemeral though they were, had turned to disillusionment while the reaction following the change of government inspired fury. The records of the prosecutions which now took place reveal the widespread disappointment and the rancour which were experienced, as well as the critical situation of the poorest classes, who seem to have been most numerous in the quarters of Santa Croce and the Santo Spirito. One may cite, as an example of their distress, the moving statement of a father: "I live by the work of my hands . . . to feed my four children who are all small. I am a poor *popolano*, obliged to earn my living by my own labour, and am not strong enough to resist *him*." He was referring to a member of the rich family of the Bardi who had violated the poor man's wife.

Historians differ in their estimate of the number of poor in Florence. Some calculate that there were about 15,000 out of a total population of 80,000 or 90,000. According to Giovanni Villani, the commune had had to assist between three and four fifths of the whole population, during the famine of 1347; even so, 4,000 died of hunger, and the government freed the prisoners so as not to have to feed them. Was it not thus merely providing further troops for rioting, which was then frequent? Villani interrupts his brilliant description of Florentine prosperity in order to describe the distress of the unfortunate. The famine of 1347 had followed a dearth in 1346 and a famine in 1344; while the famine of 1344 had been preceded by an outbreak of plague in 1340. Taxation was very onerous, not to speak of other troubles, such as the resounding bankruptcy of the Bardi and the Peruzzi in 1346.

In such conditions one can well understand why social tension persisted, even after the repression that followed the fall of Gautier de Brienne. There was a renewal of agitation nearly every year. In 1344 the population of La Lastra threatened the Bishop of Florence, and even called for his death; they also attacked the canons of San Lorenzo. In 1345 several attempts to effect a change were nipped in the bud. One, which aimed at establishing a fraternity of the wool-workers, was imputed to a carder of Santa Croce; his arrest provoked a strike and a demand for higher wages; even so, he was hanged. At about the same time nine persons on one side and two on the other were accused of inciting to riot. Finally in 1347 sixteen wool-sorters were condemned for having assaulted the house of a great wool-merchant and for having driven him out with the rest of the household and staff.

Siena experienced more serious troubles in this same year. Communal institutions had not changed since 1310, in spite of perpetual agitation; but the stability of the aristocratic government barely sufficed to restrain the social tension. During the great famine of 1347, the populace armed itself, and led by three members of the Tolomei family, took to the streets, with cries of "Long live the people! Death to the dogs who are starving us!" Several people were killed; thirty-two were condemned, and the list of their trades shows how modest was their business and social status. They were wool-carders, hosiers, tailors, basket-makers and cutlers. Their doings had been the object of a joint inquiry by the authorities of Florence and Siena, because both cities shared the evils of disorder and famine. The *Signoria* of Siena feared that the fugitive rebels might reassemble in Florentine territory—the Florentines feared the contagion of disorder.

*　　*　　*

Since the early fourteenth century new elements had come into play. The growth in the size of states and the increasing number of wars had raised the financial requirements of governments and made the state of inequality, already observable in the thirteenth century, harder to bear. After the townsmen, the peasants had begun to agitate in certain regions, the most technically advanced, and the stagnation in the prices for cereals had something to do with this. At the same time famines and dearths, which were increasingly numerous, had given rise to a few riots, and one may suppose that social antagonism had everywhere been revived. Our documents refer on occasion to the more or less epidemic maladies which these famines had caused, and it is certain that the population of central and western Europe, which was underfed, provided conditions favourable to the spread of the great epidemics. It was in these conditions that the "Black Death" broke out.

The facts, in general, are known and contemporaries of the scourge, appalled by the experience, have left records which modern historians are trying to interpret. It was a question of bubonic plague. The first symptom is the appearance or swellings, or "humps", mainly in the groin or under the arms. The patient is rapidly seized with a violent fever, becomes delirious and dies in two or three days. His body turns black, which is supposedly the origin of the name. But the pulmonary and septicaemic varieties without swellings, although less spectacular, are no less fatal. It is even the specifically "bubonic" form which, in the long run, when the body has in some sort immunized itself, became less serious; more and more patients survived, but with a lower vitality which left them at the mercy of many other infections.

The scourge had come, quite definitely, from eastern and central Asia. Genoese vessels, sailing from the Crimea, brought the germs of this plague to the ports of the Adriatic and of Sicily (autumn of 1347). From there the wave spread over most of Europe, and the mention of it by chroniclers enables one to follow its progress with a precision which authorizes the historian to attempt a chart of it. In the summer of 1348 the epidemic had covered the whole of Italy, the greater part of France as far as the environs of Paris, and the eastern flank of the Iberian peninsula. A year later England was ravaged and all south-west Germany. The last records, at the end of 1350, concern the shores of the Baltic. Hope was reborn everywhere after a few months lived in the nightmare of successive deaths, of deserted houses, of corpses piled in the streets, domestic animals running loose and expiring in the fields, and the universal stench of the plague. "The epidemic, pestilence and mortality coming to an end," says Guillaume de Nangis' *Chronique latine*, "the men and women who had survived vied with each other in getting married." And no doubt this frenzy of renewed life would soon have effaced the traces of the scourge, if a new epidemic, in 1361 and 1362, had not come to crush the energy which had but just been regained. It was everywhere called the "children's plague," because it mowed down the young generation born on the morrow of the first attack. From that time and for centuries to come Europe grew accustomed to living under this perpetual menace.

Such is the general picture. Studies of detail have brought out the variety and the nuances of the plague's effects. In one region the ravage was terrible in 1348–9, while later attacks simply completed the sinister work. Elsewhere the Black Death of 1348–9 was comparatively mild, while it was the subsequent epidemics which proved mortal. This happened in Bohemia and the surrounding lands. Navarre, which had already suffered severely, was even more gravely affected by the plague of 1422. Some regions, like Béarn and Flanders, were relatively spared. A systematic study of the sources will reveal this diversity, but will not alter the essential fact: that in about two years nearly the whole of Europe was submerged by the same wave. All this illustrates the cohesion which the increase of population and the development of international contacts had imparted to the Continent; and it also introduces the factor of synchronism, which we shall observe in the history of social disturbances.

"O happy peoples of the future!" cried Petrarch, "peoples who will not have known these miseries and will perhaps count our testimony as a fable!" The statements of contemporaries have in fact awakened doubt. According to various witnesses, half, or three-fifths or even nine-tenths of the population perished, but such estimates have been considered improbable—or rather too easily explained by the impression of terror which followed the scourge. But the analysis of objective documents, such as the tables summarizing the number of "hearths" which were drawn up for fiscal purposes in most places, if it allows us to discount certain exaggerations, nevertheless marks the amplitude of the disaster. When the number of hearths recorded for a city decreases by half, or even two-thirds—which frequently happened—it is always possible to ascribe the fact as much to the flight of survivors as to the death of the stricken. But studies which, when possible, cover a whole region, enable us to appreciate the full bearing of the disaster. Now vast areas, like the kingdom of Navarre, lost between half and two-thirds of their population. The parochial register of Givry in Burgundy—a unique predecessor of a valuable kind of documents which were to become general only in the sixteenth century—brings out the importance of the losses in a rural centre: in 1348, 649 deaths, as against an average of twenty in normal years. All the studies of rural districts confirm a fact which has long been doubted; namely that the countryside suffered no less than the towns in which, however, bad hygiene must have facilitated contagion. To sum up: we may suppose that, after the first epidemic, the subsequent attacks produced results at least as serious, because they prevented the losses from being made good; and an estimate of the total losses at one-third of the population seems a very likely minimum, and it was probably often exceeded.

The psychological shock was proportional to the catastrophe. Processions of "Flagellants" are recorded more particularly in the Rhineland, the Netherlands and London. They moved along the streets, stripped to the waist, and striking each other with nail-studded ropes; they were led by fanatical monks who thundered against the vices of the age; and they lived by begging. The sick were brought to them to be healed; while the blood which flowed from their wounds was collected as a relic on strips of linen. Many other symptoms of mental disorder could be recorded; but we are naturally most interested in the effects of the scourge on the social conflicts of the time.

The historians who have studied the effect of epidemics in modern times have been impressed by their social aspects. Death did not affect the rich and the poor in equal measure, even if it touched both of them. The former were better fed, they lived in healthier homes and more in the open; they could, and often did, take refuge in country-houses. The subject of Boccaccio's *Decameron* consists of the stories which young Florentines of good family, who have taken refuge outside the city, relate to each other to while away the hours. In the rare cases when it has been attempted, a differential analysis has brought out the "selective" nature of the mortality. Thus among the house-owners of Lübeck, the death-rate was about 25 per cent, as against an average of 50 per cent for the German cities as a whole. R. Cazelles, noting the same figures for the northern half of France, speaks of a "proletarian epidemic".

This explains the prevalence of an intense "class-hatred in times of epidemic". R. Baehrel, in his study of the cholera of 1832, uses this expression. He finds that the rich accused the poor of spreading the contagion, while the poor reproached the rich with thinking only of themselves. Medieval documents do not furnish as much detailed information, but it is reasonable to see expressions of class hatred in the pogroms which in many places accompanied the epidemic, particularly in Spain and in the Rhine valley. In the whole of Catalonia the Jews, regarded as disseminators of plague, were massacred as soon as the scourge appeared, to cries of *Muyren los traydors* (Death to the traitors). This happened at Barcelona, then at Cervera, Tarrega, Gerona and Lerida. Now the Jews were the property of the King, who drew valuable revenue from them, and who strove more or less successfully to protect them. In Alsace, even before the plague broke out but when its coming was announced, the ghettos were invaded, and as many as two thousand persons are said to have perished in Strasbourg. It was rumoured that the Jews were poisoning the wells and springs, and also mixing a suspicious powder in foodstuffs. That their death-rate was relatively as high as that of other classes had nothing to do with the matter; a notion was spread abroad that they did not suffer much from the plague. But beyond these special victims, the rich were to be the object of increased hatred.

What precisely were the economic consequences of the plague? Historians have proved that the signs of crisis and economic recession preceded the plague—and the present work has been written on this assumption. The Marxists have been particularly irritated when the essential cause for the "contraction" has been ascribed to disease, and on the whole their reaction is sound. The plague wrought such ravages only because it was attacking an organism already sick. All the same, a phenomenon of such gravity could not but leave effects which were added to factors already existing. In very rare instances it is possible to compare two tables or lists of patrimonies in a single city, one drawn up before the plague, the other after. Geneviève Prat, who has made a study of this kind for Albi, concludes that the property of the dead was divided pretty equally among the survivors. No social disturbance resulted; and inequality did not increase. This situation however— even if it were possible to record it for a large number of places —was not to last. Not only did the concentration of wealth operate inevitably to the advantage of the rich; but everything did not depend on the accumulation of properties or goods: it was still necessary to be able to exploit them. The rich, who could have recourse to paid labour, were in a better position for this purpose. A number of properties were abandoned for lack of labour, and were added to all those which lawsuits relating to inheritance prevented the heirs from receiving, for lengthy periods. The result was a marked growth of poverty. Fiscal documents testify almost everywhere to an increase in the number of the poor.

The epidemic may also have caused a sudden change in habits of spending. The menace of death, an early death, was constantly present. What good was there in saving? Life was short. It was better to enjoy it straight away. Such an atmosphere, perceptible in the *Decameron* and elsewhere, may well have led all those who had the means to expend more on luxuries. Thus the demand for the best agricultural products (meat, fruit and vegetables), and for manufactured articles, so far from decreasing with the decrease of population, seems to have been stimulated. A call for labour therefore took place in certain sectors of industry with the inevitable result of a rise in wages, which was not long in causing concern to governments. Princes almost everywhere in Europe adopted measures to combat it, but nowhere, it seems, were these measures as systematically conceived and applied as in England.

On 18 June 1349, when the plague was at its worst in the land, Edward III dispatched a decree to the sheriffs of the counties, in which he notes that "certain persons, observing the need experienced by the lords and the shortage of labour, wish to serve only on condition of receiving excessive wages, while others prefer to remain idle and beg rather than earn their living by work". Consequently, all able-bodied men and women under the age of sixty must accept the work which they may be required to perform. The lords will have priority in using the labour of their tenants, but this they must exercise only as they strictly need. The obligation to work was completed by a wage-freeze, the rates in 1346 and the preceding years being taken as the standard. No one may exact, and no one may offer or pay wages or salaries higher than those which were then customary in the region in question. The same rule applied to the urban workers (the decree enumerates the principal trades and crafts) as to the peasants. Able-bodied men are forbidden to beg, and no one may give them alms, "so that they may be obliged to work in order to live".

This programme was supported by severe sanctions. Any person convicted of contravening the regulations was to remain in prison until he provided surety guaranteeing his work. Any beneficiary of a rise in wages, or any employer agreeing to provide such rise, would have to pay a fine double the wage in question. The ill-will of employers is foreseen in the decree. If they or their agents in any way opposed its operation, they could be denounced in the royal courts and the due fine would then be tripled.

If one tried to freeze wages, it was normal that one should do the same for prices. Here however the decree was less peremptory. It simply demanded that suppliers of foodstuffs should ask "a reasonable price", in harmony with the price usual in the region, so that they may obtain a "moderate, not excessive profit". The vagueness of the formula allowed of many interpretations. But here too delation, that is "informing", was encouraged, and the tripling of fines for contravention was of a kind to combat the ill-will of the municipal authorities. Even so, the problem remained disquieting.

The judges were very soon overwhelmed with complaints and denunciations, and all this affected the application of the decree, so that Parliament, which proved more rigorous than the King, completed the text and promulgated it as a statute (9 February 1351). Commissions of judges for workers were appointed, and a few records of their sessions which have come down to us give some idea of their activity. This was encouraged by the fact that the fines which they collected were deducted from the amount of the subsidy due to the King from the county concerned. Now for the years 1352 to 1354, it has been calculated that 6 per cent of the tax was covered in this way—not a negligible figure. It was mainly wage-earners who paid the fines; condemnation of employers was comparatively rare. The result was thus, in a certain measure, to throw the weight of taxation on the poor.

Application of the statute was certainly not enough to prevent a rise in wages and in prices. Employers themselves too often tried to obtain labour at any cost, while a number of wage-earners escaped prosecution by continually moving from place to place. All the same a brake was put on these wagerises up to a certain point; the counterpart of all this was the strain involved by this gigantic effort. It no doubt contributed in no small measure to degrade social relations, and it was not foreign to the violent and surprising explosion of discontent represented by the Peasants' Revolt in 1381.

There was no such rigorous policy elsewhere. In France, where the royal administration was less strictly organized, similar measures were applied only in the district subject to the provost of Paris. In Spain Pedro I of Castille (known as Peter the Cruel) promulgated in the Cortes of 1351 decrees applicable to his various provinces: Old and New Castille, Andalucia, Murcia, Galicia, Asturias and Leon. They were long and detailed, fixing the prices and wages that were allowed for each category of worker or dealer. Journey men (*labradores*),

whose labour was obligatory, were to be punished for any
infraction with the whip. Artisans (*menestrales*) were fined if
their demands were excessive. But it does not appear that these
decrees were very strictly or continuously applied.

After the first frenzy of spending on the part of survivors,
especially in those domains which it had not affected, the loss of
population caused by the plague was felt as a crisis in the
labour-market. The rise in wages did not last long, except
perhaps in England and a few other places. In most cities the
regulations reflected a need to reserve local custom for local
artisans, and to limit the number of masters. Since the mid-
fourteenth century the statutes governing the crafts restricted,
both for strangers and for workmen, any access to the position
of master-craftsman. The necessity of an examination, often
the demand for a masterpiece, long and costly to produce,
always the payment of a fee, often the custom of offering a
banquet to one's colleagues, and sometimes the deposit of
caution-money—these were all barriers that made it almost
impossible for a workman to become a master, although they
were removed for the sons or sons-in-law of masters.

Social conflicts were henceforth to be waged in a new moral
climate, embittered by the horror of repeated epidemics, by
the weight of growing poverty, and by increasing hatreds.

*   *   *

In 1358 a revolutionary movement in Paris coinciding with
social conflict in the neighbouring countryside, constituted a
rare phenomenon. These events, short-lived though they were,
left a deep mark on contemporaries, and historians have
judged them variously. Prior to the nineteenth century
Etienne Marcel and the peasants of the Jacquerie were condemned as rebels, destructive of the established order, but with
different degrees of guilt. The peasants incarnated the blind
force of ignorance and brutality and thereby compromised the
image of the poor; Marcel incarnated the ambition of the
envious bourgeois, disloyal to his King. Both were guilty of
aggravating the country's misfortunes. The Romantic historians

on the other hand turned them into distant and heroic ancestors
of the Revolution: Marcel representing the efficient and far-
sighted bourgeois, while the peasants were the brave martyrs
of resistance to oppression. They next appeared as precursors
of the Commune: while Marxist historians have seen in the
events of 1358 a foreshadowing of the class war.

Contemporaries naturally wrote at great length about the
troubles of 1356, 1357 and 1358. In the first rank we have the
witness of Jean Froissart, most perspicacious of fourteenth-
century chroniclers. Although not an eye-witness of the events,
he was well-informed and personally acquainted with many of
the actors in the drama. Admiration for the nobles and low
esteem of commoners do not prevent his narrative from being
fairly impartial. The *Grandes Chroniques de France* are, on the
the other hand, an official history written about twenty years
after the event; the narrative here has been ascribed to Pierre
d'Orgemont, Chancellor of Charles V, one of the class most
bitterly attacked by the peasants and by Marcel.

Other records which, by exception, are unfavourable to the
ruling class and sympathetic to the popular cause, are due to
two clerics, one from Liége, the other a Norman. The former,
Jean de Venette, owed his direct knowledge of the people for
whose sufferings he felt sympathy, to his own humble birth
and membership of the Mendicant order of the Carmelites. As
an eye-witness of some of the circumstances which he relates,
he was a partisan of Etienne Marcel, but after the riots and
bloodshed of 1358 he went over to the Dauphin. The Norman
has also left evidence favourable to the people in the *Chronique
des Quatre Premiers Valois*.

More impartial is the narrative of Jean le Bel, a canon of
Saint-Lambert de Liége, a record based on the testimony of
eye-witnesses. It is surprising on the other hand, to find nothing
about the disturbances in France in the English chronicles of
the time.

The popular imagination was greatly struck by the events of
1356–8. In oral tradition the peasants were no doubt remembered in much the same way as the *Grand Ferré*, the hero
of peasant resistance to the English. Pierre Cochon in his

Chronique Normande has recorded some of these collective impressions.

Of the documents that contain a direct witness by those who took the most active part in the agitation, we find little in the administrative archives. A few letters from Etienne Marcel have been preserved. The documents which restore to us, often with the crude flavour of common speech, the statements of the humblest folk, are the letters of pardon issued by the chancellery; statements of those whose voices are but rarely heard.

Popular feeling was awakened by news of the defeat at Poitiers and the captivity of King John (13 September 1356); discontent however was not with the prince who was protected by the mystical halo of royalty. It was his councillors who were reproached with having given him bad advice, the barons who had failed in their military duties and all those who had squandered the money recently raised by heavier taxation. The political confusion thus found expression in the social domain.

There was no immediate outburst of anger on the part of the peasants, but very real resentment and contempt were felt for the feudal nobility. Froissart writes that after the defeat "the knights were blamed and hated"; he adds that the "nobles were betraying and bringing shame on the kingdom". Jean de Venette goes further when, apropos of the exactions of the armed men, that is the knights associated with pillagers, he relates the fable of the wolf and the dog. "It was thus", he said, "that this accursed dog contrived to conceal his malice, and so thoroughly that, with his companion's help, he ended by wickedly devouring his master's sheep." Those whose professional duty was to defend the King were accused of cowardice and those who spent the money so painfully furnished by the war-levies in adorning themselves with jewels were accused of dishonesty. A popular song echoes Jean de Venette's accusations:

Bragging, vainglory and indecent raiment,
Gilded belts and feathers in their hats,
Beards like those of he-goats, those unclean beasts,
That is how they stun you, as with thunder and lightning.

See how pride and overweening conceit
And haughty manners, advance them in honour!

The great treason which they have long meditated
Was clearly proved in the army we spoke of.

The discontent, while remaining latent in the countryside, quickly came to a head in the cities and especially in Paris. Agitation first arose in the assembly of the Estates, and then in the streets. Charles, Duke of Normandy, the King's eldest son, on whom power now devolved, had been able only to summon representatives of the three Estates of the Languedoïl regions to meet in Paris in November 1356. The Estates remonstrated against "the guilty private agreements between people who ought to have been working in the King's service". They also denounced the inequality of fortune between those who were "rich and fortunate and the people [who were] very poor". The class thus aimed at was the business community, in Paris above all, where the Court gave them opportunities for great profit, and real influence also. Yet it was from this class that the leader of the agitation emerged.

Etienne Marcel had been elected to the Estates of 1355, as spokesman for the cities, and he was playing a leading part by the end of 1356. As Provost of the Merchants he controlled not only the various crafts but the whole commerce of Paris, which was regulated by the association of the *Marchands de l'Eau*.[1] The collection of taxes for the maintenance of highways came also within his province; and, as was general in the Middle Ages, jurisdiction over ports and markets, dependent on the *Parloir aux Bourgeois*, fell likewise under his administration. Etienne Marcel's social influence derived from his belonging to the upper middle class of Paris and being connected with the powerful fraternities of Notre-Dame and Saint-Jacques-le-Pèlerin. On his father's side he descended from drapers and money-changers; on his mother's, from royal officials. Not having inherited as much of the family's wealth

---

[1] Because much, if not most of the trade—supply of timber, building materials, even foodstuffs—was effected by river-transport. (Translator.)

as he might have expected, he may well have conceived a certain jealousy of his kinsfolk. Two marriages into wealthy merchant families would have completely associated him with the ruling class favoured by the court, if a new problem of inheritance had not brought him into conflict with the Des Essarts, his second wife's family. We shall often find him acting against them with the assistance of a few nobles who were jealous of parvenus and of the lower class who were hostile to the newly rich. Now it was the latter who were to crystallize the discontent and compass the fall of a man whom they regarded as a traitor to their class. Such were the social and personal circumstances in which the revolutionary leader of 1358 was to act, and which, in some degree, explained and directed his behaviour.

The stages of his political action may be divided into two periods: during the first, he proceeded as a reformer, during the second, by direct action. In the first stage, the Estates General acted under the influence of the Merchants' Provost, supported by an ambitious prelate who like him was animated by private rancour. This was Robert le Coq, Bishop of Laon, who could not forgive another prelate, Pierre de la Forêt, Archbishop of Rouen, for having—as he felt—deprived him of the office of Chancellor of France. The Estates began by inculpating the men in authority, then the institutions of the state. They demanded the dismissal of many of the King's councillors, members of the upper bourgeoisie and regarded as responsible for the financial troubles. Next, on 3 March 1357, a *Grande Ordonnance* tended to subordinate to the control of the Estates, not only the levying of aids, but also the work of the council and the sovereign courts. Was France now going to obtain her Magna Carta? Was the Capetian monarchy to come under control? The idea of a reform of the state was haunting men's minds and had even reached the lower classes, who had remembered nostalgically the times of "good king Saint Louis". The *Roman de Fauvel*, which was much in vogue in the first half of the fourteenth century, stigmatized the greed for wealth and power among those who, allegorically, flattered the horse Fauvel, a symbol of vice. Interested as it was in a reform, the people could not but be attracted by certain articles of the *ordonnance*, such as the proposal to repress the exactions of royal officials, and the measures to protect the "poor folk" from the abuses of requisition (*droit de prise*). On this latter point, the *ordonnance* went as far as recognizing that, owing to the failure of government to prevent arbitrary dealing, it was legitimate to "assemble . . . to resist" the requisitioners; and if the latter tried to "beat, use shamefully, or force their way, then to reply by similar means". Necessity was leading the Estates to authorize the use of force.

Two months earlier, in Paris itself, Etienne Marcel had given an example of direct action in support of the programme of reform. This was a prelude to the second phase of his movement. On 19 and 20 January, he had resisted a revaluation of the currency by organizing a strike and the arming of the population. As the *Grandes Chroniques* put it: "The Provost and other men . . . were so much moved that they caused the craftsmen (*menestreux*) to stop work all over the city, and the said Provost commanded that throughout the city everyone should arm himself." Rebellion was taking to the streets.

It remained there on and off for a year. 1357 went by without notable events other than isolated symptoms of deterioration. Etienne Marcel's alliance with the Dauphin's cousin and brother-in-law, Charles, Count of Evreux and King of Navarre—known as Charles the Bad—opened the way to demagoguery. Already, on 30 April, Marcel had had nearly all the city gates closed on his own authority, with a view to obliging the Dauphin to convene the Estates. Seven months later he brought the King of Navarre into Paris, accomplices having contrived Charles's escape from the state-prison in Picardy where he had been held for the past two years. The Provost had him acclaimed at the Pré-aux-Clercs by a crowd of 10,000, it is said, which he "sermonized at great length, so long that everyone had dined in Paris when he stopped" (30 November 1357). The Dauphin got his own back on 11 January by haranguing a "great swarm of people" in the *Halles*, and the day after by imposing his presence on a vast assembly at Saint-Jacques-de-l'Hôpital. At the same time he was gathering troops in readiness near Paris. He was on the eve of a trial of strength of which the people became the arbiter.

The climax of the drama was due to a single incident, namely the assassination of a treasurer of the Dauphin by the servant of a money-changer to whom he owed money. This brought the excitement to a head and, as Marcel feared that the Dauphin might escape from his influence, he organized a great demonstration to intimidate him.

It will be seen from all that has gone before that the revolutionary disorders did not begin with the eruption into the royal palace, on 28 February 1358, of 3,000 artisans who had been organized by Etienne Marcel and whom he personally led from the Enclos Saint-Eloy to the Ile de la Cité, where the royal palace stood; it no more began then than the French Revolution was to begin with a similar event on 20 June 1792. The Dauphin Charles, finding himself as helpless in face of this insurrection as Louis XVI was to be, had to don the hood of the Merchants' Provost, the hood of red and blue which are the colours of Paris and were then an emblem of insurrection. Two of his marshals, who were particularly hated, were murdered before his eyes in his own room.

But violence solved nothing since the Dauphin gained time by making apparent concessions; he then left Paris and assumed the title of Regent in order to strengthen his authority. Time was working on his behalf, because Marcel, having won dominion over Paris, found himself on the defensive, and was now in a more difficult position than may appear. For a certain period he still had the support of the Parisian craftsmen, but to achieve his object, which was to transform the monarchy by bringing it under the control of the Estates representing the communes, of which he had been the promoter and the advocate, he needed more time. He tried to win the support of other cities. In a Paris still seething after the recent disorders, he presided on 23 February over an assembly of delegates of the communes. The grievances of the townsfolk against the royal administration were the same, from Arras in the north to Toulouse in the far south. Back in March 1356

the lower class (*les menus*) in Arras had risen against the nobles
and killed seventeen of them. In Toulouse, where resistance
to taxation was very strong, the king's officials were threatened
with death by the people insurgent against the *capage* (a poll-
tax). The men of Rouen, who had been disturbed in 1356
by the arrest of Charles the Bad, went further in June 1358:

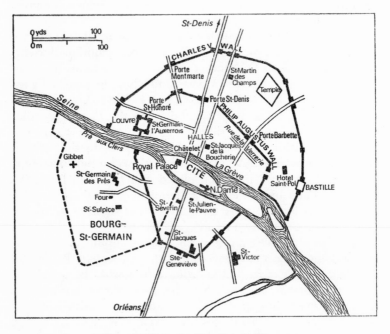

Fig. 1 Paris in the Fourteenth Century

excited by the King of Navarre's harangues, they took possession of the castle. At Amiens, in a brawl provoked by fiscal
trouble in 1357, the furriers had taken the lead. These examples show that certain cities were open to revolutionary
propaganda. One would like to know just what was Etienne
Marcel's propaganda. He wrote long letters to the city of
Ypres, being sure that he would find sympathy in the Flemish

communes, where he certainly had business and commercial
relations. He also wrote to Dreux, to Arras and to Amiens;
while his friends acted on the spot. In Laon, the episcopal see
of Robert Le Coq, the city attorney "compassed the death of
the rich men (*les gros*)", it appears, "and induced the commune
to adopt the Parisian hood", as Amiens had done. This
movement did not go far, the country not being ripe for
revolution.

Finding little support therefore in other cities, Etienne
Marcel thought of enlisting the Jacquerie on his side. The first
known episode of this revolt occurred suddenly, on 29 May
1358, at Saint-Leu-d'Esserent near Creil. It followed an
exchange of insults between men-at-arms and peasants who
were wearied by the exactions of the bands roaming the
countryside. In the scuffle that followed the rustics had the
upper hand, and this fortuitous affair was enough to spread
the example. The movement was essentially of peasant origin,
and its name was derived from the sobriquet traditionally
applied to the villains, that of Jacques Bonhomme; "Jacques"
probably because of the short garment or blouse which they
wore, the jacque.[1] Now if the word "Jacquerie" no longer
corresponds to the original sense of the word in folklore, it is
because the revolt of 1358 was, despite its brevity, one of the
most violent of rural insurrections. Even so there were in the
assemblies of "Jacques", according to the *Grandes Chroniques*,
"labourers mostly, but also rich men, bourgeois and others".
Were these men instigators? We know that before the rioters
set out, there were meetings in the village squares at which
popular orators reported the most alarming rumours. Jean le
Bel evokes most vividly the way in which "fright" was spread
round Creil; each belfry sounding the alarm to the next, and
"for no other reason" bringing on to the highways men "without other weapons than knives and iron-shod staves".

The movement as a whole was as incoherent as it was spontaneous, and has naturally been compared with the Grande
Peur of 1789. The violence, murders and blind destruction

[1] Our word "jacket" derives from French *jaquette*, which was a diminutive of
jaque. (Translator.)

wrought by the "Jacques" have been described by Jean de Venette:

"They assaulted a strong castle, seized the knight and bound him hand and foot, and, before his eyes, violated his lady and their daughter, then killed the lady who was with child, and the daughter, then the knight and all the children, and set fire to the castle. They did likewise in several castles and good houses. . . . Knights and ladies, squires and damsels everywhere fled where they could, often carrying small children on their backs for distances of ten or twenty leagues. Thus did these folk, having assembled without leaders, burn and rob, and kill gentlemen and noble ladies and their children, and violate ladies and maidens without mercy."

Although guideless at the outset, the Jacques after a time chose leaders, either the noisiest demagogue or the man who was supposed to know the trade of arms. If the allegation was not forged after the event, in order to obtain pardon, certain men asserted that they had been compelled to take the lead of a group by denying their gentle birth because, being nobles, they were held to know the art of war. The best-known leader was Guillaume Carle: "a man of knowledge, a good speaker, handsome and well-formed", according to the chronicler of the first four Valois kings who, however, did not like him. He possessed a certain gift for organization, appointed a chancellery, and divided his followers into troops, each subdivided into groups of ten. He had a feeling for tactics. Left to themselves, the facques had pillaged at random. Guillaume Carle selected the castles and strong places which would furnish support at key-points, and he was not without political sense. Instead of permitting arbitrary acts of vengeance, he saw the value of an alliance between the peasants and the discontented townsmen; he wished to make terms with Paris, saying: "We shall have the help of those in the city." We have no other knowledge of his objects, because he wrote nothing and left no records, and his political sense was limited because he fell into a trap set for him by the King of Navarre.

His troops were never very numerous: five or six thousand
men, inexperienced and undisciplined, according to Jean de
Venette. Some of them may have been former men-at-arms;
some former royal or manorial agents; a few were probably
priests who had abandoned their duties: all such had broken

Fig. 2 The Jacquerie: 1358

their ban; but the majority were peasants in revolt against
taxation, inspired by personal rancour or exasperated by
penury. Certain of them had been forcibly enrolled, or had
lacked the courage to resist the collective rising. There were

even some who, seeing banners "painted with the fleurs de lis", thought that they were serving the King.

From the area of the Plain of France and the Beauvaisis, the movement spread east and south of Paris; northward over the whole of Picardy, and from there into Normandy on one side, into Champagne and Lorraine on the other. Disorder was recorded round Bray, in the region of Amiens, in Artois, Ponthieu and Pertois; and the contagion touched Auxerre in the south. The climax was reached in the first ten days of June. Etienne Marcel had responded to Carle's advances. Pursuing an action similar to that of the Jacques, he organized punitive expeditions into the country round the capital, under pretext of a need to "raze to the ground . . . fortresses and houses, prejudicial to the city of Paris". The most notable of the dwellings thus attacked was the noble manor at Gonesse belonging to Pierre d'Orgemont, a president in the *Parlement*, which was completely sacked. But, unlike the Jacques, the Parisians committed no murders.

Meanwhile the Merchants' Provost sent a contingent of 300 men, bourgeois and unemployed labourers, to join Guillaume Carle who was near Senlis. This was effected on 7 June, but the alliance did not last. The King of Navarre had responded to the interests of his own class, that is, to an appeal from the nobles of the Parisian region, by leading a company of armed knights and marching against the Jacques. The Parisians had now to choose.

They dissociated themselves from the Jacques and proceeded towards Meaux, reinforced by peasants as they advanced. The fortified area in the market-place at Meaux was very nearly taken, and had it been, the capture, massacre or violation of noble ladies, including the Dauphin's wife, who had taken refuge there would have contravened the laws of knightly honour. But this did not happen and, on the same day, 10 June, Charles the Bad massacred a number of Jacques. Guillaume Carle had been treacherously induced to meet him by an offer of negotiation, and had then been arrested and put to death. The Jacquerie was now a lost cause, and the reprisals which followed were as violent as the deeds they were meant to

punish; letters of general remission granted two months later
by the Regent show that acts of vengeance were similar on both
sides.

In the middle of June the saviour of public order was neither
the Dauphin nor the Merchants' Provost, but Charles the Bad.
Etienne Marcel no longer had any room for manœuvre or
initiative; or even much choice. By inviting the King of
Navarre into Paris and having him elected Captain-General,
he had in fact lost control of events; he yielded to the wishes of
a fraction of the bourgeoisie, contrary to those of a population
which now began to desert him. It was then that he appealed
to the solidarity of the Flemish cities which, in the new situation, had not declared themselves. He could no longer count on
the King of Navarre to assist in negotiating with the English,
and from that moment he was alone, and lost. The population
being disquieted "murmured greatly". If Marcel had detached
himself from his own people, the latter repaid him in the same
coin; thus we know that among the associates of Jean Maillart,
a bourgeois with whom he had the altercation that preceded
his murder, was Pepin des Essarts, his cousin by marriage. It
would be too simple to reduce Etienne Marcel's adventure to
the level of a family quarrel, for this had been only the start of
it. Our present business is rather to examine some of the
problems raised by the Parisian revolution and the Jacquerie, *chapter theme*
and more especially their origins and their natures.

At the root of these troubles we find the conjunction of
political circumstances with an economic and social situation of
peculiar difficulty, further aggravated by the after-effects of the
plague. Fiscal problems were again a source of discontent. But
it seems to us an exaggeration to describe the situation in Paris
as one of clear-cut oppositions, such as the contrast between the
industrial and commercial power of the capital and the
depression of the neighbouring country districts.

A certain concentration of manufacture and trade was no
doubt an advantage to the business aristocracy which Etienne
Marcel represented. Over against this class was a lower class of
merchants and shopkeepers jealous of an economic independence of which the newly-rich were beginning to deprive

them; and below this class again the multitude of small artisans and labourers had, owing to the fiscal, military and economic difficulties of the time, been swollen by a considerable number of workmen and vagabonds moving back into the capital.

In the countryside, especially since the plague, social disparities were more marked, while the ancestral relations between man and man were distended. The development of the short-term system in the farming-out of agricultural work contributed as much to this as the custom of paying rent in kind and the frequent absence of the lord who was fighting in the King's service. The recent wage-legislation of 1351, by taxing the maximum sum at which service was hired and by trying to pin down labour to the places where work was needed, was running counter to circumstances. All this explains the social character of the Jacquerie. "Very well! So be it", said a Jacques. "Let everything go as it will, and let us all be masters." Another Jacques, reputedly responsible for the movement in Lower Normandy, walked about Caen wearing a hat adorned, provocatively, with a little wooden plough. Froissart needed only a few lines to stigmatize the "commotion of the non-nobles against the nobles"; in their violence, he writes, they "robbed and burned everything, and killed all the gentlemen whom they found, all ladies and maidens, without pity or mercy, like mad dogs".

Such rancour would not fully explain why the Jacquerie arose and developed in some of the richest agricultural districts. Guy Fourquin has investigated the economic causes of the uprising in the corn-growing parts of the plains round Paris and of the Beauvaisis. The persistent weakness of agricultural prices, especially of seed-grain, played a leading part. "The disparity between industrial prices and cereal prices," he writes, a disparity "due to the crisis of 1315, still persisted. The Jacquerie was a rebellion against the after-effects of the wheat-crisis at the beginning of the century."

The increase of fiscal burdens was added to the latent discontent in the towns and country. Now this discontent was increasing the more as the upper class of business men who had been admitted to the King's council was richer and more influential. Nothing would have been more natural than to think of purging the council; but who thought of it?

Writers have often referred to the awakening of political consciousness in the *grande bourgeoisie* and its ambition to obtain a share in government; but this is inadequate. Historians have recently, and rightly, insisted on the political programme of that fraction of the nobility which desired constitutional reform. They were less disregarded by public opinion than has been stated, and were constantly present in the council, where their share in government was of capital importance. These nobles shared the people's hostility to the parvenus and embezzlers, as much as they continued the action undertaken by the nobles of the generation preceding the death of Philippe le Bel. Revolutionaries in their way, they proposed to stabilize the part played by the council as a moderating influence on the King; and it was among them that real political consciousness was to be found. Etienne Marcel's intentions were not however theirs; and the clamours of the Jacques were of no use to them. Their understanding with Marcel could only be temporary; their disagreement with the Jacques was naturally total. Marcel was no more at ease than they. It cannot be denied that his intentions were those of a reformer and that he thought of uniting the communes of France within the framework of a sort of limited monarchy, but time was pressing and he had to make choices, perhaps unwillingly.

The idea of associating the Parisian revolution with the Jacquerie cannot have been inspired by class-consciousness. The Jacquerie had arisen independently of the Parisian movement. Marcel could not foresee it and had no means of taking it in hand. How could he, *grand bourgeois* as he was, experience anything but scorn and perhaps fear of these unbridled and violent rustics? If he was in contact with them for a very short time, the initiative seems to have come from Guillaume Carle. Marcel may, at the most, have thought of "using" the Jacques in order to scare the Dauphin and incline him in his favour. Did he think it possible to organize them in some way? We do not know. He never really joined forces with them. In his last letter to the aldermen of Ypres, written three weeks before his death, he sought their help "to defend the good people, the good labourers and the good merchants"; but this did not prevent his totally disavowing the Jacques a few lines further on. We can have no illusions regarding his attitude. When he roused the artisans of Paris to insurrection and when he felt a slight inclination to assist Guillaume Carle, his cause was neither that of the artisans nor of the peasants.

Characteristic both of the Parisian revolution and of the Jacquerie was the alternation of verbosity and violence. Oratory reigned supreme after the meeting of the Estates and during the most troubled and noisy period of the Parisian rising. Oratory also had its influence on the peasants who, like all unsophisticated communities, were sensitive to the magic of words. It was not surprising that a cleric like the Bishop of Laon should have known how to dominate a great assembly; but it was still more remarkable that the Dauphin, then little more than a boy, contrived to sway over to his side the crowd assembled in the Halles on 11 November 1358—so much so that the Merchants' Provost judged it necessary to hold another meeting, which proved very tumultuous, the very next day. It was again thanks to his eloquence and cleverness that the Dauphin Charles held a popular meeting at the town hall: first, on 4 August, a few days after the Provost's assassination, he justified the crushing of the conspiracy; and again, in October, he harangued the crowd from the top of the steps of the cross in the Place de Grève, to reassure it. The "sapience" of the future "wise King" would not have sufficed; he also needed, and possessed, the art of handling words and swaying multitudes. In those days the art of rabble-rousing ran riot. Charles the Bad was equally proficient in it, but great is the fickleness of the crowd; the Dauphin had learned it to his cost on 22 July, nine days before Marcel's assassination. The clamour that rose from the street to the balcony of the Maison aux Piliers made him see very clearly that his collusion with the English was no longer to the popular taste and that his famous success as an orator at the Pré-aux-Clercs on 30 November 1356 was now a thing of the past.

Etienne Marcel was no more deficient than he as a popular

orator. He does not seem to have acquired this art at school, though he was doubtless not devoid of culture. He was above all a man of action who knew how to manipulate crowds, win them over by promises, excite them by means of catch-words (his device was: *A bonne fin*) and symbols (the red and blue hood), involve them in demonstrations peaceful or violent, dominate the tumult and—a more difficult task—arrest it. He had the double gift, rare at that time, of planning a scheme of action, preparing for it and knowing how to lead men. Thus the day of the "massacre of the marshals" had been planned from far ahead. Charles the Bad, who paid little heed to the character of his followers, had forced the Dauphin to open the prisons and liberate their inmates. Etienne Marcel contrived to use them side by side with the naturally peaceable artisans whom he assembled in the Enclos Saint-Eloy.

In the Jacquerie direct action counted of course for more than oratory; but the latter was not absent. Guillaume Carle expressed himself well, while the village orators, not to speak of some Parisian emissaries, knew how to inveigle the peasants.

To sum up: the two movements were distinct, in spite of some common features. Both were the outcome of the same general situation. The political bearing of the Parisian events and the gravity of the social problems underlying the Jacquerie are evident; neither can be neglected. The two movements failed, but the causes which had provoked them did not disappear with them.

*   *   *

The generation born after the plague had not reached maturity, that is about the age of thirty, without seeing the problems which had arisen in its childhood, and had matured with it, coming to a head. As always on the morrow of great ordeals, there first came a period not of equilibrium or of quiet, but of a sense of respite and expectation. It was the same all over Europe, with varied fortunes because, almost everywhere, temporary remedies were applied in unequal doses to situations unequally critical.

France had been sufficiently shaken by war and revolution to be spared in the course of the two decades of the strong government of Charles V. The re-establishment of political and administrative order and a certain economic revival did not however prevent the financial department from mortgaging the future. On the other side, the traditional social bonds continued to grow weaker. The industrial districts were inevitably more sensitive to the ups and downs of the situation, in the north of the kingdom and more particularly in Flanders. The number of the poor increased, especially when recurrences of plague in 1369 and of famine in 1375 accumulated their ravages. The usual charitable institutions were no longer adequate for their purpose. Towards 1363 the Bishop of Paris was deploring the deficiencies of the hospitals. The charity works for the poor, as for example the *Commune Aumône* of Mons in 1371, have left evidence both of their efforts and their inadequacy.

In the centres of the Flemish cloth industry, the social situation remained tense. At Douai, Ypres and Saint-Omer the struggle for survival of the old urban cloth industry did not create an atmosphere likely to improve relations between the craftsmen and the great merchants. At Ghent the fullers nourished bitter memories of their defeat in 1359. Reduced to being no more than second-class citizens, they no longer had the right to elect a dean, and the head of their craft was appointed by the magistrate. On the other hand, unlike the situation in crafts where the masters alone had a voice in the organization, the workmen in the weaving-trade could express themselves with the same freedom as the other members of the craft; thus their right of intervention contributed to place their craft in the van of agitation. The establishment of pious foundations proved little more than a palliative for the difficulties. More serious was the situation which arose when the Count of Flanders imposed a tax on apprenticeship which assisted the poor weavers while excluding former rebels from the benefit involved. Social tension could only be prolonged. At Ghent access to the mastership was again closed in 1367 to those weavers who were not burghers or sons of burghers. In

1372 the magistrates cancelled the right of fullers to refuse to work or to leave the city. Now the stagnation of wage-rates continued to provoke annual disputes. It was much the same with the dyers, though these were more fortunate because, being perhaps more feared, they won a slight rise in wages in 1374.

Tension was no less severe in other regions. In Italy social problems remained extremely acute in Florence and Siena. A method had been devised in Florence for facilitating the fusion of social groups, at least in the political domain. The *magnati* could now, as individuals, abandon their status and demand inscription as *popolani*. But this was a lure, and few asked for it. Furthermore, although such men who changed their status were forbidden access to the *Signoria* within less than twenty years, the procedure could very well facilitate the ambitions of certain demagogues; and it was against ex-*magnati* that in 1363 the first serious troubles since the Plague now broke out. The men who set fire to the houses of the Scali family were animated by social hatred and by the accusation of treason in the war against Pisa.

Fiscal inequity was one of the most usual motives of discontent with the rich. The war was costly. Apropos of this struggle with Pisa (1362–4) Giovanni Villani records the following remark: "The rich man should be obliged to pay and it ought to be an established principle that war should not be paid for out of the pockets of the poor, but rather by those who are in possession of power."

Towards 1368–9 problems of work and pay once more became serious. Various causes were alleged for this: increasing competition from the English cloth industry, higher costs of production, inadequacy of wages, and rise in the cost of foodstuffs due to a succession of bad harvests since 1360. In 1368, 500 men rioted against the corn-merchants, pillaged the stocks, and demonstrated in front of the Palazzo della Signoria with cries of "*Viva il popolo minuto!*" Sixteen were executed—a fruitless penalty.

We know that among the Florentine craftsmen the dyers were some of the most active and as such considered most

dangerous. For long past they had vainly demanded autonomy for their craft. They rose in rebellion in 1370, stopped
work and demanded higher wages, the possibility of refusing
to work for the *lanaioli* and freedom to delay completing the
work. This was refused, but in 1371 the authorities virtually
admitted their impotence by repealing the laws which forbade
the dyers to form an association. Nothing in fact caused such
anxiety to the *grassi* as to see the *sottoposti* uniting, even in
religious fraternities. But the exodus of workmen from the city
worried them even more. This threatened to ruin one of the
fundamental principles of the "Art of Wool", and the strength
of the *popolo minuto* grew in proportion.

Towards 1370 the popular party experienced a new access of
strength. The success of the party of the Ricci in 1367 had
caused a renewal of the struggle against the *noveaux riches* (*la
gente nuova*). The cause of the *minuti* coincided at this time with
hostility to the Guelphs, and the following saying of one of
them has been recorded: "If I had any dealing with the party
of the Guelphs, I should like to turn its mansion (*palazzo*)
into a ditch into which I should throw all the excrements of
Florence." Men's passions were growing more heated. Faction-
fights and the war of the "Eight Saints" with the Holy See
were added to the accumulation of material difficulties and
hardened the attitudes of conflicting parties. And more serious
conflicts were in preparation. Those men who were bent on
pursuing a popular policy and purging the governing body
took an oath of membership in a secret society, Salvestro dei
Medici being one of them.

In the course of the decades following the plague Siena was
repeatedly harassed by very grave troubles. The enemies of the
government, namely the nobles and the minor Arts, were
merely awaiting a chance to destroy it. The prestige and
influence of the ruling bourgeois had just been weakened by the
bankruptcy of their richest members. The Emperor Charles
IV's arrival on 23 March 1355 was marked by violent episodes,
both nobles and *popolani* wishing to secure his support against
the patricians. He had scarcely had time to settle down in the
palazzo where he was to lodge, before clamour broke out.

Cries of "Long live the Emperor" mingled with cries of "Death to the Jews." Demonstrators attacked the *palazzo communale* where the nine priors, who had not had time to rally the militia, had taken refuge. For two days the city was given over to rioting. The bourgeois were hunted and their mansions looted and burned. On the 25th the Emperor contrived to free the nine priors and received their more or less unwilling resignation of office; and before he left, on the 28th, he entrusted a committee of twelve with the duty of reforming the constitution. This had been done when he returned on 9 April.

The revolution in Siena had put an end to the closed patrician regime. In spite of affrays on 8 May, the new system which was open to the *popolani* began to operate. The twelve "governors and administrators of the republic" who were invested with powers of government were henceforth to be *popolani*, while twelve nobles, who had to belong to separate families, formed another council. In the general Council of the Commune the *popolani* had a majority of seats, 250 as against 150 for the nobles. Finally the Captain and the *Gonfaloniere di Giustizia* were appointed by the general council from among the *popolani*, with the duty of maintaining public order and justice. It went without saying that former members of the government were excluded. The reorganization of the crafts granted a larger place to the minor Arts which had formerly been kept aside, but the new machinery soon began to creak, because the understanding between the nobility and the *popolo* was merely superficial. Among the nobles, Guelphs and Ghibellines hated each other. Among the *popolani*, the major Arts, the minor Arts and the *sottoposti* all opposed each other. Discord continued to prevail.

Many were the incidents to which it gave rise, one of which, during the first year of the new regime, has been described by a Sienese religious, Fra Filippo. On the pretext of wishing to remove from the near-by convent of Selva del Lago some banished patricians who had taken refuge in it, a punitive expedition had set out with the real intention of burning down the monastery. The suspects were seized, but at the moment when they were going to be condemned and when fire was to be set to the building, the Prior secured a miracle: a torrential rainstorm cooled the spirits of the demonstrators who now declared the prisoners absolved.

However, all the episodes did not end so agreeably, the seriousness of the problems scarcely permitted it. Apart from social contentions, economic and financial difficulties, and also the demands of mercenary troops, maintained an atmosphere of anxiety and discontent. Particularly violent disturbances occurred in 1368 and 1371. An attempt on the part of the nobles to restore the regime of the Nine took place on 2 September 1368, and for twenty-two days they remained in possession of the *palazzo communale*. The *popolani* recovered power but had difficulty in retaining it. The Emperor having returned barely escaped being made prisoner by the rioters who assailed his lodging. Neri di Donato, in the *Chronicle* of Siena, comments thus on the violence of the riot: "The Emperor remained quite alone, a prey to the greatest fear ever experienced by a wicked man." The people had won the day, the *minuti* now obtaining a majority (eight out of fifteen) of the increased number of seats on the Council of Government.

In 1371 events assumed a different aspect. The economic situation and the social atmosphere had become really bad. There were unemployment and business troubles; employers were assigning and paying for work as they liked. The disparity between wage-rates and the cost of commodities had increased in 1370 by reason of a dearth which raised the price of wheat to a record level. On 14 July, under pressure of hunger, three hundred weavers formed an illegal association, the *Compagnia dei Branco*, rose in insurrection and pillaged the houses of the rich. The chronicle, just quoted, says that "they wished to be the masters", though their real object was a rise in wages. However, the *Chronicle* continues: "their attack on the Signoria was a failure. If they made great clamour and uttered threats, these men who wanted to kill the masters of the city were themselves victims of repression". Although the *popolani* had a majority in the communal government, they could do no more than attenuate the effect of this rigour. The rebellion was mastered, but its working-class nature, its demand for higher wages and the violence of its behaviour reveal the events of 1371 in Siena as giving a foretaste of the "Tumult of the Ciompi" in 1378 in Florence.

It is now clear that the revolutionary tempest which was to mark the years from 1378 to 1382 did not come like a clap of thunder from a clear sky. If the years following the Jacquerie of 1358 were not marked by any major insurrection—a fact which may be ascribed to the languor produced by the epidemic of 1361–2 and to the slowness of a revival—they were not perfectly calm. Urban conflicts continued to occur in the Empire, as in Italy, the insurrection at Augsburg in 1368 being a spectacular example of them. In England peasant agitation, consisting of hundreds of isolated incidents, grew more and more violent. Serfs who had been arrested by their lords were freed by force; agitators encouraged others to refuse their services; while the judges who administered the Statute of Labourers had several times to seek protection by the forces of the Crown. On every hand, perils were clearly threatening.

[Chapter Four]
The Years of Revolution (1378–82)

FROM THE SPRING of 1378 to the first months of 1383 a large part of Europe was shaken by social conflicts of unexampled seriousness, and almost simultaneous occurrence. While we cannot say that they were strictly synchronized, the closeness of their occurrence, as illustrated by the accompanying chart, is no less striking.

These revolutions had some influence on each other, as we shall show; but if there was a "symphony", it was not at all played to time. The troubles seem to have broken out without any connecting links, and the authorities were able to repress them one after the other. News did not yet travel quickly enough for there to have been a real revolutionary contagion. Nevertheless the Black Death, thirty years before, had revealed a new cohesion between the peoples of a Europe in which connections of every kind were growing numerous. Thirty years mark a generation. Is it unreasonable to see a connection between the wave of pestilence which overwhelmed one country after another and the years of revolution which were also to come so closely together?

The outbreaks of trouble were, on the other hand, diverse in character, each of them hingeing on a local or regional tradition. We have indicated their antecedents, and should also describe their individual features. But, without losing sight of

138]

CHRONOLOGY OF EVENTS BETWEEN 1378 and 1382

DATE	FRANCE	NETHERLANDS	ENGLAND	ITALY, THE EMPIRE
1378	April: riot at Le Puy, agitation at Nîmes.			July: revolt of the Ciompi at Florence. Agitation at Dantzig.
1379	October: insurrection at Montpellier and environs. November: insurrection at Alès.	1 September: beginning of disturbances at Ghent.		
1380	September–October: university agitation in Paris. 16 September: death of Charles V.	1 December: concession from the Count of Flanders. Early months: new insurrection in Flanders. 29 May: defeat of the weavers of Bruges. June: siege of Ghent.		13 August: submission of the ruling class in Brunswick.

CHRONOLOGY OF EVENTS BETWEEN 1378 and 1382—contd.

DATE	FRANCE	NETHERLANDS	ENGLAND	ITALY, THE EMPIRE
	3 October: agitation against the *aides* (taxes) at Saint Quentin, Compiègne and Laon. 15 November: demonstration in Paris against the *aides*. Anti-Jewish riot.		End of the year: poll-tax voted.	December: trial of strength at Lübeck.
1381	May: riot at Saint Quentin.	Spring: new revolt at Ghent.	End of May: beginning of the revolt in Essex. 2 June: revolt in Kent. 10 June: taking of Canterbury. 13 June: the rebels enter London. 15 June: death of Wat Tyler. July–August: repression.	
1382	8 September: riot at Béziers.	26 January: Philip van Artevelde, Captain-General of Ghent.		January: final defeat of the Ciompi.

Year			
	24 February: Harelle at Rouen (and agitation at Amiens and in Normandy). 1 March: the Maillotins in Paris. 15 March: suppression of the Maillotins. 29 March: Charles VI at Rouen.	3 May: capture of Bruges by the men of Ghent.	17 September: arrest of the conspirators of Lübeck.
1383	1 August: second Harelle at Rouen. Autumn: agitation in Paris.	27 November: battle at Roosebeke.	
1384	January–February: repression in Paris. March: repression in Rouen.	July: success of Franz Ackerman in Flanders. 30 January: death of Louis de Male, Count of Flanders.	
1385		18 December: peace of Tournai.	

certain similarities or of the closeness of their occurrence in time, it seems better now to describe these revolutions separately.

Florence was the first city to be affected. Everything concurs in explaining this: the level of economic development which had been attained by the Tuscan metropolis, the degree of its political consciousness, the difficulties of every kind which afflicted it in the years preceding the great outbreak, and especially the war against the Holy See, known as the War of the Eight Saints (*Otto Santi*), that is, the eight magistrates who had been invested with plenary powers to wage it.

REVOLT

The very name of the *Tumulto dei Ciompi*, traditionally used to describe the events of June, July and August 1378, not only expresses their violence and the part played in them by the humblest of the lower strata (*sottoposti*) of Florentine industry; it also illustrates their confusion, and the fact that they were improvised and had no aftermath.

Towards 1340–2, as we have seen, Florence had already experienced great agitations and, after that, some difficult times between 1360 and 1368. The taxes, especially the personal tax of the *catasto*, the jurisdiction in the service of the *grassi* of the *ufficiale forestiere*, the problems of food supply and of wages, the claims made by the new Arts for the benefit of the dyers and other crafts of the second rank—all these factors made up a sum of grievances on the part of the *popolani minuti* against the employers. Were the events of 1378 the outcome of a worsening situation and an accumulation of motives of discontent? Did their explosion result from the initiative and action of a few individuals? What were their objects, what were the results? And what was the bearing of these events?

The information we dispose of reflects, usually, a similar point of view. Contemporary chroniclers, whose works have been mostly published, are nearly all hostile to the Ciompi. They wrote after the rising and even after the reaction, and their feelings were of retrospective fear and of a hatred untempered by fear. One is struck by the manner in which one of the most famous chronicles, ascribed first to Gino di Neri

Capponi and later to Alamanno Acciaiuoli who witnessed the *Tumulto* when he was young, subsequently described the rebels: "Ruffians, malefactors, thieves ... useless men, of base condition." For him, "Ciompi means nothing but what is fat, dirty and ill-clad". He insists on their violence, he judges and condemns. Marchione di Coppo Stefani is a quieter chronicler; he does not apply prejorative adjectives to the Ciompi but words indicating their trades. In a desire to be impartial he observes that the insurgents set fire to the houses of the rich "so that it should not be said that they were stealing". Chronicles favourable to the Ciompi, of which the best known is that of the *Squittinatore*, are rare; but we also have unpublished fragments of the journal of a cloth-cropper named Paolo di Guido.

Archives are also fragmentary. We have at least the record of a few deliberations of the Signoria and the *Balìa* of 1378, protocols of the *Mercanzia* and the Art of Wool, tax lists, and accounts; not forgetting private archives, such as those of the Strozzi and of Francesco Datini, a great merchant. These documents allow us to modify the views which the chroniclers present, perhaps too simply, in their tragic or picturesque vision of the past. On the above foundations, followed by the researches of A. Doren, G. Renard and N. Rodolico, the works of A. Sapori, F. Melis, V. Rutenberg, E. Werner and G. A. Brucker throw the light of varied sources and colours on the causes of the "Tumult", on its actors and its historical bearing.

The succession of events in Florence may be summarized in three phases: a reforming stage in May and June; a revolutionary explosion in mid-July; and towards the end of August the beginning of a reaction which grew inexorably over the years that followed.

As to whether the beginning of the difficulties should be ascribed to a worsening of the economic situation, interpretations differ. It is evident that the social and industrial structure already described—a system involving the existence of a great number of ill-paid *sottoposti* whose way of life was precarious—

still subsisted. Their wages were modest, paid in copper coinage which had been devalued in relation to the currency in gold and silver, and subject to the rule of a maximum. The number of feast days, about 122 in the year, further reduced their income, and one must also take account of some unemployment. Indebtedness was widespread. Since 1371 any advance on wages had to be repaid by work. Insolvency brought the debtor before the court of the *ufficiale forestiere*, who was

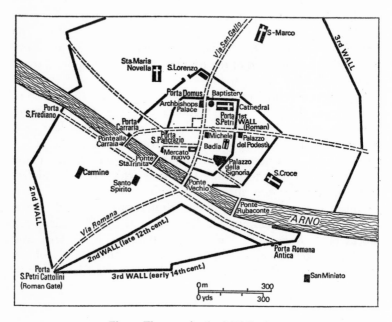

Fig. 3 Florence in the Middle Ages

inclined to severity since he pocketed 25 per cent of the fines. Moreover the *sottoposti* could not legally act together to defend themselves, all forms of association being prohibited.

It was contingent circumstances that caused the complications of May and June 1378; mainly the consequences of the war with the Holy See. Already in 1375 central Italy, like other regions, had suffered from a serious dearth in the corn supply. The interdict issued by Gregory XI was of a kind to interfere with the provisioning of Florence, to hamper the importing of English wool, and to close certain markets for the export of cloth: in short, to disturb the economy and the social order. According to some historians, the production of textiles suffered a notable decline in 1377, falling to some 24,000 pieces of cloth, in marked contrast with the prosperity which Villani describes as prevailing before 1340. Other authors, notably G. A. Brucker, who base their views on the archives of the Art of Wool, deny the opinion that a severe economic depression followed the War of the Eight Saints. Merchants less scrupulous than the English in regard to the interdict, are held to have supplied Florence with wool, while neither Pisa, nor Siena, nor Venice, nor Hungary, nor the Levant would seem to have discontinued buying cloth. The effect of unemployment should not be exaggerated, and the rise in prices was probably not as great as suggested. One should therefore look elsewhere for the real cause of the political crisis.

The Ciompi did not intervene at the outset and the outburst of discontent first came from "middle-class" groups, from political motives. If in fact it be admitted that during the first months of 1378 discontent was neither more nor less great than before, it evidently increased in the spring. In April the consuls of the Art of Wool decided to make it more difficult for the *lanaioli* to obtain office and quadrupled the fee for matriculation; and this inopportune measure turned the upper class of *sottoposti* into opponents of the regime by disappointing their hopes of social and professional advancement. But, generally speaking, it was the "Guelphic terror", with its proscriptions (*ammonizioni*), that unleashed the tension. The penalty was very heavy because it included the loss of social "status", thus depriving the victim of any influence or possibility of access to office; and it was hereditary, into the bargain. These *ammonizioni* affected every social category, which explains why the most varied kinds of people joined in opposition to the regime. The entry into the *Signoria*, on 1 May 1378, of Salvestro dei Medici, a man already known for his demagogical attitudes, could only in such circumstances appear as a provocation.

As *Gonfaloniere di Giustizia*, Salvestro did not delay two days in challenging the policy of *ammonizione*; even among the Guelphs abuse of the system was provoking protests. We may suppose that some bargaining and a compromise attenuated the system of proscriptions; but six weeks later, on 14 June, when the captains of the Guelphic party accused a dyer and a tanner of being Ghibellines, the very class which it would have been wise to conciliate was roused to indignation. Four days later the agitation began. Salvestro dei Medici supported by arguments of a demagogical kind a proposal to renew the application of the Ordinances of Justice. He won wide support by declaring himself the spokesman of the merchants, the artisans, the poor and the weak who "desire to live and work in peace", in order to "be able to live in security and freedom, and so that justice in the city may be restored". The proposal, regarded as an ultimatum, was so strongly opposed that Salvestro threatened to resign from the Signoria and he stirred up the crowd in the square who responded with cries of "Long live liberty! Death to the traitors!"

One should read the chronicle in which Alamanno Acciaiuoli, one of the priors and therefore an eye-witness, recorded at the time the way in which the riot started, on 18 June 1378. First, the words and theatrical movements of Salvestro:

"Wise men of the council, I wish to heal this city of the maleficent tyranny of the great and powerful, and I am not allowed to act. . . . I am not believed. . . . Therefore, since people do not follow me, I consider that I can do nothing more as prior or as *gonfaloniere di giustizia*. Consequently, I decide to withdraw to my home. Appoint another *gonfaloniere* and make your arrangements with God."

While Salvestro, draped in his dignity, was reaching the stairway, the other members of the council played their part:

"Some retained him and brought him back into the hall . . . where they began to recriminate violently. . . . It was then that

Benedetto di Nerozzo degli Alberti . . . presented himself at the
window and began to shout: 'Long live the people' and to call
to all those who were assembled in the square: 'Cry: Long live
the people!' That was why a great rumour immediately arose
throughout the city, the shops were closed . . . and people
began to arm themselves."

The days of moderation and compromise were over. Most
of the chronicles place the responsibility on Salvestro dei
Medici and his followers, who were accused by Ser Nofri of
being the "promoters of so many evils and scandals". On
22 June, the rioters, with the furriers in the lead, reinforced
by prisoners who had been liberated, set fire to a dozen
palazzi, one after the other, and began to attack the monasteries. The communal treasury narrowly escaped pillage; this
was prevented by the pork-butchers who seized five strangers,
said to be Flemings, and hanged them at the cross-roads: a
sign of xenophobia inspired by immigrants who were specialists
in a craft then in a state of crisis.

Instead of attempting repression, the Signoria appointed a
balia, a commission of eighty members entrusted with reforms,
and adopted measures of appeasement: on the one hand,
purgation of the governing body and sanctions against some of
the most powerful; on the other, rehabilitation of a few
Ghibellines, and the right of appeal against *ammonizione*. The
situation however remained tense. Some people were so disquieted that they removed their goods from the city and closed
their shops and work-rooms. While the militia patrolled the
streets and stood guard at key-points, a few patrician families
recruited body-guards in the *contado*. At the beginning of July,
Florence seemed to be expecting a civil war.

The shilly-shallying of the Signoria and the half-measures
adopted led to the second phase, the phase of revolutionary
explosion. The minor Arts took the initiative by presenting a
petition supported by a crowd in arms on 8 July. The
movement was evolving step by step in a democratic direction.
The petition did not tend to reverse the established order, those
who had written it being as hostile to the arrogance of the

grassi as they were to the audacity of the Ciompi; they wished
to promote, within the traditional corporative structure, civic
equality between the small shopkeepers and business men
concerned with international trade, the people living on private
means, and the magnates. In their view, the representatives
of the twenty-one Arts should, without exception, share in the
voting for the Signoria; on the other hand, those who exercised no professional work should not have access to communal
office. The petition, although no doubt conservative in tenor,
reflected the revolt of the artisans against the monopolizing
by their employers of communal offices and of the control of
crafts. The fundamental claim logically implicit in the petition
was, as in the days of Gautier de Brienne, the establishment of
supplementary "Arts" for the dyers, the makers of doublets and
the lower class of Ciompi who could not be assimilated to the
various specialized crafts.

The step over into illegality had been secretly prepared by
a few conspirators bound by an oath, during meetings held
in a church in the Via San Gallo, then in a place called Ronco
in the quarter of the Santo Spirito. Agitation broke out next
day simultaneously in four places, mainly in the popular
quarters of Santo Stefano and San Giovanni. The chronicle
ascribed to Alamanno Acciaiuoli contains a detailed account
of what followed. The Signoria had had wind of the conspiracy and had arrested a few suspects, including one of the
leaders, a certain Simoncino. At the head of the movement,
with him, were a rich cord-maker, a druggist and two artisans.
Simoncino admitted that the cloth-workers wanted, above all,
to be freed from the "Art of Wool". "They were", he said,
"badly treated by the officials of the craft, who punished them
for peccadilloes, and by the employers who paid them badly.
For a piece of work worth twelve *soldi* they give eight. . . . We
wish to have no dealings either with the *lanaioli* or with their
officials. We wish to share in the government of the city."

The movement was growing wider. The crowd had been
stirred to riot by the revelation of a clock-maker who, having
come to the Palazzo Vecchio to wind up the clock, involuntarily witnessed the questioning of the prisoner, under torture.

On 20 July several thousand armed men besieged the Signoria, demanding the liberation of Simoncino. The priors in the Palazzo Vecchio passed that day in a critical situation. Only from certain quarters did the militia answer the summons of the *gonfalonieri*, and the priors had to wait until the evening for reinforcements, which had been urgently called for, to arrive from the *contado*. The Ciompi had assembled near the Palazzo Vecchio. The night was illumined by the burning of mansions to which the rioters had set fire. There was, says Stefani's chronicle, "the most incredible disorder".

Despite a violent storm, the trouble continued next day. The palace of the Podestà, a strategic point, was taken by storm, the stocks of grain at Or San Michele were plundered, the archives of the justice and fiscal departments and of the Art of Wool were burned, and the public executioner was hanged by the feet in front of the Palazzo Vecchio: this, paradoxically, was the only murder recorded. The seizure of the civic standard might be regarded as a revolutionary act but also as a traditional gesture. After the period of rioting the coalition of the Ciompi and the minor Arts tried to get practical effect given to the programme of reforms elaborated at San Lorenzo during the night of 21–2 July.

This programme was presented to the priors in the form of two petitions and in the name of the minor Arts and the *popolo minuto*. The requests were comparatively moderate and reveal no clear egalitarian pretensions. In asking for the creation of an *Arte del Popolo Minuto* they were no doubt demanding the same rights as the others, but most of their claims were for reforms rather than innovations: the rehabilitation of victims of the Guelphic proscription; an amnesty for those who had taken part in the June disorders; reform of the system of penalties; suspension of arrest for debt; no forced loans for the next six months; and abolition of the *ufficiale forestiere*. The programme had the merit of being clear, though most of the measures proposed were due to temporary circumstances.

Nevertheless the manner in which it was imposed on the Signoria revealed not only a change in the kind of people

involved, but also definite political resolution and a social
transformation of those who were in possession of political
power; for the priors capitulated in the afternoon of 22 July.
They had tried, though in vain, to gain time. The crowd which
assembled in front of the Palazzo Vecchio tolerated no delay.
"The priors", wrote Alamanno Acciaiuoli, "rushed this way
and that, not knowing what to do. They stared at each other;
some weeping, others wringing their hands, others smiting their
faces. They were completely disorientated. . . . A clamour was
coming up from the square where the multitude was demanding
the resignation of the priors. If they refused to leave, the city
would be consigned to the flames . . . and their wives and
children would be arrested and killed before their eyes."
Finally the priors withdrew one by one, followed by the only
two who had declared that they meant to remain at their post.

"When they had gone", continues the chronicler, "the gate
of the palace was opened and the people entered. A certain
Michele di Lando, a foreman of the wool-carders, was carrying
the banner of the *popolo minuto* which he had found in the executioner's house. . . ." Then, according to an anonymous
narrator, "the crowd poured in after him . . . entering all the
rooms; they found the ropes which had been prepared for
hanging the poor men who had pillaged buildings. . . . Several
youths climbed up the tower and rang the bells to celebrate,
to the honour of God, the victorious seizure of the palace."
After which, Alamanno Acciaiuoli draws the following conclusion, at once melancholy and humorous: "What a succession
of strains and novelties! God in Heaven, what a miracle thou
hast made us behold!" And he expressed amazement that a
simple wool-carder, son of a work-woman, should suddenly
have become *Gonfaloniere di Giustizia*.

Of the actions which consecrated the popular victory, some
were symbolic, others were politically effective. In order to
confirm popular sovereignty and to signalize the promotion of
the *popolani* to a social rank hitherto closed to them, sixty of them
were dubbed knights, Salvestro dei Medici figuring among the
foremost. A similar interest in legitimate procedure appeared
in the ceremonial handing of the banners to the companies of

the sixteen quarters of the city; the procession being preceded
by a band of musicians which gave it the festive character of
all revolutions. On 22 July in fact a new authority had been
improvised, not without an eye to effect. The new *balia* of
thirty-seven members, chosen by acclamation, contained
representatives of the major Arts, of the minor Arts and of the
three arts which had been demanded by the insurgents and
established for the *minuti*. Thirty-two of the members were new
men, five only belonging to families which had already occupied communal office. Lastly, on 29 July, with a view to
making permanent the movement of the commune towards
democracy, the Ciompi burned the "purses" containing the
names of candidates for the magistrature which were to be
drawn by lot. New and enlarged lists had to be drawn up.

On 4 August a religious ceremony was held to celebrate
the raising of the interdict. This might have been intepreted as
a sign of civic reconciliation and harmony if difficulties of every
kind had not led the new Signoria to adopt a policy which put
a brake on the revolution. The Ciompi were not slow to oppose
this new trend.

The most urgent problems of course related to public order
and economic life. The *balia* strove to reassure the population
which had been confused by persistent rumours and troubled
by the continual tramping of armed men through the streets.
On 25 July a civic militia of 1,500 archers was formed with
the object of bringing the popular troops under official control
while procuring regular pay for them. And during the last
days of the month a systematic search was undertaken with a
view to disarming the population.

Even so, a certain number of shops and work rooms were still
closed at the beginning of August. The need for repeated
measures to require their reopening (24 and 27 July and 1
August) reveals the difficulty of effecting it. On 15 August
resumption of work in the cloth industry was not fully effective.
A graph of the taxes received on the signing of contracts enables
us to estimate the length of the business recession. From 395
florins on 19 July, receipts fell to 13 on the 26th, were only
84 on 2 August, and 113 on the 9th. They rose to 689 on

the 16th; but the normal figure as observed at the beginning of July was regained only in December. One of the main causes of this economic recession seems to have been the flight of employers into the *contado* and the removal of some of the merchandise from the city and as far afield as Pisa and even Bologna. In reality circumstances had amplified the seasonal migration of those Florentines who had means of escaping the great heat of summer. The *balia* decided on a few measures, fixed six weeks as the period of delay permitted for the re-opening of businesses, but, following tradition, exercised no coercion. It is true that the population would doubtless not have assented to it, since wage-earners seem to have preferred a direct bargain with their employers to the intervention of the *balia*. The only decision it took was to fix at a minimum of two thousand the number of pieces of cloth which each *lanaiolo* was to produce monthly, under pain of sanctions.

There was a risk that problems of food-supply would be added to the questions of employment—and unemployment—raised by the *balia's* decree on business. It suppressed the tax on the milling of corn and supervised the maintenance of sufficient reserves of grain by ordering (9 August) that all stocks possessed by Florentines in the *contado* should be brought into the city within the next week. This order had to be repeated; it had doubtless not been strictly applied. On 30 August the *balia* made a free distribution of corn to the indigent. Yet there seems to have been no dearth in August. The chronicles record no popular feeling in this matter, while the accounts of the flour-mills show that the latter were working normally and that prices remained stable at between ten and sixteen *soldi* for a bushel, whereas in times of famine they rose to forty *soldi*. On the other hand the *balia* had to face serious fiscal problems. The disorders had added to the difficulties due to the war with the Holy See. These had involved new expenses (for the militia, and new elections), while causing a diminution of public revenue (suppression of the tax on milled grain, and a reduction of the salt-tax). In such circumstances the *balia* was reduced to adopting conservative measures and to applying only partially the programme of the Ciompi. There were no doubt measures of financial purification: an enquiry into the usurpations by individuals of public funds with a view to recovering the amounts taken; a few auction-sales (27 August), suspension of interest-payments on the public debt (the *monte*), above all a revision of the basis (*estimo*) on which direct taxation was assessed. This was the only decision which survived from the measures of the revolutionary programme drawn up at the Ronco on 19 July. This programme had envisaged radical measures such as the total liquidation of the public debt within twelve years. So great however was the debt that no government could have undertaken the operation without risk of bankruptcy. But the *balia* further disappointed the Ciompi by decreeing a forced loan, a thing which it had undertaken not to do for six months. Care was taken, in August, to touch only the richest taxpayers. Yet the small ones had some motives for dissatisfaction with the men who were not carrying out the reforms with which they had been entrusted. Thus, observes one of our chronicles, "the poor have always carried the burden of expenses, while the rich have always had the profits".

On the political plane also the *balia* was not keeping the promises of July. The form and procedure, and the very nature of its decisions, bore the stamp of tradition. Certainly some thirty of the *grassi* were exiled, the victims of the Guelphs were restored to enjoyment of civil rights, and an amnesty was declared for those who had been condemned for fraud or for crimes against the State. The list of citizens eligible for the magistrature was considerably enlarged in favour of the *minuti*. But in fact, apart from a few dismissals, the administrative staff of the old government was maintained; and scarcely a sixth of the 13,000 members of the three new Arts of the *sottoposti* were found to be eligible, that is, to have fulfilled the conditions required for inscription among the taxpayers subject to the *prestanze*. The Ciompi movement, though proletarian in appearance, was leading to a system based on property qualification. Should one ascribe the art of contriving smooth transitions to that innate sense of *nuances* which the Florentines possess? Or simply suppose that the *balia* did what it thought practicable in difficult circumstances? Or should its members be accused of treachery as regards the revolutionary cause? These are delicate questions. A sociological analysis of the *balia* shows that among the thirty-two new members, scarcely half were Ciompi. All the others were men of middle rank, and of varied professions: a notary, some merchants and heads of small businesses. They were conservative by instinct; and the only motive for their conversion to the revolutionary side was jealousy of the patricians and the desire to prevent the political system from being closed to the advantage of the latter. There were, besides, among the Ciompi, men of every social origin, and one should not forget that in spite of demagogic speeches, the old habit of clientèle led to the formation, hardly demo-cratic, of cliques around men like Salvestro dei Medici, Giorgio Scali and Alberto Strozzi. Nothing, in short, was perfectly clear and malcontents could with reason complain of a policy already reactionary before reaction became an open fact.

Such are the circumstances which explain the last and violent upheaval of the revolution at the end of August 1378. A mere incident or pretext was enough to catalyse the disap-pointment and the aspirations of the *minuti*. The judicial records of the repression which followed the new disorders throw a pitiful light on the credulity of the crowd in face of the mirage of apocalyptic prophecies; and on the naïveté of its revolutionary dreams, devoid of any political sense. Thus Antonio di Ronco, one of the Ciompi, said: "The time will come when I shall no more wander about like a beggar, because I expect to be rich for the rest of my life; and if you will join me, you too will become rich and we shall enjoy a brilliant situa-tion in Florence." And here are the words of a cloth-worker to a friend: "We will turn the city upside down, we will kill and despoil the rich men who have despised us; we shall become masters of the city; we shall govern it as we like and we shall be rich."

The Ciompi were shocked to see their former comrades who had entered the *balia* now accepting payment for their duties. The reaction of the most sincere was due to honesty as much as to disenchantment. Now, as before, most of the demonstrators poured out of the working-class districts of the Santo Spirito and San Giovanni, and some five thousand assembled in front of the Church of San Marco. At their head were men "elect" in the full sense of the word, since they were called "The Eight Saints of the People of God". Stimulated by this appeal to a revolutionary mysticism, the multitude marched on the Signoria. Curiously enough, it was a nobleman who had joined the popular cause, Luca da Panzano, who presented the demands of the Ciompi. With a theatrical gesture, he removed the golden spurs which he wore as a noble and asked the *minuti* to make him a knight of the people. As in July, the wool-carders were the most active of the rebels, and they at once came into conflict with the wool-carder who had led the July insurrection and was now considered to have betrayed them.

The *popolo di Dio* required, first, the purification of the new Signoria, that is, abolition of the exorbitant privileges enjoyed by its members, such as Salvestro dei Medici and especially Michele di Lando. It was said that the latter had agreed to sell himself for some hundreds of florins and the baubles of the aristocracy. A pennon, a buckler and armour, at the expense of the Commune had been offered him. Especially did the Ciompi desire the abolition of the *consorteria della libertà* which, under cover of its high-sounding name, involved the members of the *balia* in the same compromising situation. The Ciompi next demanded that the *Otto Santi del popolo di Dio* should become a permanent institution, instead of the Eight Saints of the war with the Pope, who were now useless. Finally, and more specifically, the *minuti* demanded a moratorium on debts and the liquidation of the *monte*.

Finding itself now in a false position in face of these demands, the *balia* on 22 July decided first to evade the question. It reserved its reply as to making the Eight Saints of the people of God a permanent institution, but, pending a new consultation of the electoral corps, accepted the other claims in principle. This was a means of gaining time. Michele di Lando, on whom the issue depended, lost none. On the one hand he worked at neutralizing those representatives of the Ciompi in the *balia* who were uncompromising; on the other, at discrediting the rebels. By taking a solemn oath he joined those of his colleagues who shared his point of view. Rumours most injurious to the Ciompi now circulated through the City; they were accused, as forty years before in the time of Gautier de Brienne, of wanting to put power in the hands of a popular tyrant. The stakes were down, and the last act took place on 31 August, in two phases, which are described in the journal of the *Squittinatore* and the anonymous chronicle. Two rebellious Ciompi had come from their headquarters at Santa Maria Novella to the Palazzo Vecchio to seek from the magistrates a reply to their demands. After a lively altercation, Michele di Lando drew his sword, threatened his former friends and, sounding the alarm, drove them into the street to the cry of "Death to those who want a lord of the city!" This time the encounter was violent and the fighting, which began in the Piazza della Signoria, ended with the rebels being hunted through the popular quarters. As in most of the riots at the end of the Middle Ages the corporation of butchers distinguished itself by its relentless fury. The passion and mutual hatred of "haves" and "have-nots" made this day one of the bloodiest in Florentine history.

The destruction of the Ciompi revolution was to continue for several years. Reaction was progressive. It inevitably involved condemnations to death—160 in five years—and banishments. Salvestro dei Medici and Michele di Lando were exiled, although they had abandoned the Ciompi; the property of the Alberti was confiscated. On 2 September the establishment of a committee of vigilance (the *Otto di Guardia*) provided the regime with a political police which was formally joined to the Signoria in 1382. The concessions made to the *minuti* were revoked; the XXIVth Art—that of the Ciompi—was immediately suppressed; then, in 1382, it was the turn of the two others which had been founded in 1378. Little by little the major Arts recovered half of the seats of the priors, the office of Gonfalonier, and a majority in the councils. Reaction continued inexorably, and was completed by a reform in the mode of elections in 1387 and, in 1393, the reorganization of a reliable militia. The haunting fear of social subversion strengthened an oligarchical form of democracy.

Now that the events have been related, we should try to define their historical significance which has been so often discussed and so diversely interpreted. The complexity of the facts is such as to exclude any simple explanation. One wonders, first, how the regime established after the fall of Gautier de Brienne could have survived until 1378. The condition of the Ciompi had not improved; on the contrary, the causes of discontent had persisted and worsened, so much so that very little was needed to provoke the explosion of 1378. On the other hand, if we admit the seriousness of the social problem, how are we to explain why the Ciompi movement was so short-lived and why it failed?

We must take account of all the factors. We know that beyond the economic difficulties, of which the gravity has been open to question, the social structure was also a factor, even if contemporaries were not fully aware of it. But to what extent? It does not appear that the Ciompi revolution was anything but an urban movement. Yet this does not mean that there was no economic and social unbalance in country districts. What most strikes us is a pre-capitalist development in the urban cloth industry; but this has perhaps been exaggerated since the publication of A. Doren's work (1908) and the more recent researches of F. Melis and R. de Roover. Historians tend to generalize the importance of the men on whom they are best informed; now industrial enterprises like those of Francesco Datini and Giovanni dei Medici, while appearing the most important, did not actually employ such a large number of workers. In 1380 Florence possessed 279 businesses, of which the annual production varied from a few to 200 pieces of cloth. Concentration had not gone as far as supposed.

That the *sottoposti* included in their ranks a considerable number of real proletarians, the Ciompi, there is not the slightest doubt. But an analysis of the lower strata of society reveals their social diversity. Very numerous were those whom an average daily wage of five *soldi* for a working-day of from sixteen to eighteen hours was not enough to sustain. Among these were a certain number of peasants who had been drawn into the city by the hope of wages. In 1378 Florence contained from nine to twelve thousand Ciompi, and nearly 30 per cent of the population were exempt from paying taxes on the ground that they possessed nothing. However, the *sottoposti* included some people whose economic situation put them on a footing of equality with the members of the Arts. They contributed to the *catasto* and subscribed to the public debt, as is proved for example by fragments of the accounts of two wool-combers. Moreover there were cases of permeation between social groups. Small impecunious business men were members of the Arts, while men belonging to comfortably-off families figured among the *sottoposti*. Finally, to increase the complexity of contrasts between the categories, relative though they were, we see dyers constantly and bitterly complaining of the control exercised over them by the Art of Wool, but also, as employers themselves, sharing the views of the *lanaioli* regarding the work of their own employees. Sociologically, it is impossible to regard the *sottoposti* as a whole, including the Ciompi, as a homogeneous class in the modern sense of the term. All this, it seems, provides one explanation of the resistance offered by the traditional system before 1378 and during that year.

Now if the economic structure and the absence of homogeneity among the *popolo minuto* help to explain the course of events, other factors played a part. As against the juridical and economic interests which the *sottoposti* had in common, the traditional bonds which bound person to person seem often to have prevailed over common interests. We have observed how, during the events in the summer of 1378, the habits of clientèles determined the behaviour of individuals who followed a few leaders like Salvestro dei Medici, although themselves originally strangers to his class. Del Bene's correspondence between 1378 and 1381 contains interesting evidence of these personal bonds between masters, artisans and workmen. It was in this way that Benedetto Alberti and Tommaso Strozzi succeeded in turning the policy of the *balia* in the direction of moderation in August 1378.

The Ciompi might have been able to associate their cause with that of the peasants, as it appears that the Londoners did more or less in 1381, by making a pact with the insurrection of the country labourers. This was perhaps what the Florentine patricians were afraid of. As early as 20 June the Signoria had ordered the peasants who were in the city to return to the *contado*. In August the *balìa* reduced income tax by a third and lowered the price of salt, measures favourable to the country-folk. But the Ciompi's programme was purely urban and of no interest to the peasants. The country-women who spun wool were suffering from the closing of town workshops, which had provided them with additional resources; and in September as in July, it was from the *contado* that the patricians could expect the assistance of armed men whom they had summoned to their help. The Ciompi thus found themselves isolated.

Thus did the revolutionary spirit of the Ciompi gather no impetus after the events of 1343. The group, as we have seen, was not absolutely homogeneous; it had no doctrine and no urge for innovation. It does not seem that, apart from being open to prophecies and rabble-rousing, the movement underwent any marked ideological influence. The sect of the "Free Spirit" had adepts in Florence, and its messianic spirit may have impregnated certain minds; but of this nothing more is known. There is no evidence that the *Fraticelli*, though very near to the *popolo minuto*, had any adherents among the Ciompi, because the latter did not share their ideal of absolute poverty; nor did they listen to the preaching of the *Fraticelli* until later, when reaction had triumphed. If we have no clear knowledge of the spiritual aspect of the Ciompi movement, its irrational impulses were active and more than once caused events to deviate in a sense different from what economic conditions suggested.

The absence of any feeling for innovation is fairly striking. We have seen how difficult it was for the most ardent of the Ciompi to conceive a programme outside the traditional framework; which helps to explain the conservatism of most of the decisions taken in August 1378. The Ciompi acted within the institutional framework of those they had overcome and even adopted their moral attitudes.

The very destiny of those who had led the movement illustrates its poverty of inventive imagination. Michele di Lando was accused of treason; and in fact this former clerk of a *penaiolo*, whose wife was a pork-butcher's assistant, appears to have been intoxicated by power or else, owing to inexperience, to have let himself be circumvented by his associates. He was spared, before being exiled in 1382, but he did not rebel or seek revenge. He grew rich, gave a generous dowry with his daughter, became Captain of the People at Volterra, and ended his career in Modena as a respectable bourgeois and *lanaiolo*. Did he really betray the cause, or follow a natural direction which others would have followed, if they had had the chance? According to certain records the Ciompi had other, and more effective, leaders but did these men, after their defeat, follow a very different route? Luca del Melano, a former workman in the cloth industry, was exiled after the riot of 31 August; but he came back in 1382, set up as a poulterer in the Mercato Vecchio and the last trace we find of him is a lawsuit which, as an employer, he brought against a former employee for debt and breach of contract. As to the men of patrician origin who had by chance taken a lead in the Ciompi movement—Aribaldo Strozzi, Guerriante Marignolli and Mezza Attiviani—they hatched from outside the city commonplace conspiracies against the regime which had banished them. Thus we should consider the Ciompi movement in some of its aspects as an imbroglio, fairly typical of Florence, partly destructive, partly original.

However, the myth of a deadly subversion, a myth maintained by the reaction, does not merely correspond with a deep dread of a recurrence of the events of 1378. These events were quite clearly the outcome of more than disorder and tumult, as one can detect certain features of a revolutionary mentality. It would be an exaggeration to apply the word "programme" to a movement of which the main object was to replace one set of men with another. What was new and original in July and August was that the Ciompi adopted an organization of their own and acted on their own initiative with a view to seizing power. New, no doubt, but was it, after all, original? To answer this question we must examine what was happening elsewhere during the same years, and ask ourselves whether similar causes produced similar effects.

*   *   *

In the year following the "Tumult of the Ciompi" agitation broke out in France and continued in one city and province after another, at a time when the work of reaction was complete in Florence and weighing heavily on England. The disorders in Flanders presented original features, as usual, and had nothing in common with the southern turbulence known by the name of Tuchins; but their connection with the urban insurrections in the Parisian region, in Normandy and Picardy, lead us to consider all these rebellions collectively, so that we do not lose sight of the dramatic intensity arising from their being simultaneous.

We have already seen that the increase of "perils", after the middle period of the plague, was as threatening in Flanders as in Tuscany. Social problems took the same forms in both regions, that is, in terms of wages, working-hours, rivalry between crafts, opposition between rich and poor, and between the dominant and the dominated. Competition for control of the civic government took place in both regions, mainly within the textile crafts. And in Flanders as in Florence, industrial competition was raging: Florence, the rival of Siena, competing with Lucca and Pisa; Ghent, jealous of Bruges and Ypres. Without exaggerating comparisons, we may observe that the strife between Guelphs and Ghibellines corresponds with that between the "good" (*Goeden*) and the "bad" (*Kwaden*), formerly the *Leliaerts* and the *Clauwaerts*. The Flemish situation was complicated by a political factor, namely its being within the territorial framework of the county of Flanders and the feudal jurisdiction of the King of France. Apart from all this, it appears that the deeper motives underlying these revolutionary disorders offer striking analogies between Flanders and Florence. Ypres did not wait for the example of the Ciompi before acting: the weavers there were agitating as early as 1377.

In other parts of the French kingdom, the disorders present features corresponding with the two regional manners of the north and the south, and perhaps with different forms of economic and social development. On the one hand working-class insurrections in the cities predominated; on the other, rural revolts, not without analogies with the Jacquerie, accompanied urban agitation. One motive, however, was common to all these movements, namely strong discontent with the system of royal taxation: in that matter they are related, at least by their respective causes, to the insurrection of the English labourers. Thus the flames of rebellion broke out both in the north and far south of France in 1378 and 1379. The first sparks in the south were revolts about taxation at Le Puy-en-Velay in 1378 and at Montpellier in 1379. In Flanders the conflagration, so to speak, was immediate.

A revolutionary tradition had been growing up for a century past in Flanders, especially at Ghent. In 1379 when the first outburst took place, the rebels had an organization, methods, a leader and precise objects; they had for long known who were their adversaries: the rich men and the Count; and they knew where to strike. In Flanders people did not beat about the bush. Pirenne thought that Wat Tyler's doctrines had been formulated in the working-class quarters of Ghent, Bruges and Ypres several years before they were disseminated among the English labourers: in an economically advanced region the ground was certainly favourable for them. However, the immediate cause of the insurrection at Ghent in 1379 was not social.

The cause was connected with the long-standing opposition of interest between Bruges and Ghent. To put an end to an old quarrel Count Louis de Male, in 1379, authorized the digging of a canal to connect the Lys and the Reie, the river on which Bruges stands, which would have short-circuited the river traffic of Ghent, which stands at the confluence of the Lys and the Scheldt. Hardly had the work begun on territory subject to the castle of Ghent, when the watermen of that city, armed with picks and shovels, attacked the navvies to prevent

their completing the work, and also to fill in the canal which
on the territory subject to Bruges, had been nearly finished.
This was enough to bring the weavers to the assistance of the
watermen. The insurgents opened the prisons, set fire to one
of the Count's castles near the city and murdered the bailiff.

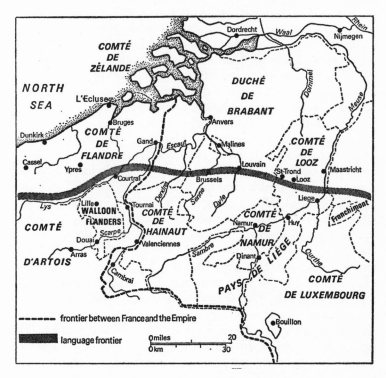

Fig. 4 The Netherlands in the Fourteenth Century

This episode, local at the outset, rapidly grew into a social and
political insurrection. It at once found a leader in the dean of
the watermen, an active and authoritative person named
John Yoens; and a dynamic party in the weavers of Ghent
who, in turn, incited their colleagues at Bruges and Ypres to
join the rising. The rebels had a definite programme: the

defence of municipal liberties and an attack on the patricians, who supported the power of the Count. They improvised an army to which the villagers, who were dominated by the townsfolk, were obliged willy-nilly to supply contingents. By the autumn subversion seemed complete. The Count's agents had fled, leaving the field clear for the rebel leaders established by Yoens. The rich had barricaded themselves in their homes and dared not appear outside; or had fled for refuge to Oudenarde, where the people's militia laid siege to them. On 1 December Louis de Male resigned himself to confirming the urban franchises and appointing a committee of inquiry. This solved nothing, but it enabled the Count to gain time in face of adversaries who were divided among themselves.

Most of the chronicles are hostile to the rebels, and they insist on the political aspect of the rising. The monk of Saint-Denys sees in it little more than rebellion against the lawful authority of the Count, and of the King, his lord. Froissart is not more favourable; but his having come from Valenciennes and his natural gift for observation enable him better to describe the events. He saw that the matter was very complex: it was a *grande diablerie*. Devilry is an adequate term, because the Great Schism had just (1378) destroyed the unity of Christendom, and the Flemings like the English had decided to obey Urban VI, the Pope of Rome. The problem however was essentially social. The *Chronique rimée des troubles de Flandre*, the *Istore et chronique de Flandre*, the *chronique des Comtes*—the documents as a whole—leave no doubt in the matter. The agreement between the cities for the defence of their liberties was only apparent: the strongest bonds were on the social level.

At Bruges as at Ghent and Ypres the notables constituted the party of order and supported the Count. Louis de Male, at the very beginning of the revolt, admitted it. To the patricians of Ghent who came to protest their devotion, he replied: "I well believe that you have not caused these outrages and misdeeds, in which evil men have not observed justice and there has been no more use of reason than among brute beasts." The author of the *Chronique rimée*, for his part, insists on the

sordid motives behind the violence: "covetousness is its foundation" and pride its source. He sums up his opinion of the
common folk as follows: "Their mouths still hunger after
filling themselves with the good things belonging to the lords."
They are all, he adds, nought but "mean knaves, ribald
fellows, muck".

In opposition to the solidarity of the powerful, that of the
commoners appears to have been less homogeneous, or rather
there were several united groups. The weavers formed one of
the strongest unions. It had been effective from the beginning,
between the weavers of Ghent, Bruges and Ypres. It was strong
again in 1380 when the Count's partisans roughly handled the
watermen of Ghent, and the truce of December was broken.
The solidarity of the weavers persisted in city after city, although at Bruges it conflicted with another kind of union,
that of the other crafts who were more numerous there and
impatient to throw off the control of the weavers of Ghent. The
Bruges weavers called those of Ghent to their aid, but in vain:
in a conflict with the butchers, fishmongers, furriers and
brokers, the weavers had the worst of it (29 May 1380). This
division among the craftsmen could only weaken their cause.
Although Ghent was then encouraged by an insurrection at
Malines, itself encouraged by Liége, the Flemish capital was
to lie under siege for three years, which made it one of the
liveliest centres of a general agitation; while its desperate resistance became a symbol and an example for other cities.
Ghent had started the struggle, Ghent maintained it and, when
needed, as at Bruges, renewed it. Meanwhile the other cities
of the French Kingdom which were also in rebellion found
encouragement in the example of Ghent. "Long live Ghent!"
was a general cry.

The circumstances which kindled agitation in Paris and several
other French cities were connected with the King's demise. A
certain relaxation following the change-over from a strong
government to that of a king who was still a minor, was
natural; though the first street-disorders in Paris were due to a
puerile but significant dispute over precedence during the

funeral ceremonies for Charles V, on 24 September 1380. An altercation broke out between Hugues Aubriot the Provost, a rather unpopular man, and the Rector of the university. The latter wished to have precedence in the procession over the chapters of Notre-Dame and the Sainte-Chapelle. "Do you pretend to a rank equal to that of prelates?" the Provost asked. "It is enough for us to be in our customary rank", replied the Rector. Whereupon Hugues Aubriot seized him by the chin and began to say: "Kill, kill them all." This aroused fury on both sides, and they came to blows. The Provost's officers drove back the "scholars"; several were wounded, one died three days later, and thirty-six were arrested; while the Rector nearly fell into the Seine. There was something picturesque about the ensuing panic, when the members of the university left their copes, belts and hoods on the ground and fled in every direction; some swimming across the river to regain the Latin Quarter. When refusing to receive a delegation next day, Aubriot is reported as exclaiming: "Ha! pack of braggarts and beggars. ... I'm sorry that worse didn't befall them!" But the university took its revenge in the following spring. By basing its argument on its traditional privileges it persuaded the regents to disavow the Provost's action, and Aubriot was compelled to make amends, bareheaded and on his knees, in front of the cathedral, for having infringed the privileges of the scholars' corporation. The affair, ridiculous in itself, thus ended by humiliating the authority which was responsible for public order, which, at this difficult moment, was very unfortunate. It also greatly encouraged the pretensions of the university people to whom the divisions due to the Schism had given many opportunities for asserting themselves. Thirty years later, at the time of the "Caboche" affair, they were to regard themselves as still better qualified to make their voice heard, even in the streets, and this time in the political domain.

The episode of 24 September 1380 would not have been very important if it had not occurred at a time when the general atmosphere was tense with growing discontent. There was a rumour that the dead King had limited the power of his successor, contrary to custom, by suppressing the *aides*. This was enough for the taxpayers to believe that Charles V had really wished to do such a thing. From early October 1381 people were refusing to pay the tax, for example at Compiègne, at Laon and at Saint-Quentin. When, on 14 November, a general assembly was held in Paris, the crowd demonstrated in front of the royal palace to obtain a formal abolition of the *aides*. The older people remembered Etienne Marcel, the younger ones had heard of him. This time the Merchants' Provost did not lead the crowd; it was the crowd that pushed him forward. His spokesman was Jean des Mares, a barrister in the *Parlement*; we shall see him repenting, later on, of having sought to revive the magic effects of rhetoric in politics. On this day however the most serious symptom of disorder was not an anti-fiscal demonstration but an explosion of anti-semitism. The Parisians asked for the expulsion of the Jews and amid cries of "Up and at them", pillaged some forty of their houses. A rabbi was killed. This renewal of anti-Judaism was significant of the reaction following the death of Charles V. During the fourteenth century a latent hostility to the Jews had broken out several times in France and elsewhere. Charles V himself had been tolerant, and Hugues Aubriot had supported him in this. At the time of the anti-Jewish riot of November 1380, which we have just mentioned, a number of Jewish children had been seized by the Christians with the object of having them baptized: the Provost, despite his reputation for harshness, had these children restored to their families. Now this move constituted a grievance, added to the other accusations that were soon afterwards brought against him, at his trial. The regents, however— Louis d'Anjou and Philippe le Hardi—followed his example and the late King's, their brother, in trying to disarm public opinion; but their efforts were useless. Nearly all the subsequent popular agitations included anti-Jewish outbursts, and in the end, as Charles VI's insanity made it impossible to oppose them, an order was signed to expel the Jews in 1394. It is true that France enjoyed no monopoly of such commotions and that they had reached a peculiar pitch of intensity in Spain.

Thus from the first months of Charles VI's unhappy reign,

all the kinds of agitation and disorder which it was to experience had shown themselves. The movement swelled, and from one end of the kingdom to the other, storm-clouds were piling up. Northern France was then often ill-informed as to what was happening in the Midi; but could it have been unaware that the southern cities were, like the moors of Languedoc, scenes of grave disturbance? In any case, fresh riots broke out at Saint-Quentin in the spring of 1381; but it was Flanders, where trouble had been continuous, that again attracted most attention. The insurrection found a leader, naturally in Ghent, and he was naturally a man whose name had borne an aura of prestige for the preceding generation: a name that inspired all the nostalgia and all the hopes which could minister to the independent and democratic spirit of the Flemings: Philip van Artevelde. Born in 1340, the son of Jacques van Artevelde, he could remember nothing of his father's deeds save what legend or filial piety retained. But he contrived at once to make the same moves without even waiting for the Flemings to assert their confidence by investing him with the power and title of First Captain of the Commune of Ghent (24 January 1382). He had already in 1381 got in touch with the court in England and worked for cohesion in the rebellion. Like his father, forty years before, he sought to unite everyone against the common foe. Thus his four lieutenants were selected from rival groups, two being *poorters*, one a weaver and one a waterman. An article of his decrees summarized the democratic spirit of his programme: "When we hold a conference, everyone can come and give counsel, the poor as well as the rich." He, in fact, had to lean for support on the lower classes, from necessity as much as policy. Closely beset at times by the besieging forces, Ghent had difficulty in feeding the host of refugees and unemployed peasants whom the scorched-earth tactics of the Count's forces had driven from the surrounding plain. The Captain of Ghent spoke one day of the "30,000 folk in this city who ate no bread for two weeks". It was a "great pity to see and hear the poor folk". The bakers had to be provided with armed guards, for otherwise the people who were dying of hunger would have forced their way in. Artevelde "caused the granaries of the abbeys and the rich men to be opened and the corn to be distributed at a certain [fixed] price". He also acted at Ypres to settle the dispute about wage-rates between the fullers and the weavers.

If they were to succeed, the weavers of Ghent needed those of Bruges to draw their city into the rebellion, and Artevelde worked for this end. Very astutely he took his enemies by surprise, attacking the place on a feast day in spring (3 May 1382). On that day the men of Bruges were used to venerating the relic of the holy blood of Christ, which Thierry d'Alsace, Count of Flanders, had brought from Jerusalem in the twelfth century. The assailants nearly captured Count Louis de Male, who managed to escape only by swimming across the city-moat and fleeing to Lille. The social nature of the revolt is clear. The *Istore et Chronique de Flandre* tells us how the union between the weavers of Bruges and of Ghent was expressed: "When weavers, fullers and craftsmen saw the [Count's] discomfiture, they went to the men of Ghent, crying 'All as one!' " It was a union of interests, but also an agreement in hatreds and vengeance; for, continues the chronicle, the craftsmen "slew all the butchers, cutlers, glaziers and fish-mongers whom they could find, because these men were said to belong to the prince's party. . . ." Thanks to this terrible settling of accounts Ghent acquired the mastery over Bruges and a great part of Flanders until the autumn.

The revolt had meanwhile spread like wild-fire as far as the Seine and even as the Cotentin Peninsula. It had been provoked everywhere by a decree decided on 15 January 1382 and applicable on 1 March, for the collection of *aides*. The facts are again known to us only from chronicles hostile to the insurrection and from the documents that record the repression. However, an analysis of the details and nuances, particularly in the letters of remission which have been used by Léon Mirot in his study of the *Insurrections urbaines au début du règne de Charles VI*, will enable us to detect the social character of the agitation.

To begin with the facts: Normandy gave the signal without waiting for the date when the new *aides* were to be collected.

The collectors of *aides* had barely fixed the amount due from the province before disorder broke out, on 24 February, in Rouen. About two hundred "mechanics", mainly from the textile industry, rioted in front of the town hall, sounded the alarm by ringing the bells in the belfry, and then assembled in the Old Market Place. Prisons were opened and pillaging went on for three days. The rioters attacked the King's officers, the wealthy bourgeois, the former mayors, the cathedral chapter, the monks of Saint-Ouen and the Jews. Agitation had been anti-fiscal at the outset, and the name by which it has since been called, the *Harelle*, is connected with the cry of *Haro!*, a form of judicial protest customary in Normandy. While the original motive had been anti-fiscal, the insurrection took a social turn by attacking the wealthy and challenging the validity of certain feudal titles which were slashed to pieces at Saint-Ouen. The rebels went further when they appealed to the privileges granted by the Charter of Normandy and swore to have it respected by the Royal authority; although, after three days of agitation, they were afraid of provoking its wrath. So they sent deputations, which received the reply that the King would come to Rouen a little later; he would then "know who had eaten the bacon". For the moment the government had other business in hand.

The week was hardly over and calm had scarce returned to the streets of Rouen before Paris suffered the insurrection of the "Maillotins". On 1 March, when the King was at Saint-Denis and on his way to Rouen, he heard of what was happening in Paris and returned to Vincennes. A very minor incident had provoked the rebellion in the populous quarters on the right bank of the Seine. Buonaccorso Pitti who was an eye-witness and, as a foreigner, impartial, has given the following circumstantial account:

"The common people rebelled in Paris. At the origin of this revolt was a green-grocer, because a tax-collector tried to seize her merchandise to collect the excise (*gabelle*) on her fruit and vegetables. She began to cry: 'Down with the tax', that is, the excise. This is why all the people rose and attacked the excise men's houses, looting them and killing the men. And as the people had no arms, one of their number guided them to the new Châtelet where Messire Bertrand du Guesclin, the former Constable of France, had stored 3,000 leaded mallets (*maillets*), which he had had made with a view to fighting the English. The rioters broke in the doors of the tower where these mallets were kept, and that is why they were called *Maillotins*. Having seized these weapons, they roamed through the streets, pillaging the goods of the King's officers and killing many of them. The rich people, that is, the good citizens who are called bourgeois, feared that the common people, who were like the Ciompi of Florence, might loot their houses too, armed themselves and appeared so strong that the Maillotins agreed to obey them. This was why the bourgeois undertook to act in conformity with the people's demands and to take part in the revolt against the King's lords. For this reason the King and these lords withdrew to Vincennes and deliberated."

The news from Rouen had evidently influenced the Parisians, but the latter were more violent. The chronicles and the letters of remission give exact details, so that we can, in imagination, follow the crowd whose numbers were swollen by idlers and demonstrators, through streets of which the names still subsist. They went from the Marais to the Temple through the Jewish quarter, then to the Châtelet and Saint-Jacques de la Boucherie; next towards the cemetery of the Innocents by way of the streets of the Verrerie, the Tixeranderie and the Ferronerie. From there they moved back towards Saint-Martin-des-Champs and the Porte Saint-Denis. Others went to shut the gates of the Porte Saint-Honoré, looting the quarter of Saint-Germain-l'Auxerrois on their way. Thus the whole right bank was in their hands. They numbered perhaps four thousand. Whereas there had been two deaths in Rouen, there were perhaps thirty in Paris, including sixteen Jews.

At Vincennes the government was waiting. It thought of agreeing to free the prisoners, but the rebels did this, and pillaged the Châtelet. As however the insurrection had grown more violent than ever, the citizens reacted now in self-defence by arming themselves to put an end to the disorder. A party in connection with the university and a liberal magistrate, Jean des Mares, whom we met with in 1380, attempted conciliation; and the government made certain formal concessions. It agreed to return to the old system of taxation, the system "of the time of Saint Louis", as it was said, in a formula full of echoes pleasing to the popular mind. But repression was immediate and severe, between fifteen and twenty people being executed in four days. The dukes, who were governing in the name of their young nephew, had good reason to think that they had no time to lose.

Following the example of Rouen and Paris, risings had taken place in several cities, so that disorder became general during the first half of March 1382; though the whole situation remained uncertain until the autumn. In Normandy the tax was resisted not only in Rouen but in Caen, where the royal commissary, who had been appointed to deal with the *aides*, came into conflict with a yelling crowd, while his agents were molested. Resistance spread to the little towns and villages, such as Falaise, Mortain, Vire, Condé-sur-Noireau, Avranches, Carentan, Coutances, Thorigny, Saint-Sauveur-Lendelin, Lisieux, Deauville, Pontautou, Pont-Audemer, Beaumont-le-Roger, Breteuil, Conches, Gaillon, Maineval, Vernon and Dieppe. In the provinces of Vermandois, Champagne and Picardy, *aides* were refused at Laon and Rheims where the inhabitants held meetings; and more particularly at Amiens. Here there was agitation amid significant cries of "Long live Ghent, long live Paris, our mother!" Assemblies held in the markets were tumultuous; their object was to appoint delegates to Estates that were held at Compiègne in April, and these too protested against the *aides*. The struggle against this tax was thus being organized, and without giving rise to serious action everywhere, nevertheless expressed social as much as fiscal discontent, and tended to become general. Orleans had also rebelled and even at Lyon, in the south, the inhabitants who had been assembled by the lord of the Castle declared bluntly that they would pay nothing.

As soon as they believed they had finished with Paris the

regents escorted the young King to punish Rouen and make
an example of it. On 29 March Charles VI made his entry
into the Norman capital. which seemed to be in festive mood
to receive him. It was Holy Week, and the court made it clear
to the inhabitants that the time had not come for rejoicing.
The doors under the great gate were thrown down, and the
court entered as into a conquered city. Twelve persons were
executed, the population was disarmed and heavily fined;
lastly, the city lost its privileges as a commune and fell under
the direct control of the King's officers. And as a symbol of this
subjection, the bells which had rung out the call to rebellion
were brought down from the bell-tower. After that, the population was amnestied.

News from Flanders, the victory in May of the men of Ghent
at Bruges, were not however of a kind to discourage rebellion;
and in fact it broke out again in August. There were people at
Rouen who were not disposed to let the matter rest, and who
regarded as weakness the decision in July of the Estates of
Normandy to accept the levying of an *aide*. At the beginning
of August several of the inhabitants of the city and its suburbs
demonstrated in the Cloth-Hall under the leadership of a
butcher. They put to flight the officials of the *aides* and sacked
their offices. The matter did not go further, but the relapse
into violence was disquieting.

Certain Parisians, for their part, did not hesitate to conspire.
Animated by memories of the revolt in March, a certain number of cloth-workers held secret meetings at Montmartre, at
Saint-Eloy and at Saint-Julien-le-Pauvre. Repeating the gestures
of the communal movement they swore an oath over mallets
(as a symbol) that they would assist each other in refusal to
pay the tax, and even that they would riot and murder the
Provost of the Merchants. The conspirators also met at the
Pré-aux-Clercs, under pretext of playing bowls and skittles,
and of "flying the dragon", that is, flying kites. A secret shared
by too many people is soon discovered. It became known that a
meeting was being held in a house near Saint-Sulpice; the
plot was unmasked and the conspirators arrested. Others,
however, continued to conspire; they corresponded with the

men of Ghent and even tried to intercept government convoys at the time of the royal intervention in Flanders, of which it will soon be a question. Paris therefore was not to be counted on; but the government was taking the difficulties one by one and awaiting the hour to inflict punishment.

The situation elsewhere was not more favourable. Thus Amiens remained a source of worry. Here, as in other places, it proved difficult to re-establish the collection of *aides*. Two of the leaders in opposition to the tax had been elected as magistrates. The dismissal of one of them provoked a renewal of violence and a long lawsuit between the patricians and the popular party.

Charles VI's uncles were, in short, right in believing that order would not be definitely restored, in Paris or in the other cities of France, until the Flemish revolution was subdued. Ghent was acquiring the prestige of a myth: thus the King's decision, taken in council in August 1382, to answer the Count of Flanders's appeal for help, seems to have been very quickly followed by a renewal of plotting in Paris. This is not the place to describe the campaign which ended with Charles VI's victory at Roosebeke, south of Bruges, on 27 November. Philip van Artevelde perished in the mêlée and Bruges had to submit. On that day the chivalry of France wiped out the humiliation of Courtrai and forced the herd of common infantry to drink the dregs of humiliation. Charles VI went next to remove the golden spurs which, since 1302, had been hanging on the wall of Notre-Dame de Courtrai. Then, being unable to lay siege to Ghent in winter, or to persuade the city to negotiate, he returned home.

Paris now, in its turn, learned the cost of revolts, rebellions and conspiracies. The King arrived by the Porte Saint-Denis on 11 January, went straight to Notre-Dame and then to the palace. The repression began next day and went on for a month. The tribunals worked rapidly. Some attitudes in the past failed to win pardon. Though Jean de Mares had acted as mediator in 1381, his efforts had not blotted out the memory of his earlier rhetoric as a demagogue. There were vengeances that went far back in time. Nicolas le Flament, now an old man, had taken part in the massacre of the marshals in 1358, and at that time the Dauphin had spared him: he was executed in 1383. A detail like this clearly brings out the way in which rancours, aspirations and fears really persisted from one generation to the next. After Rouen which had lost its commune, Paris now lost the office of Provost of the Merchants. Just as had happened thirty years before, the failure of the rebellion turned to the advantage of the monarchy.

Ghent however was still unconquered, and the city resisted all the court's efforts to reduce it for two more years. The city had found a successor to Philip van Artevelde in Francis Ackerman. This struggle became more and more involved with Anglo-French rivalry, and the problem of the Papal Schism tended now to pass from the sphere of social revolution to the domain of politics proper. The king dispatched two further expeditions to Flanders, without however attacking Ghent. The new master of Flanders was the King's uncle, Philippe le Hardi, Duke of Burgundy. The men of Ghent made peace with him at Tournai on 18 December 1385, but they "never deigned to bend the knee".

Before concluding, we should seek to understand the bearing of the very complex events which took place in the French kingdom between 1378 and 1385. What was at stake? Who led the revolts? And how did the course of events deviate?

One may argue about the object of the 1382 disorders. Like the agitation of 1356–7, that of 1382 profited from the weakness of the government and the quasi-vacancy in the throne; but the existence and the form of the monarchical state were no more challenged in 1382 than in 1358. The troubles in 1382 represent in large measure a relaxation, natural enough after the authoritative rule of Charles V. What was contested was above all the fiscal system, which was the government's weak point. England had just experienced the same thing, apropos of the poll-tax. But in reality refusal to pay the tax, if it was not an expression of political opposition, revealed other forms of a deeper malaise, psychological, economic and social. We shall not linger over the first aspect of the trouble, although the coincidence of the events with the beginning of the Great

Schism deserves to be recalled. It was the economic and social problems which required attention. If we take altogether the observations we made at Ghent, and at Paris, Rouen, Amiens and Languedoc, we shall easily grasp the importance of the social problems. An attentive study of the documents throws some light on these.

A first observation arises from the succession of events. Almost everywhere, rebellion against the tax began spontaneously among the common people, who were rather seriously affected by the coincidence of fiscal burdens with the cumulative effects of successive economic crises and repeated dearths. The most serious perhaps had afflicted Languedoc in 1375. Here we encounter various problems which are to be analysed later: increase of poverty in the second half of the fourteenth century; living conditions among the workers; in the cities, workmen, companions and even masters forced to hire out their labour to others; in the countryside, an exodus from the land, perceptible though still not well known, which brought an unusual number of vagabonds on to the highroads; and in the cities, labour which was untrained and hence destined to unemployment or low wages. This can be clearly seen in Paris and Rouen. Such then were the people who actually agitated in the first stages of the trouble: at Ghent and Ypres, workmen in the lower and despised levels of the textile industry, weavers, fullers and dyers. At Rouen, it was the "composite and unarmed crowd" of men of low estate (*homines vilis status*—or *infimi*), "coppersmiths, cloth-workers and dealers in coarse stuffs", hands (*famuli*) "engaged in work shops". In Paris the crowd that demonstrated on behalf of the greengrocer who was being tormented by the excise men was composed of modest artisans (cloth-croppers, curriers, sellers of tripe, ironmongers and navvies) and rustics (*populi rusticani*) uprooted from the land.

The first social group seems to have been rapidly outnumbered by other elements whom the chroniclers, sensitive as they were to distinctions, treat with scorn and repugnance. In fact, for Paris as for Rouen, the chronicle seems quickly to change its tone, speaking less of the humble folk as such or, in neutral terms, as the "small" people or the common people. Those who now appear on the stage are malefactors, mendicants, beggars and other rabble, "an oddly assorted crowd", who were joined on 1 March 1382 by a number of "youths standing about and looking on". These were the Maillotins, the men who at Rouen rifled the cellars of the rich, and at Bruges and at Béziers burned down their houses; and who had their counterpart among the Tuchins. Protests were succeeded by violence; the rabble now had recourse to force, it needed only leaders to organize it.

During the third phase the poor folk who had demonstrated at the outset were not merely overwhelmed by numbers, but compromised and frustrated. They became hostages for troublemakers and victims of the reaction. It was the same everywhere. The terms used by the chronicles again change with the change of events. Here, first, are the demagogues and exploiters of disorder. They are named. A few nobles mixed with the Maillotins, as did some bourgeois (*cives*) hitherto considered peaceable; one of them was pardoned, because it was through "fear of the people and in order to please them", he explained that he had used subversive language. Others, malcontents, thought they would justify themselves by alleging they had wished "by means of mallets and the Commune of the city of Paris to defend the liberties of their city and of the whole kingdom of France". At Rouen on 24 February 1382 "certain rich merchants and vintners covertly supported the riot". Ghent did not lack well-to-do people, in good positions, to direct the revolution, men for whom the lot of the poor was of less import than their personal fortune and the city's privileges. There were, moreover, among the demonstrators at Rouen men able enough to oblige the Abbot of Saint-Omer to sign concessions in the diplomatic formula of the time. In the negotiations with the court at Vincennes, the insurgents' delegation was led by people sufficiently versed in the procedure of the chancellery to refuse a charter sealed with red wax on a simple parchment tongue to the document, instead of with green wax and silk cord. There were, then, some brains among the rebels. This does not mean that, except at Ghent, there existed at this time a revolutionary doctrine and programme properly so called. There were rebellions concerted with a view to limited, and often even private interests, in the fiscal, professional or social domains, but no real revolution.

Finally, it was the little men, those who had revolted at the outset, who most often bore the brunt of the repression: judicial records and lists of condemnations bear witness to this. It will be noted at Béziers in 1381; it was the same in Paris, in Normandy and in Flanders. For these poor folk, the worst consequence was the appearance in men's minds of the notion of dangerous classes. Chroniclers, moralists and judges seem to have experienced a panic fear of total subversion. One wonders how far they believed in the existence of class-consciousness in the lower ranks of society, a consciousness with which the latter were not, and could not then be animated. At least, contemporaries seem to have been very deeply disturbed by the simultaneousness of the agitation in their own town or country, and the agitation in other regions; and sometimes by the connections between them. We have already mentioned Buonaccorso Pitti's comparison of the revolt of the Maillotins with the "Tumult of the Ciompi." It was not the only one. An equally perspicacious remark comes from the pen of the monk of Saint-Denis, who was not always so clear-sighted: "Nearly all the people of France had rebelled and were agitated with great fury and, according to general rumour, they were excited by messengers from the Flemings, who were themselves being worked upon by the plague of a similar rebellion, stimulated by the example of the English." Florence, England, Flanders, France: the simultaneous nature of the disturbances raises many other problems which touch on the structure of these societies and affected the depths of men's consciousness.

*   *   *

Northern France and southern France were like two worlds apart; relations between them were scanty and news did not circulate well. The disturbances in Languedoc seem to have

developed independently of outside influence; whether because, being far distant, they did not directly threaten the
monarchy, or because the movement lacked vigour, unity and
real strength. In any case, historians are unaware of them or
leave them in the shadow; thus it is indeed difficult to give a
balanced account of the situation. Our sources come mainly
from the towns. The Tuchins, like the Jacques with whom
they may be compared, left no written documents, and the
other documents we have are generally hostile. The letters of
remission, on the other hand, provide a less biased picture. It
remains true, none the less, that owing to the number of
unfortunates whose anger they record, owing also to the geographical extension of the disorders, and to their duration, the
trouble in the Midi was really serious and significant.

The Tuchins began by pillaging. Contemporaries in the Ile-
de-France were for long unaware of this and were astonished
at its suddenness. The chronicler of Saint-Denis depicts this
"multitude of abject folk called Tuchins, by reason of their
secret practices, a multitude which rose up unexpectedly like
earth-worms which wriggle on the surface of the soil. Having
abandoned their work as townsmen or peasants, they swore to
support each other, under terrible oaths, by never more sub-
mitting to any fiscal burden and by fighting for the ancient
liberty of their country." People have wondered what the
name "Tuchins" means. It may doubtless be connected with
the word *touche*, which meant "woodland, moor or maquis"—
so that we may conclude that they were what we now call the
maquisards. It was in fact a question of ex-peasants and former
artisans who were now, in upper Auvergne, living by brigandage,
with the complicity of the common people in such towns as
Aurillac and Saint-Flour. The formation of these wandering
groups may certainly be connected with the presence in the
mountains of Auvergne of disbanded soldiers whom Bertrand
du Guesclin had not managed to destroy. One may also suspect
the influence of Jean de Roquetaillade, a Franciscan of Aurillac, a visionary and sort of tribune, whose prestige among the
common people inspired the hostility of the rich. One of the
first mentions of the Tuchins concerns Saint-Flour and dates

from 1363. Saint-Flour was then troubled by opposition between the merchant patricians who controlled the consulate, and the lower class of craftsmen. The common people expressed their discontent by refusing to pay the tax or by joining the maquis. However, the activities of the Tuchins, although further provoked by a recurrence of plague, by the famine of 1375 and by an increase in taxation, were for a long time very local.

The urban rebellions were a different matter. A succession of these occurred after 1378, especially in eastern Languedoc. The signal had been given by the town of Le Puy where subsidies granted to the King were still being levied in the form of indirect taxes. Inventories of the stocks were just being drawn up when "during the celebration of Mass the statue of the Holy Virgin, covered by reason of Lent, was unveiled according to custom. Then arose an immense cry mingled with tears and lamentations. . . . Many people cried aloud: 'O blessed Virgin Mary, help us! How shall we live, how shall we be able to feed our children, since we cannot support the heavy taxes established to our prejudice through the influence of the rich and to reduce their own taxes?' " The letter of remission which contains this passage vividly evokes the spectacular nature of the popular feeling, and its religious aspect. There were among those present in church, "a great number of workmen of various nations, vagabonds now, and assembled here by reason of the pilgrimage." The crowd in its exasperation destroyed several houses belonging to the consuls, but without killing anyone. "A son of iniquity had even caused the ringing of the alarm-bell." Whereupon, dread of the punishment which could be expected from the King's agents, inspired a kind of union of classes. The consuls took it on themselves to "content the King in another way, according to each man's means and property". And the Duke of Anjou, the King's Lieutenant in Languedoc, and, later on, Charles V himself pardoned the outbreak.

The trouble at Le Puy was not however the only one. Nîmes rose in rebellion. Next, in October 1379, several of the King's officers were massacred at Montpellier. Disorders broke out at Alès and Clermont-l'Hérault. However, the trouble at Clermont does not seem to have been due to any conflict between poor and rich. The letter of remission granted to Déodat Guilhem, Lord of Clermont l'Hérault, leads us to understand that there were quarrels between rival "bands", one of which accused the other of complicity with the English. Déodat Guilhem had suppressed the outbreak, but only after violating the King's safeguard and protection covering a "royal" bourgeois, two sergeants and other men who were victims of his summary justice. To obtain pardon more easily, he assumed the attitude of a destroyer of popular tumults.

"In practically the whole land [he asserted] the wave of disorder was continually swelling, to such a point that the members of the King's courts, the temporal lords and the other good men of the country and the cities were in great peril for their lives, the more so as the common people of various places were shouting: 'Let us kill, kill all the rich men, do as was done by the men of Montpellier and Clermont!'—[these lords and good men] rightly fearing that if the infamous insolence of the rabble of Clermont was not severely repressed, the worst might follow. . . ."

These civic riots were easily held down. But it was then that Charles V recalled his brother, Louis d'Anjou, from Languedoc. Rumour had it that he was planning to appoint Gaston Phébus, the popular Comte de Foix,[1] in his place; but he died before he could do so, and very soon Jean, Duke of Berry, well known for rapacity, was given the post of King's Lieutenant in Languedoc. True, Toulouse and other communities in the region hesitated for some time between the two men. Toulouse even opened its gates to Gaston Phébus. Jean de Berry, who had been delayed by other business, arrived at last on the scene, and the Comte de Foix, reluctant to push the matter to extremes, yielded place to him in September 1381. This political uncertainty which had continued for more than a year facilitated the spread of disorder.

[1] Gaston III, better known perhaps as a patron of arts and letters, author of a work on hunting (*Le Livre de chasse*), and a pleasant character in an age which did not produce many. He entertained the agreeable Froissart at Orthez in 1388. (Translator.)

Of the new troubles the insurrection of Béziers is the best known owing to letters of remission and to the conscientious account written by Jaime Mascaro, Secretary to the Consulate, in his *Libre de Memorias*. It was a sudden flare-up of rage, unorganized and without aftermath. On 8 September 1381 while consuls and councillors were deliberating as to how best to receive the Duke of Berry, "men of evil mind" assembled, broke in the gates of the town hall, and set fire to the tower, so that several bourgeois were burnt to death or forced to jump from the windows to fall crushed far below. The rioters then scoured the city, killing and looting. Mascaro gives us the names of the victims, of whom there were ten at the town hall and nine in the city. He then lists the executions, suggesting that repression came rapidly. Four men were beheaded "in the city-square, on a wine-press", and forty-one were hanged, including sixteen weavers, thirteen labourers and various artisans. It does not appear that the revolt had a leader. The name of Bernard Pourquier, a carpenter, who was pardoned, has come down to us, but nothing allows us to suppose that he played any particular part.

According to a chronicle of Montpellier entitled the *Petit Thalamus*, "on the Sunday before Christmas, which was 22 December, a plot, hatched by about four hundred common folk of Béziers, was discovered. These men planned to kill all the citizens who were worth more than a hundred *livres*, on St Stephen's day; and forty of the said plotters were to kill their own wives and then marry the richest and fairest wives of the said rich men who had been killed." A pretty absurd project! Mascaro, the best-informed of local chroniclers, says nothing of it, and there is every reason to treat it as a tall story, like many that were certainly current during these disorders.

At the beginning of January 1382 the Duke of Berry entered Béziers and took the events of September 1381 as a pretext for imposing a heavy fine on the city. Yet two facts lead us to suppose that the revolt produced some positive gains. In 1382 a reform of the consulate made it a shade more "democratic"; while in 1384 the consuls drew up a book of "estimates" with a view to a better assessment for direct taxation. Béziers had been slow to achieve these advantages, already acquired by so many cities, which explains perhaps why it had remained a centre of great unrest; but after this, it returned to the normal situation.

This affair also reveals the unpopularity inspired by the mere name of the Duc de Berry, and the reason why he needed some months to establish his authority. Owing to all the above circumstances the Tuchin revolt rapidly spread over the whole of Languedoc. During 1382 and 1383 the province was the scene of a sort of Jacquerie, known to us by the problems in which it involved the cities, themselves in difficulties, and the complicity it met with. 1382 was the year of "tribulation" for Toulouse. To meet urgent needs the *capitouls* (local name for *consuls*) had the silver table-ware of several citizens seized; dispatched an expedition against the disbanded mercenaries; and sent help to Saint-Antonin in Rouergue. After this the instigators of disorder, fearing to be confused with the Tuchins, went into hiding. At Carcassonne, while "a species of folk called Tuchins dominated the said country" a doctor in canon law, Maître Pierre Boyer, gave advice to the communities which were resisting the King's agents, acted as intermediary to obtain "harness, armour and food" for the Tuchins themselves, and on several occasions received their leaders at his lordship of Aragon. This man was not therefore any poor devil; and if the part he played is known to us through a letter of remission, everything suggests that he was not an isolated case. At Nîmes which "took sides with the Tuchins", an esquire named Huguet de Mirabel, fearing (he said) the hostility which the common people were showing towards the nobles, preferred to make terms with them. He took part in the mounted assault they made on Saint-Gilles—where a number of oxen, valuable for the food supply, were being kept —and fought in their ranks to the end.

These few records, collected from end to end of Languedoc, suggest the wide extent of the rebellion, the support it won and the general uncertainty. But this was not to last. In 1384 the Duke of Berry or one of his lieutenants crushed the armed bands of the Tuchins. Charles VI granted a general pardon, in return for an enormous fine of 800,000 gold francs, payable in four years—which for many years stifled any desire for rebellion.

What strikes us in these agitations is their disorderliness, the absence of any programme or even mutual understanding. A few of the rebellious cities, like Béziers and Le Puy, were those in which such reforms as a "democratizing" of the consulate and direct taxation imposed on everyone, had been least achieved, and the troubles promoted their adoption. But the Tuchins leave us perplexed, records of their activities being inadequate.

Without being really organized, the Tuchins had leaders often of noble or bourgeois origin. A Pierre de Brugère is said to have ordered his men to kill any traveller "whose hands should appear too fine or merely without callouses, and all those whose movements, bearing and language had anything noble or bourgeois about them." It is said too that the Tuchins hated churchmen; though not more than did the disbanded soldiery whose behaviour the Tuchins repeated. The latter in fact were composed of famished and uprooted people whose only object was to survive at the expense of the established order: a fact which deprived their movement of any political efficacy, without however removing its historical importance in a picture of the miseries and rebellions of the age.

*   *   *

Among the popular movements of the fourteenth and fifteenth centuries, the insurrection of the English labourers in 1381 achieved several notable "records". It was the only movement which could really be called national. Not that the whole kingdom was affected; but an important part, including the nerve centres round the capital, was galvanized into action. While most of the rebels came from country districts, a great number of towns were gravely affected. The shock was tremendous; for some days it looked as if the monarchy were being carried away on a torrent of fury. William Stubbs, the Oxford historian, was to call it "the most monstrous phenomenon in English history".

In the second place, the organization and programme of the rebels appear to us with a clarity which, though far from really satisfying us, far surpasses anything to which we are accustomed. Their leaders, even if we do not exactly possess their biographies, live again vividly before the eyes of imagination. The rebels themselves presented the King with a veritable book of claims.

The relative wealth of documentation is another advantage to the historian of this revolt. Not that we should accept all the data with the same degree of confidence; but two series of sources, the narratives and the judicial records, are both abundant and can be usefully combined. It is worth reviewing them briefly, so as to make clear what our narrative and interpretation of events are based on.

The narrative sources furnish the most living and coherent picture of the whole. The French first have recourse to the work of Sire Jean Froissart. Book X of his *Chroniques* contains a narrative picturesque, sometimes poetical, always attractive. One must always be on guard against this attractiveness. Froissart, a skilled and intelligent writer, may at times have seen inside the rebels' mind; but they none the less remain for him "evil men"; and one of his prime objects is to denounce their "pestilence" (as he calls it), to serve as an object lesson. On the other hand he was not an eye-witness of the events; he was in France at the time and stayed in England only in 1394–5, when he met few of the old acquaintances whom he had made when living there between 1361 and 1370. We are not sure who informed him of the events: perhaps Sir Richard Stury who entertained him for a long time in his manor of Eltham; or possibly Robert de Namur, Lord of Beaufort and Chièvres in Hainault, who was a companion of Richard II during those tragic days. But Froissart does not specially emphasize the part played by this protector in connection with the young King, as he would doubtless not have failed to do. In any event, his information appears accurate on the whole, sometimes a little vague, and always enlivened by the artful touches of the professional writer.

We must give priority to less literary writings: especially

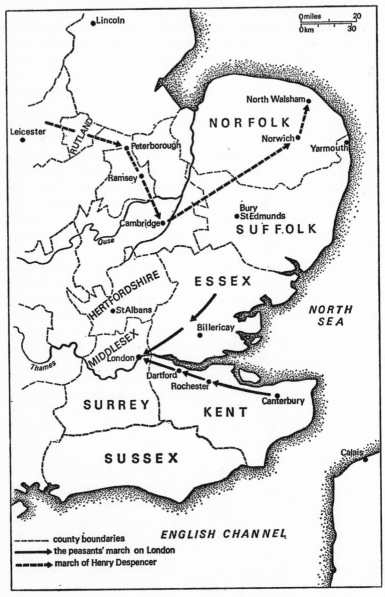

Fig. 5 The Peasants' Revolt of 1381

to the *Chronique Française Anonyme* which was recopied at the end of the sixteenth century and which the copyist represents as the work of a cleric of St Mary's Church at York. Written in a confused kind of Anglo-French, it does not deal with events around York but describes what happened in London with a precision and liveliness that can only be the work of an eye-witness. This is relatively impartial and is witness number one. Number two is the chronicle ascribed to the monk of Evesham, a rather personal work which however incorporates certain documents of the time. A useful continuation, to the year 1381, of Higden's *Polychronicon*, was written by John Malverne, a monk of Worcester. One should distrust the *Chronique d'Angleterre* of Thomas of Walsingham, a monk of St Albans, and also the chronicle of Henry of Knighton, Canon of Leicester. These two men were mainly acquainted with what took place in their own districts; for the rest, they wrote from hearsay. They are carried away by hatred of the rebels, and they denounce their connivance with Wyclif and the Lollards.

These and a few other texts are to be combined, and also with judicial sources of information. Several law-reports, recording the condemnation of rebels, have been preserved. These acquaint us with a number of men and doings which were not in the front rank and of which the chroniclers were unaware—or which they neglected; but the sum of them conveys a picture, in depth and extension so to speak, of the insurrection. Thanks to them, we can check the probable accuracy of the chroniclers when they disagree about a date; thanks to them we can measure the geographical limits of the affair; and also detect the motives of individual rebels, which are very soberly reported. Here too one must remain critically alert. When a judicial enquiry has been made, the declaration of the jurymen may have been biased in a particular direction —in London, for example, to throw responsibility on a few individuals for complicity with the peasants of Kent and Essex, when in reality a great number of Londoners were responsible; the object of the jurymen being to avoid collective punishment.

In any case, and by comparison with the Continent, our dossier of records is very substantial. Yet again we must be on our guard. In addition to hostile documents, we have others which are recommended by an appearance of impartiality. But we have none which represent the rebels' point of view, their real motives and the way they lived during the days of uproar. Accusation may be moderate, but is still accusation. How can we put ourselves in the place of the accused?

We shall first try to trace the course of events, beginning with the immediate causes. The narrative itself will show that these causes fail to explain everything. Yet in the light of the said causes, an explanation may be attempted.

Problems and difficulties abounded in the England of 1381. Edward III, glorious ancestor of a time when England won the battles and lost the wars, died at the age of sixty-six, after reigning for nearly fifty years. His son, the Black Prince, being already dead, it was his grandson Richard, a child of ten, born at Bordeaux, who succeeded him. He was to be surrounded by intrigues and incessant conflicts between his own councillors and his relatives, especially his uncle, John of Gaunt.

The bright days of easily successful war were now well over. Under Charles V the French had waged a guerilla war of ambushes in which Bertrand du Guesclin distinguished himself, and which reconquered nearly all the lands ceded to the Plantagenets by the Treaty of Bretigny in 1360. The French were struggling less successfully to complete the work; but the English had to bar the way, raise and equip troops and find money: a heavy task, because a defensive war brought in no profits. Among several possible alternatives the Parliament of 1377 chose a poll-tax of a groat (four pence) levied on every man or woman of at least fourteen years of age. The plan was unjust but less so than it appears, because wealthy households, containing a great number of domestics were more heavily taxed, while the indigent obtained exemption. The moderate rate of the tax made it bearable. When the poll-tax was again levied, in 1379, an attempt was made to grade it in proportion to people's means, though the outcome was deceptive. The Parliament of 1380 decided therefore to return to the flat rate, this time at a shilling a head, that is three times the 1370 rate. Each community was to pay a lump sum calculated on this basis, according to the number of inhabitants, less the number of beggars. However, within each community, the sum payable was levied and collected in proportion to the tax-payer's means. A poor man might pay only a groat for himself and his wife; a rich man, sixty groats (one pound).

This was just only in appearance, because everything depended on the means of the inhabitants, as a comparison of two villages in Suffolk will show. Among seventy adults at Brockley there was one gentleman taxed at 18 groats (6s) and five rich farmers each of whom paid 7½ groats (2s 6d); the poor, therefore, had to pay only a groat. But at Chevington near-by, out of seventy-eight adults, there was no resident landowner and only one important farmer; the villains—that is the serfs—had each to pay 3 groats (1s). This was an important figure, equal to a labourer's wages for three days, and higher than any previous tax.

Rumblings of discontent soon made themselves heard; and under the pressure of public opinion the constables of the communities closed their eyes to fiscal evasion. A new census of the taxable population was taken, but produced no more than two-thirds of the 1377 roll. The most usual procedure had been to omit women, or at least widows and young girls. As soon as the results of the census reached the council, they provoked stupefaction and criticism. On 16 March a general inquiry into the situation in fifteen counties was ordered, and entrusted to new commissioners. John Legge, a sergeant-at-arms who was supposed to be one of the authors of the new census, was, for that reason, to be decapitated later by the rebels. Meanwhile the new commissioners set to work in April and May and discovered enormous abuses. At Norwich, 600 taxable persons did not appear on the tax-rolls, and in the whole of Norfolk, 8,000.

What followed was inevitable. On 30 May at Brentwood in Essex, a commissioner named Thomas Bampton, with no armed force behind him, clashed with recalcitrant peasants and had to flee. This was the first spark. Within a few days the fire spread over Essex and into Kent, contacts being established on both sides of the Thames estuary. On 2 June several members of a judicial commission had their heads cut off by the rebels. On the 5th a rebel band seized the citadel at Dartford; on the 6th the castle at Rochester was taken; and on the 7th Wat Tyler appeared.

We still know little about this man, who was to be the principal leader of the insurrection. He came from Essex and may, as Froissart asserts, have had some experience as a soldier in France. In any event, he was not only a fine speaker, he knew how to organize and command, and impose his authority on everyone. The insurgents whose numbers had swollen elected him leader at Maidstone.

On the 8th and 9th the rebellion affected the whole of Kent and Essex. Castles and manor-houses were destroyed, manorial documents burned, and gentlemen required to swear loyalty "to King Richard and the Commons of England". On the 10th Tyler marched on Canterbury. The city was occupied without resistance, the archbishop's palace looted and the county archives set on fire.

Amid all this tumult, an itinerant preacher, a sort of prophet with the gift of the gab, was freed from prison. This was John Ball, of whom Froissart has drawn a memorable portrait:

". . . This John Ball (Jean Balle) had been used, on Sundays after Mass, when all the people came out of church, to go to the cloisters or the graveyard, and there preach and assemble the people round him. And he would say: 'Good folk, things cannot go well in England, nor will they, until goods are held in common, and until there are neither villains nor gentlemen, and we are all the same. What have they done, those we call lords, to be greater lords than we? Wherein have they deserved it? Why do they hold us in servitude? And if we all come from one father and one mother, Adam and Eve, wherein can they say or show that they are better lords than we, unless it be that they make us till their lands and gain for them what they spend? They are clad in velvet and silk[1] trimmed with squirrel-fur;

[1] "Camocas", a silk stuff something like satin. (Translator.)

and we are clad in poor cloth. They have wines, and spices, and good bread; and we have rye-bread, and remnants and straw, and we drink water. They have good homes and fine manors; and we have pain and toil, and till the fields in the rain and wind; and it is from us and our labour that must come the wherewithal to maintain their estate. We are called serfs and beaten if we do not, at once, do their service. And yet we have no sovereign to whom we can complain or who would listen to us or do us justice. Let us go to the King; he is young. We will show him our servitude, and tell him that we want things to be different, or we will ourselves provide a remedy. Now if we indeed go, and all of us together, then all manner of people who are named serfs and held in servitude, will follow us, in order to be freed. And when the King sees us or hears us, whether fairly or otherwise, he will provide a remedy.'

"This John Ball spoke in these, and similar words, on Sundays, by custom, when people came out of Mass in the villages; for which too many common folk would praise him. Some who meant no good would say: 'He speaks truth!' And they would murmur and remind each other, when in the fields or going their way from one village to another, or in their houses: 'Such things says John Ball, and he speaks truth.'

"The Archbishop of Canterbury, when informed of this, had John Ball taken and put in prison, and held there for two or three months, to punish him. And it would be better if, the very first time, John Ball had been condemned to be always in prison, or to be put to death, than what he [the Archbishop] did with him; for he had him freed and scrupled to put him to death. And when the said John was out of the Archbishop's prison, he was at his old tricks as before."

The only means the peasants had of preventing a swift repression from falling on the two counties, now a prey to almost total agitation, was to march on London. While the insurrection was still spreading, the rebels marched on 11 and 12 June. On the evening of the 12th the Kentish insurgents (50,000 according to the anonymous chronicle) camped on Blackheath, in the southern suburbs. Several pushed as far as Southwark and Lambeth, where they found a number of Londoners in sympathy with them. The Bishop's palace was pillaged, prisons were opened. The drawbridge giving access to London Bridge had been raised, and for the moment entry to the City was forbidden. But bands of rebels from Essex were on the march north of the river.

The government was in confusion. In the presence of the young King, who was now fourteen, the councils met without taking any decision. They needed a military leader. Of the King's uncles, John of Gaunt was in Edinburgh, another was in Wales, a third on his way by sea to Portugal. Could not some other leader come to the fore? William Walworth, the Lord Mayor, appeared very much decided, but he had to count with the feelings of so many Londoners who favoured the insurgents. Even on the municipal council attitudes differed. John Horne, one of the three alderman who had been sent to summon the insurgents to retire, promised Wat Tyler that London would help him. Was this treason, as suggested later? Yet the insurgents were loudly proclaiming their respect for the King. In any case the King had at his disposal only a few hundred archers and men-at-arms, the troops of his household and of his councillors.

The 13th began in an atmosphere of expectation. It was doubtless then that Ball delivered the famous sermon:

> When Adam dalf and Eve spun,
> Where was then the gentleman?

A great crowd being now massed on the right bank of the Thames, the King with a few councillors came in a boat with the idea of haranguing them. They no sooner saw him than they invited him to disembark; but in the royal barge the sense of danger this would involve was too lively, and the boat half-turned away. At least no arrows or other projectiles were fired at it.

The rebels meanwhile were beginning to be short of food, and felt they must get into London. A later inquiry threw the responsibility on three aldermen: John Horne who encouraged the crowd, Walter Sibley who lowered the drawbridge, and

William Tonge who opened Aldgate for the men of Essex. But these aldermen were simply yielding to public feeling in the city. In fact, when the rebels poured in they were offered food and drink, and many citizens made a point of paying for them. Tyler strove to maintain strict discipline among his troops. True, their first act was to assault John of Gaunt's splendid palace of the Savoy, which had been recently completed, and to destroy and burn everything; but John Malverne assures us that the pillagers were executed. Other rioters sacked the Temple, which belonged to the Knights of St John of Jerusalem, whose Prior was Robert Hales, the King's Treasurer, a man detested by the peasants. Prisons were destroyed, as were a number of houses belonging to rich Londoners. After nightfall the multitude slept round great fires which had been lit within sight of the Tower, while their principal leaders met in the house of Thomas Faringdon, a wealthy Londoner who had come over to their side, and drew up a list (we are told) of persons who should be proscribed. From his refuge in the Tower the King could contemplate the alarming spectacle of huge fires and sleeping rebels. It was "very horrible" for him, Froissart assures us.

That same evening the King's council was discussing what to do. Opinions were sharply divided, according to Froissart. Walworth, the Mayor, is said to have advised an armed sortie, taking advantage of the rebels' being asleep; the King's men "would have killed them off like so many flies". But others pointed out that the Londoners themselves were to be reckoned with, and that it was preferable to negotiate. This opinion, supported by the Earl of Salisbury, is said to have decided the King. Did things really happen like this? All we know for certain is that an interview at Mile End between Richard and the multitude was announced for the morrow. The King was hoping that his most unpopular officials, his Chancellor Simon Sudbury, Archbishop of Canterbury, and the Treasurer Robert Hales, might be able to take advantage of this move in order to escape. Sudbury in fact was to try, but he was recognized by the rebels and had to return to the Tower.

On Friday the 14th, the small royal company set out early

for Mile End, "a very fine meadow where the people come and amuse themselves in summer". But the King's entourage was weakened by the defection of his two half-brothers. Richard now found himself face to face with a great multitude: 60,000 men, according to Froissart, 100,000, according to the *Anonymous Chronicle*. Did he cut a poor figure, or appear anxious "like a lamb among wolves"? (the monk of Evesham). However that may be, he had little choice. He accepted Wat Tyler's demands. Serfdom was abolished; all tenants were to be free, and would pay a uniform annual due of fourpence per acre; all restrictions on the freedom to buy and sell were suppressed; and a general amnesty was proclaimed. These four points offer no problem for the historian, because they are to be found in other documents, particularly in the subsequent decree of revocation. But four other concessions are mentioned in various sources. Freedom of work (therefore, a revocation of the Statute of Labourers); regular punishment of traitors, according to the *Anonymous Chronicle*; the freeing of all prisoners (Adam of Usk); lastly—but this is more doubtful—a promise by the King to be counselled henceforth by the "true commons", that is, the rebels. This last detail, furnished by the monk of Evesham, would suggest a popular monarchy, governing over the head of Parliament, the rights of which are totally ignored. A discussion of these points is far from trifling. The question that arises is to know whether the rebels had a programme, and if so, what.

To show that he was taking the rebels under his protection, Richard caused a royal flag to be given to a representative of each county. Thirty clerks, writing in haste, were to draw up charters of freedom and amnesty in favour of all the districts which should claim them. It was hoped that the rebels, each group satisfied in turn, would return home.

Meanwhile, without waiting, Wat Tyler and his acolytes hastened towards the Tower. The drawbridge was lowered as a mark of confidence, and the rebels walked round freely, treating the warders familiarly and even pulling the beards of a few of the knights(?). Sudbury and Hales, who had taken refuge in the chapel and had just communicated, were beheaded, as was one of John of Gaunt's physicians and John Legge the sergeant-at-arms already mentioned. Afterwards the Tower was evacuated and the gates closed. The King however feared that some rebels might be about and took refuge elsewhere, in the robing-house, where he was actually less safe. All that afternoon clerks were copying the Mile End charters and many groups of peasants, having secured them, left the city; but not all. Murder and pillage were still going on.

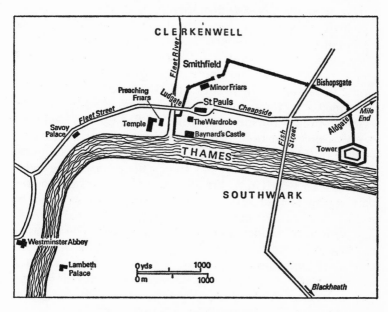

Fig. 6 London in 1381

On Saturday the 15th difficulties arose, as a part of the crowd, no doubt the most resolute, remained in London. On returning from Westminster where they had communicated, the King and his followers encountered this group and the King granted another interview, at Smithfield, a vast area outside the City proper, towards the north-west. This was to be decisive, and it is important to know just what happened, but unfortunately accounts of it are vague or divergent. Coming from the east, Richard and his followers drew up in front of St Bartholomew's Church. The crowd was assembled to the west, and between it and the royal group extended an open space, vast enough to prevent it from following the whole scene. Tyler rather audaciously advanced on horseback, dismounted and shook the King's hand. He was wearing a dagger, which showed his distrust. On Richard's asking him, he presented new demands.

The *Anonymous Chronicle* furnishes an exact list of the articles presented at Smithfield, articles divided into three classes. The legal group: no law was to survive except the Statute of Winchester which entrusted the maintenance of peace to the people (1285); which no doubt implied a suppression of the special legislation of the Statute of Labourers. This statute was also aimed at in the request for the abolition of outlawry, with a view to protect the labourers who had fled from the holdings to which they had been tied. There was a manorial group: a renewal of the demand for the abolition of serfdom; the lords were to be obliged to share out among their tenants the rights in the use of woodlands. Finally, an ecclesiastical group, the most spectacular of all: all Church properties were to be taken over and, once the subsistence of the clergy was assured, they were to be divided among the parishioners. There was to be, henceforth, only one bishop in England (and the insurgents were no doubt thinking of appointing John Ball). Richard limited himself to replying that he would concede everything that he legally could, saving the rights of the Crown; which meant nothing. Some uncertainty was apparent.

What is certain is that Wat Tyler quenched his thirst by drinking a pint of beer in the King's presence, and remounted his horse. But an altercation then arose between Tyler and a Kentish gentleman; blows were exchanged, Walworth, who was wearing a breastplate under his cloak or tunic, intervened, and Tyler was killed. Had there been provocation on his part? Intoxicated by success, did he deliberately adopt an insolent attitude in order to provoke a violent incident? This is not very probable. The important thing for him was to secure a definite promise from the King regarding the articles he had presented. Did the provocation come from the other side? Did the group of men which included Walworth, who had already favoured an armed sortie from the Tower, seek to excite Tyler, who let himself be involved? This is more likely.

The situation was embarrassing. According to the heroic version of the affair, the crowd, seeing Tyler fall stricken to the ground, is supposed to have prepared to avenge him. The young King then rode to meet the crowd and proudly harangued it: "It's I who am your leader, follow me!" And he conducted it to Clerkenwell, that is, northward. Meanwhile Walworth and his companions quickly assembled armed troops in London, found they had more men than expected, rejoined the King at Clerkenwell, and surrounded the rebels. But Richard is supposed to have asked that they should be allowed to disperse freely, and even to have had the Kentish men guided back to the right bank of the Thames.

It may be that the situation was much less clear; that the crowd did not see Tyler fall, since he was completely surrounded, and that the rebels thought he would be presented to them after being dubbed a knight. The rite and myth possessed great virtue! Once dubbed knight, Tyler would have been a legitimate leader in their eyes. The mental horizon of English labourers was bounded by the traditional and hierarchical ideas of the time. Without being aware of it, they reacted like the Ciompi, one of whose first gestures had been to create Knights of men of the people. For Tyler, this was not to be; his destiny was cut short, too soon, though not perhaps blindly.

It is certain that the army assembled in London—seven to eight thousand men led by Sir Robert Knolles, a famous veteran of the war in France—must have been made ready in advance, and this was perhaps part of a plot against Tyler. However that may be, Richard adopted a moderate attitude, contrary to that of Knolles who is said to have wanted to massacre the rebels. The King knighted Walworth and three other men on the spot, then returned to London where a succession of arrests was made. Thus June the 15th was decisive. Fate, so favourable to the rebels for the past two weeks, now turned against them.

Such was the principal scene of the revolt; but there were secondary ones. The rebels of Kent and Essex had converged on London, had come into direct contact with the King, and had been defeated in the capital. But all the counties of the south-east were affected, and even Lincolnshire and Leicestershire to the north. A connection, more or less close, has been established between all these disturbances and the principal one. St Albans had rebelled against the Abbot on several occasions, since he conceded no franchise. He was even accused of concealing a charter of privileges going back to the time of King Offa! Here an energetic leader named William Grindcobbe put himself at the head of a small delegation, was present at the Mile End conferences, obtained a charter and conferred with Tyler. In the whole of Middlesex, Surrey and Hertfordshire, when the peasants heard what was happening in London, they seized the manors, burned the documents and sometimes the manors too. John Wraw, a poor priest who happened to be in London, made his way to Suffolk where he had been a vicar for many years. He issued a proclamation, assembled a band of men and entered Bury St Edmunds, which was at odds with its Abbot (13 June). In Norfolk an active and intelligent dyer named Geoffrey Litster headed the insurrection, enrolling as his lieutenants certain knights, of whom Sir Roger Bacon was the most notable. Litster's force entered Norwich on the 17th and Yarmouth on the 18th, and he sent delegates to the King. In Cambridgeshire emissaries of Wraw appeared, and also men from London who said they were bringing royal orders, like the bucket-maker John Stanford. On the evening of the 15th and during the 16th Cambridge town rose against the university and several colleges were pillaged. Disturbances broke out further afield, at York and in Cheshire: of these we have knowledge mainly through judicial archives.

Repression clearly originated in London, but it was assisted by a local reaction due to Henry Despencer, the active Bishop of Norwich, a character more militant than truly religious. He happened to be in Rutland when he heard of the insurrection in his own diocese. He immediately set out with a little band of followers, gradually increased by the gentlemen who joined him. On the 17th he nipped in the bud an insurrection at Peterborough. At Ramsey on the 18th he captured a band of men led by one of Wraw's emissaries. On the 19th and 20th, at Cambridge, he severely punished the town and its leaders. On the 22nd he intercepted Litster's delegates; and on the 24th he entered Norwich. Then, at North Walsham, he crushed Litster's forces. Calm was quickly restored to the whole of East Anglia, without the King's having to intervene.

In London reaction was being organized on the evening of the 15th. Walworth directed the arrests. Leaders like Jack Straw were executed without trial; others like Faringdon, Horne and Sibley were merely imprisoned. The city lay quiet, and the forces of repression could assemble at their leisure. On the 18th the King issued a proclamation ordering "all sheriffs, mayors and bailiffs" to arrest malefactors. On the 20th he sent armed troops into Kent and Suffolk where they restored order in the course of a month. He himself left for Essex where the largest bands of rebels were giving trouble. To remove any doubt in the matter, he denied fellowship with the rebels in a proclamation of the 23rd. When on the 24th he encountered a delegation which begged him to confirm the promises made at Mile End, he repulsed it roughly. "Villains you are, and villains you will remain", he is supposed to have said. An attempt at resistance was organized, but the principal rebel band was defeated near Billericay (28 June), others were dispersed. At Chelmsford on 2 July Richard was able to issue his final proclamation. All the charters granted at Mile End were expressly revoked, and local commissions were entrusted with a regular enquiry. The commissioners then travelled through the counties, executing judgement according to the external forms. On 30 August their work was practically finished, and what remained was transferred to the King's Bench. On 14 December Richard proclaimed a general amnesty, from which only 247 fugitives were excluded.

Parliament met in November and until February 1382 spoke of also excluding several towns which had rebelled; in the end only Bury St Edmunds suffered this fate. The new Treasurer asserted that the King had revoked the charters which he had conceded only under pressure of force, and without the usual consultation with Parliament. He had however heard that certain lords were ready to free their serfs, and he was disposed to agree. One wonders if this was a sincere move in favour of the villains, or a hypocritical act designed to throw the responsibility on Parliament. In either case Parliament immediately negatived the suggestion, and the matter seemed to be closed.

We have related the story of the revolt simply, as from the outside, while striving to combine and co-ordinate the sources. It is now worth reflecting on the deeper causes of the insurrection.

Causes

The immediate cause was the levy of the poll-tax. Our best source, the *Anonymous Chronicle,* enables us to follow the sequence of events in detail. The injustice of this tax was like the drop of water which makes the vase overflow; the more so as it was ordained by unpopular men who were accused of betraying the kingdom. The hatred they had aroused showed itself clearly during the rebellion. Sudbury and Hales, who were responsible for royal policy, paid for it with their lives, and one can see that they expected this. The hatred inspired by the Duke of Lancaster was no less clearly expressed, and his absence saved his life; but the sack of the Savoy Palace might be regarded as a "punishment". Once the revolt had been suppressed, the government took care not to collect this tax again, and it was forgotten for practical purposes. Beyond the above cause, it was the failures of the royal policy and the war in France, involving heavier fiscal burdens, which explain the *political* motive behind the insurrection. It was natural that public opinion, as frequently happens in such cases, should believe there had been treason. In reality, no serious accusation of this kind could be brought against the ministers. What explained the English reverses were the technical conditions of the war, the guerilla tactics adopted by the French under Charles V. Was the country then to abandon the ambitious policy of conquest which had led to the Treaty of Bretigny? Richard was to think so later, and in the end it was what the English did.

However, public opinion was not yet ready to resign itself to such a peaceful solution.

It would be vain however to insist only on fiscal and political reasons. The rebels' programme certainly included the punishment of "traitors", but it put forward other demands connected with rural and social life. Froissart, writing a few years later with the advantage of a better perspective, con-considers only these. And in fact these were the grievances most keenly resented: "There is a custom in England [he writes] and in several other countries, whereby the nobles have great freedom over their men and hold them in serfdom." At the beginning of his narrative Froissart goes straight to this explana-tion. It is fundamental. In the greater part of France, for example, the economic expansion of the twelfth and thirteenth centuries had been accompanied by the freeing of grea numbers of serfs, though they had usually had to pay a certair sum. Towards 1300 the vast majority of French peasant consisted of tenants, working for the local lords, but personally free, and exempt from the incapacities and fiscal burdens characteristic of serfdom.

It was not so in England where the serfs—or villains, as they were called—remained very numerous, especially in the regions affected by the rebellion. They were perhaps even increasing in number. The villain paid a particular due known as *chevage*, quite small in general, but humiliating because it was regarded as the sign and reminder of his condition. He could not leave his holding unless permitted. If his descendants wished to take holy orders, they had to solicit permission; the principle being that one could not give oneself to God if one belonged to a man and was not, therefore, free. The villain could not give his daughter, sometimes even his son, in mar-riage without licence from the lord. This was normally granted, but against payment of a due, the *merchet*; which could however be avoided if the daughter was established as a concubine. But if she was with child, she became subject to another tax, the *leyrwite*. Otherwise, the *merchet* would have been evaded too easily. Moreover bastard children were generally considered free, on the ground of being unworthy to profit from the guarantees accorded to the serf, that is, protection by the lord and by custom. This sounds a paradox, but it would have risked affording a means of evading serfdom.

When a villain died, his movable goods which, like his person, were regarded as the lord's property, could pass to his heirs only after his best animal, his best garment and sometimes even the best tools had been set apart. This was the *heriot* or succession duty. For the same reasons he could not, in his lifetime, sell his animals; the object being to oblige him to preserve the beasts with which he worked on the lord's reserve.

Again, whereas the free tenant could, as he liked, transfer his lands, give them, exchange or sell them, the villain—because his goods belonged to the lord—had first to hand them over in the manorial court, that is, at the lord's tribunal, under the control of the steward, and he always ran the risk of not being able to conclude the transaction.

In the manor all the tenants had to pay certain taxes considered as the rent for the holding they occupied; besides this, they had to provide the lord with service for exploitation of the lands which he reserved for himself, what we today often call the demesne. In the case of free tenants, these services were fixed by custom, but the villains were dependent on the arbitrary decision of the lord. It would be an exaggeration, though not a great one, to say that the villain was never sure one night what he would have to do on the morrow, and from this uncertainty the organization of work on his own holding obviously suffered.

A descendant of villains was a villain. This hereditary condition doubtless rested on a rudimentary conception of transmission by blood. Servile status in the mother was enough to transfer villainage to the child she was going to bear. When a villain, one remained as such. But one could also become a villain when, by some means or other, one received a piece of land hitherto worked by serfs. Thus a real was added to a personal villainage. Of course the system did not function with perfect clarity. Peasants might take advantage of a relaxation of control to discontinue paying *chevage*, and declare that they were free. Conversely, the lords might try to impose new services, and then class as villains the tenants who had not dared to refuse.

The lords were the more strongly tempted to impose increased services after the epidemics of plague had created a crisis in the labour-force and caused a rise in wages. The free tenants were affected by this, because the lord always had the right to exact "customary" services which he had previously commuted into dues; but they were affected even more than the villains, because the lord preferred to call on them as liable to statute-labour than to pay them as wage-earners. The crisis in the labour-market therefore raised the problem of serfdom anew and with greater force. We have already seen that an unparalleled effort had been made in England to prevent a rise in wages and prices. At the most, a brake had been put on it; but many kinds of resentment had resulted from it. The fire had smouldered for many years; now it was crackling in the wind.

Miss Levett has shown that the weakening of the manorial system counted for something in the outbreak of the crisis. In particular the manorial courts which, as guardians of custom, constituted a protection for the tenants, were meeting less and less often, and the royal courts were depriving them of an increasing amount of business. Great landowners found it advantageous to establish itinerant baronial councils, composed of professional jurists, which were replacing the manorial courts for all difficult cases, and judged according to Roman or Canon Law. *Summum jus, summa injuria!* The case is very clear. The Abbot of St Albans had established a council of this kind which, when in full session in 1381, was put to flight by the peasants, who refused "to be judged in future according to Civil or Canon Law". This illustates a new aspect of the trouble: a crisis in the growth of the State, which was beginning to unify juridical practice at the expense of local custom and of everything that the manorial system, with its personal relationships, offered in the way of advantages to the average peasant.

Another question concerns the share taken by the towns in

an insurrection mainly rural. Some of these towns were archaic lordships, the lord being generally an ecclesiastic, like the abbots of St Albans, Bury St Edmunds, etc., who had shown himself to be particularly hard and finicky, in dealing with a population which, as elsewhere, was seeking emancipation. Here it was the old struggle being renewed under generally favourable conditions. Elsewhere, a conflict arose between the common people and the upper class, the former merely seeking to shake off the omnipotence of the ruling oligarchy. It is worth noting that this took place in towns sometimes remote from the regions of peasant "contagion". Winchester, Beverley and Scarborough were examples. The problem was more complex in London and no doubt in a few big towns. Nowhere, however, was the solidarity between city workmen and country labourers more spectacularly manifest than in London. It is again Froissart who informs us of this: "The commons of London [and many there were who agreed with them] came together and asked: 'Why do they not let these good folk enter the city? They are our people and all that they are doing is for us.' So it was agreed perforce that the gates should be opened." This is not the only piece of evidence. The admission of the rebels to London was not the work of traitors but the consequences of popular pressure.

The factors that operated in London must have been numerous and varied. As in other cities there must have been a rising of the lower class against the bourgeois aristocracy. The more or less scandalous profiteering by the arms-manufacturers, revealed in 1376, had just provoked an outburst of anger among the craft-guilds. Within the latter, workmen and apprentices were beginning to oppose the masters. In 1303 and again in 1383 the workmen in the guild of bootmakers who used Spanish leather were forbidden to hold assemblies; yet in the second half of the fourteenth century associations of workmen appeared among the saddlers. But the small men were not the only people to show sympathy for the peasants, because the latter found burgesses, obviously well-to-do, to lead them. Mention has already been made of three aldermen who played a decisive part in opening London to the rebels. Now all three

belonged to the guilds which managed the food supply; and it
has been thought that these were in rivalry with the drapers
over the question of free-trade, which the drapers desired and
the others opposed. During the disturbances several foreign
artisans in the textile trades, Flemings in particular, were
killed, and this must be ascribed partly to xenophobia. One
can therefore understand how all these factors may have
operated for a time but, how then, when conflicts arose between, or within, the guilds, the reaction was strengthened.

We must also ask ourselves whether the insurrection had any
religious causes. One cannot but notice the fairly large number
of priests who took part in it; historians have even named a
list of them; but their share in the revolt is easily explained by the
sometimes miserable lot of the lower clergy and the jealousy
they felt for the aristocratic prelates who often lived in great
luxury. On the other hand, the people attacked the clerics
here and there. The Hospitallers were particularly disliked
because their Prior was the King's Treasurer. Elsewhere, an
ecclesiastical lord or well-to-do parish priest would find his
people in revolt. Two of the articles presented at Smithfield
were obviously anti-clerical: the demand that Church properties should be secularized, and that all the bishops but one
should be abolished—these were radical measures! We should
however observe that the insurrection was never anti-religious.
At St Albans the charter of liberty was read aloud to the
villains in front of a crucifix; and many such "para-religious"
scenes could be mentioned.

What strikes one perhaps above all in the rebellion—and
first of all in the sermons of John Ball, the priest whom the
Archbishop imprisoned several times, though never for long
(to Froissart's regret)—was an egalitarianism, even communism, based on the Bible. The historian Gerald Owst has
insisted on the influence of the sermons which vigorously
denounced the pride of the nobility, the vices of the clergy
themselves, the hard-heartedness of jurists and the egoism of
the rich. They continued to do so after 1381. They inspired
an important part of English literature, such as Langland's
Piers Plowman (1362) and, after 1387 Chaucer's *Canterbury*

Tales.[1] It is true that there are marked signs of an egalitarian current in medieval Christianity. But preachers also attacked the idleness and meanness of peasants and artisans. They took their stand on the moral ground and could not elaborate a programme of social reform; which was why after 1381 no one attempted to censure them.

Whether the mendicant orders can be more specially accused is a further question. Thomas Walsingham ascribes to Jack Straw, one of the rebel leaders, a kind of confession made at the foot of the scaffold, in which he complacently describes the horrible plans of the peasants, including the intention of "removing from the earth all those in possession, such as bishops, monks, canons and rectors of churches. Only the Mendicants would live, and they would suffice to celebrate the sacraments. . . ." An almost contemporary collection of texts, the *Fasciculi zizaniorum* (Bundles of Tares) contains a letter which the four Mendicant orders are supposed to have written to John of Gaunt to exculpate themselves from a reproach inspired by the "sower of discord"—the reproach of having favoured the insurrection by the very amount of their begging, which could have impoverished the people; by the example of idleness they set; and by the advice they were said to have given when confessing the faithful. Here one recognizes traditional elements of the hostility to the Mendicants, which, since the thirteenth century, had been current among the rest of the clergy, so that one is tempted to see in it only a quarrel among clerics; and yet the more "popular" character of the Mendicants is certain.

 We now have to face the last and most serious of all the problems: the question of any influence that Wyclif and his disciples may have exercised on the revolt. The coincidence in time is impressive. This Oxford M.A., a protégé of the King and of John of Gaunt, had just written his principal works on the relations between Church and State. His great theological writings date from 1378. In 1379 he broke with the Mendi-

[1] Many of his pilgrims were clerics, a fact which made it easy and relevant to denounce corruptions in the Church. Thus the monk, the friar and the pardoner are all targets for satire or ridicule. (Translator.)

cants, hitherto his partisans, and with the court. The preaching of his disciples, "the poor priests", soon to be known as Lollards, probably began in 1380. In 1382 his doctrines and his partisans were solemnly condemned; and he himself survived only two years longer. The major heresy then was contemporary with the major insurrection, and both presented features in common.

A number of the theses defended by Wyclif could have been immediately applicable. He asserted the necessity of purifying the Church by secularizing its property; that tithes were no more than alms, that they were not obligatory, and that to refuse to pay tithes to bad priests might be a duty; that the temporal power could correct the vices of unworthy clerics. Grace was the true foundation of authority; therefore any governor in a state of mortal sin lost for that very reason the right to command. The Lollards were not slow in pushing these ideas further; they even maintained that "every virtuous man, predestined to eternal life, if a layman, is nevertheless a true minister and priest ordained by God to administer all the sacraments ... even if no bishop has laid his hands on him". The condemnation pronounced in 1382 mentioned some particularly drastic articles, such as: "God cannot confer civil power on a man and his heirs in perpetuity", and "Human charters which engage the patrimony in perpetuity, are impossible things."

Contemporaries did not fail to assert that there was a link between Wyclif and the rebels. Walsingham accused John Ball of preaching Wyclif's doctrines. At the end of the century a rumour was current to the effect that, just before dying, Ball confessed to being a disciple of the great heresiarch, and spoke of a sect organized to cover the whole of England. And the Lollards were reproached with sowing discord and rousing the people to revolt.

Some undoubted facts however prevent our going far in this direction. Wyclif himself denied any collusion with the rebellion and, if he understood certain causes of it, blamed it all the same. He was above all a theologian, and not a social reformer in the least. One might also insist on his tolerance of abuses, and on the connections he maintained to the end with certain court circles, which explains why he was able to end his days in peace; finally on his deep-rooted conservatism. One might also note in the Lollards certain features which, at the beginning at least, prevented their figuring as revolutionaries: their pacifism and insistence on the duty of obedience even to a bad master. It is also certain that no "poor priest" was found among the agitators of 1381 and that the rebellion took place in regions very little affected by Lollardism.

We cannot therefore speak of direct influence. The "revolutionary" reputation of the Lollards formed part of a campaign waged against them in 1382 and after; and because they won over a number of knights and rich men, they were represented as seditious. Coincidence there certainly was between the rise of heresy and the social rebellion, but it was only a coincidence which enemies were only too glad to exploit, wrongly, against the heretics.

However—though here any precise historical evidence is necessarily lacking—indirect influence by Wyclif cannot be excluded. One may suppose, besides, that both rebels and "poor priests" were sensitive to certain abuses and vices in the social system which were the same for everyone.

We have dwelt at some length on the Peasants' Revolt. It deserved that we should do so on the ground of its national importance, and owing to the wealth of our documentation, to the complexity and seriousness of its causes, and to the gravity of the problems it raises. Our lengthy treatment of the rebellion is also justified by its international celebrity and by Wyclif's connection with the Hussite revolution, as will appear later.

Even in the Empire, which, as we have seen, was periodically disturbed by uprisings in the towns, this period seems particularly agitated. It was especially the Hanseatic areas, hitherto more or less exempt from trouble, that now sprang into activity. At Brunswick in April 1374 an increase in taxation provoked an insurrection of the craftsmen; several councillors were killed and others banished. On assuming power, the rebels wrote (during the summer no doubt) to the neighbouring Hanseatic cities to justify their action and ask that no measures should be taken against them. In vain; for in June 1375 the council of the Hansa decided to expel Brunswick. This was no doubt because the conspirators there had encouraged other disturbances in the interval. As early as the autumn of 1374 the craftsmen of Lübeck addressed a still very respectful petition to the city council; in 1374 the crafts of Nordhausen were in commotion, and those of Hamburg asked the council to reduce the principal tax and abolish various other charges. On this occasion the butchers acted as spokesmen; but the mercers, coopers and other groups supported the merchants, and the craftsmen had not only to give way but to take a new oath of loyalty. In 1376 Stade and Danzig in 1378 were agitating, while Brunswick persisted in its rebellion. Finally on 13 August 1380 the government of Brunswick had to make amends in front of the great doors of Lübeck cathedral: a humiliating ceremony which seems to have made a great impression.

It was then however that trouble began at Lübeck. Here too the butchers were the instigators, and it is often for this reason that the insurrection is called *Knochenhaueraufstand*. They were compelled to sell their meat on stalls belonging to the city, with various consequences: for example, the council let the stalls every year and collected the tax anew; the number of butchers was limited by the number of stalls; and when a stall fell vacant, the council had a major voice in selecting the new holder. It was this kind of tutelage that the butchers were trying to shake off, but they appealed to the "ancient right"—evoked as more favourable to artisan freedom—in order to lead the other craftsmen to make common cause with them. So they presented a petition to the council and December 1380 saw a trial of strength between them and the burghers, each side having come armed. The council made various concessions. The butchers would have the right of nominating their own candidate to a vacant stall; but the ultimate aims of the craftsmen, such as full corporative freedom and access to the city council, they did not achieve.

So the affair gave rise to much discontent, and this was used by a man who had probably been absent at the time of the disturbances mentioned, a certain Heinrich Paternostermaker, son of a burgher, who, as his name suggests, had grown rich by exporting amber rosaries from the Baltic; but the son was not as successful as the father, and financial troubles may have embittered him. H. von Brandt has made a close study of the conspirators who gathered round him: most of them were butchers, but other crafts were represented. They were generally fairly well-off, sometimes in financial difficulties, but not always. Most of them formed a sort of clique, united by family or business ties. Their plan was to meet at 9 o'clock on 17 September 1384 at the same time as the council, to occupy the town hall and arrest or kill all the councillors. Various nobles in the vicinity were then to intervene from outside and support the new council. But the careless talk of one of the plotters warned the authorities at the last moment. The principal suspects were thrown into prison and Paternostermaker killed himself to avoid confessing. All the craftsmen had to swear a new oath of loyalty, but the butchers' craft was dissolved and the council reserved the right to let the stalls as it pleased and to increase the taxes collected on such occasions.

If rebellion had been contagious, so was the repression that followed. In March 1385 Lübeck renewed a treaty which it had formerly concluded with Hamburg, by virtue of which each city undertook to pursue or prosecute fugitives from the other. Lübeck even asked the Hanse to apply these measures to all members of the league. This did not prevent the craftsmen of Anklam, near Stettin, from overthrowing the council in 1386, nor those of Stralsund from rebelling on several occasions, as in 1391 and 1394. Finally in 1396 Cologne, which was also a member of the Hanse and long regarded as the model of a patrician city, experienced the triumph of the craftsmen.

Thus, what confers a certain novelty on these disturbances at the end of the fourteenth century, among all those which had confusedly troubled the cities of the Empire, is that the movement affected places which had been hitherto more or less spared. Yet, apart from some gains at Brunswick, where the council remained open to the craftsmen, and also the revolution at Cologne, the results of rebellion were virtually nil.

[Chapter Five]
Conflicts Old and New

THE REPRESSION which crushed the rebels in the various lands troubled, between 1378 and 1382, by revolutionary turmoil, re-established peace for some years. In France it was a military and political crisis which, in the next century, was to set the old mechanisms in motion and cause a new outbreak of disturbances. There was, in the meantime, nothing very new about the anti-Jewish pogrom in the Iberian lands which had long remained socially tranquil. Nevertheless, even in Catalonia and various parts of Europe, a genuinely popular agitation took place: in this the lower groups several times acted separately from the middle groups and fought to achieve definite social and economic objects. Lastly and above all, the Hussite crisis was to bring to light tendencies and programmes so new that we cannot do better than describe them in completing this study.

Catalonia apart, the Iberian peninsula has furnished little to comment on up to now. True, Maria del Carmen Carlé has recorded symptoms of social trouble, even in the cities of Leon and Castille, during the later thirteenth century. However, it was often the population as a whole which opposed the nobility, and none of the episodes in question was of much note. The Portuguese rebellion which in 1383 established the Avis dynasty in power had some social features; but the rather remarkable tranquillity that reigned throughout the peninsula between 1378 and 1383, when so many parts of Europe witnessed disturbance or upheaval, is none the less striking.

A study of the documents that concern the period 1380–90 would probably reveal more than one sign of coming troubles. Thus it was at Barcelona in 1386. King Pedro IV, "the ceremonious", intervened in a dispute between the craft of the weavers, fullers and dyers on the one side, and the councillors on the other, who constituted the executive power, and he supported the former. He especially favoured a plan to reform the civic constitution, because, adds the text, "he had long known that the city was badly governed". This plan of reform was based on a division of the population into three social categories: "honoured citizens", that is burghers living on private income or by judicious investments; merchants; and artisans. Each of these groups was to be equally represented in the council (which would have six members, and not five as before) and in the deliberative assembly, the Council of the Hundred. All councillors and officials would in future be required to render account of their administration, while an inquiry was opened into the administrative work of all those responsible during the past twenty-five years. To break the resistance of the sitting councillors who were preparing to hold elections in the customary manner, the King appointed councillors and "*prud'hommes*," including artisans; but he died soon afterwards, on 5 January 1387, and Juan I, the new sovereign, hurriedly abandoned the plan of reform.

It was owing to the Jewish question that the storm was to burst five years later. All over Europe the position of the Jews had steadily deteriorated during the fourteenth century. In 1290 Edward I had expelled them from England. In France since the time of Philippe le Bel expulsions had followed periods during which the Jewish communities had been able to re-establish their business; which might be called the policy of the sponge. They were scarcely popular with the public, as was shown by the *Pastoureaux'* movement in Languedoc (1320) and by the anti-Jewish episodes in the civic disturbances of 1382. Nowhere, however, did the Jewish question exhibit the same seriousness as in the Iberian peninsula.

The number of Jews living in fourteenth-century Spain has been very variously estimated: a million and a half in the kingdom of Castille alone according to some, about twenty thousand according to others. The best way of judging is to start from the presumed number of the Jews who were expelled in 1492, and it is agreed that between 100,000 and 150,000 left Castille at that time. Prior to this, massacre, emigration and conversions had reduced their numbers in proportions difficult to estimate. It is not unreasonable to suppose that towards 1370 they may have numbered about 200,000, that is, between 3 per cent and 5 per cent of the total population. The most important communities were living in Toledo, Seville, Jerez and in Murcia; but small *aljamas* (seventy-one in Castille proper) were scattered throughout the kingdom. They were even more widely dispersed in the kingdom of Aragon, which probably contained nearly 60,000 Jews, a relatively greater number, namely 6–7 per cent of the population. One is averse however to adopting the figure which Fritz Baër proposed for Barcelona: 5,000 Jews, or 12–14 per cent of the population. If there were 1,500, this is a fair estimate, but at least we may suppose that this was the most numerous community in the kingdom.

Were these Jews as rich as has been said? Increasingly, since the thirteenth century, a prosperous minority of great financiers and administrators had become isolated from the mass of the (Jewish) community. A certain Yucaf Pichon was virtually director of the royal finances for Enrique II, King of Castille, between 1369 and 1375. The Jews monopolized the posts of tax-farmers or receivers, posts for which their means and experience commended them. Even the nobility had recourse to their services. One suspects that this contributed to making them unpopular. Doctors like Yucaf ibn Wakar, in the service of the King of Castille, who entrusted him with diplomatic missions; or the Rabbi Haym el Levi who in 1389 was physician to the Archbishop of Toledo; or again astrologers such as Hasdai Cresques, in the service of Yolanda of Aragon, rose to very high office. These rich Jews often became less devout, and the Rabbis loudly deplored the fact, but the great majority of Jews remained ardent believers, and these included usurers, but also small farmers, artisans and merchants. There were also poor Hebrews, for whom a hospital had been founded at Barcelona; but Christians in general did not make these distinctions. The Jews had won a strong social and economic position, they were rough in recovering the moneys owing to them, they refused to be assimilated and so represented a "cyst" in the State.

The conflict became particularly acute in the kingdom of Castille where passions had been inflamed by a dynastic dispute. Pedro I, whom his enemies called "the cruel", had openly leaned for support on the Jews. This encouraged immigration on the part of large numbers, people who had been made uncomfortable by the attitude of their various governments. His half-brother, Enrique de Trastamare, who led the insurrection against him, strongly reproached him with his pro-Jewish policy. This was only one of the grounds of contention. But Enrique was overtaken by his own propaganda. His troops destroyed several *aljamas*; the one at Toledo was partly sacked in 1355; and when the people of Valladolid rose against Pedro I in 1367, eight synagogues paid the price of this "emotion". When Enrique II was victorious in 1369, the Jews rallied round him, and he continued to use them, though less blatantly. One may suppose that the events of 1391 were the culmination of these conflicts.

Anti-Jewish feeling subsisted on instinct. It also adopted the old conception of the collective and hereditary responsibility of the Jews in the Passion of Christ, and for this reason showed itself most strongly in Holy Week. But definite claims, precise demands were formulated. What was demanded was, first, a moratorium, or even a reduction of the debts owing to the Jews. People sometimes went as far as asking that loans advanced at interest, which were theoretically prohibited, should be effectively forbidden. Certain crafts, such as medicine and finance, were to be closed to them. Generally speaking, a Jew's profession should give him no power over Christians. He was also to be distinguished from Christians by special signs worn on his clothes, by confinement in a ghetto, and by being forbidden to assume a christian name. In the law courts, a Christian's testimony should always prevail over a Jew's. Finally, any sign of increased activity, such as the building of new synagogues, or embellishment of old ones, was jealously watched and opposed. The *aljama* of Cordova was compelled to demolish a new religious building, and the principal synagogue in Valencia, which had been enlarged and adorned, was given by the Queen to her principal chaplain (1379). One can clearly distinguish the social and economic character of these grievances against the Jews.

They were still further exasperated by the propaganda of new converts, not then very numerous, but full of hatred for their former co-religionists; and also by fanatics among whom Ferran Martinez, archdeacon of Ecija, was outstanding. Some went as far as preaching in favour of a "definite solution" of the Jewish question. The *aljama* of Seville had several times to complain of the archdeacon of Ecija, and Juan I of Castille had to write to moderate his zeal. But the King died on 9 October 1390, leaving an heir who was a minor, and Enrique III's reign was marked from the outset by great agitation.

It was in these conditions that the pogrom started. To fix the chronology and measure the extent of this drive would be useful, though much further research in local archives will be needed. We may begin by recording what is known from— among other sources—the letter which Hasdai Cresques, the Queen of Aragon's astrologer, wrote to the community at Avignon. Violence started at Seville on 6 June 1391, directly encouraged by Ferrán Martinez. Two synagogues were converted into churches, murders and thefts followed. The contagion spread to nearly all the *aljamas* of the archdiocese. Cordova was soon the theatre of scenes as frightful, and the wave of violence moved on to Ubeda, Baeza, Jaén, Muradal, Ciudad Real, Huete and Cuenca. At Cuenca a subsequent trial was to prove that several members of the municipal council took part in the massacre. Toledo was affected on 18 June.

By way of Orihuela and Alicante the flame of hostility reached Valencia. We are fairly well informed about the

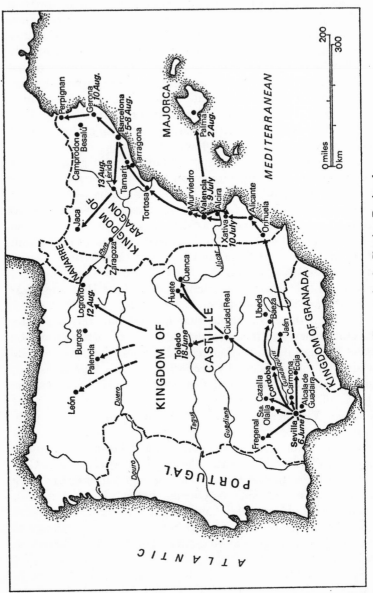

Fig. 7 The 1391 Pogrom in the Iberian Peninsula

pogrom at Valencia by an account which was written by order
of the city magistrates themselves. Despite the precautions
inspired by the disquieting news, forty to fifty young men
appeared at the gateway to the *Juderia*, uttering threats. Some
of them even managed to invade the ghetto, the Jews having
shut the gate too late. Responding to the shouts of the Christians
who had remained outside, the crowd was joined by soldiers
and vagabonds. The Infanta, escorted by the Knights and
sworn aldermen, asked the Jews to reopen the gates, in order to
reassure the crowd as to the fate of the intruders; but in vain.
While the Jews were refusing, the barrier round the ghetto
was crossed and the massacre began. Some Jews fled to the
churches and let themselves be baptized.

Repression began on 11 July, when the aldermen ordered
those who were in possession of clothes, jewels and money stolen
from the *Juderia* to bring and deposit them in front of a special
commission. They arrested nearly 100 persons, of whom about
eighty were men of the people, though ten were men "of high
lineage". This detail and several others emphasize the view
that elements of all ranks had taken part in the riot. When
however on 8 November 1392 the King granted a general
pardon, and made an exception for only twenty of the culprits
who were to be named, these were all artisans. What strikes
one, moreover, about these events is the religious enthusiasm
amid which they took place. The aldermen, in their letter to
the King, pointed to several miracles as having occurred, some
of them officially certified by notaries, and they concluded that
this could be explained only by divine intervention. Thus a
repudiation of the excesses committed at the expense of royal
property (the Jews being regarded as such) was combined, in
spite of everything, with a belief in an overruling providence;
both circumstances having led to so many conversions.

In the meantime the contagion had spread north to Catalonia. On 2 August the same atrocities were perpetrated at
Palma de Mallorca; though there a new element crept in.
After plundering the *aljama*, the mob attacked the property of
certain Christians.

Of events in Barcelona we have the means of offering a

more detailed picture. On receiving the news from Valencia, on 17 July, the council had decided to establish a force, armed and sworn in, which would prevent any possible assault on the *Call*, or Jewish quarter. Then, as all remained calm, anxiety died down. On 2 August the council seemed to be absorbed by problems of food supply; it was a question of sending two ships to Sicily, in particular two Castilian ships which happened to be in the harbour.

It was then that the four terrible days began. On Saturday 5 August, towards half past one in the afternoon, a small band, which had come from the port and included Castilian sailors, set fire to the gates of the *Call* and killed some hundred Jews. During the whole evening and night the mob shared in the pillage, while the surviving Jews took refuge in the royal Castillo Nuevo, near by. Sunday the 6th witnessed a lull in the tempest and an attempt at reaction. A number of the culprits were arrested and confined in the Provost's gaol. The royal officials, the councillors and many "honoured citizens" mounted guard round the *Call* and the Castillo Nuevo. These measures were continued on the Monday. The citizens assembled under arms, as commanded by the councillors, and a well-attended council unanimously condemned ten Castilians to be hanged. Guilhem de Sant-Climent, the royal Provost, was preparing to execute the sentence when towards half past one in the afternoon a far greater rising took place, amid cries of "Long live the King and the people!" The documents agree in making the lower class responsible. After a turmoil which left one man dead and several wounded, the rioters attacked the Provost's (*viguier*) gaol and freed the prisoners. For a short time sedition turned into a social conflict. The houses of several "honoured citizens" were threatened. Canon Mascaro, our best source of information, indicates a Knight, Pons de la Sala, as having under cover of two royal flags diverted the common people towards the royal castle and then laid siege to it. Meanwhile, the cathedral bells were sounding the alarm. In the evening the peasants belonging to the militia (the *sagramental*) flocked to the castle. During the night the archives of the *batle* (that is the bailiff) were burned. Finally,

on Tuesday 8 August, the Jews, who had taken refuge in the
new Castillo and were dying of thirst and hunger, surrendered;
and a procession, setting out from the cathedral, came to
receive them. Mascaro records the memory of a monk, standing
on the castle mound and holding up a cross. Numerous
baptisms were at once celebrated in the cathedral and in other
churches. Recalcitrants were lodged in families and instructed
in Christian dogma. Some more were converted, but many,
especially women, refused and were killed; three hundred,
according to a fairly reliable source.

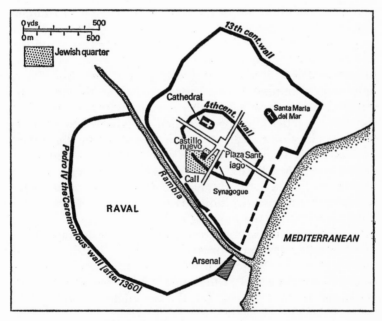

Fig. 8 Barcelona towards 1390

Then came a long period which Mascaro describes as
follows:

"They [the rioters] threatened to kill all the clerics, and
forced them to pay taxes and to contribute in everything as if

they were laymen. Next they menaced the silversmiths, merchants and rich men, without putting them to death, though
they were not far from it. During this time when a council
was held in the city all the common folk were admitted to the
general council. Various embassies were sent to the King,
containing men of the upper, middle and lower orders."

The register of the council for this period, which has been
preserved, confirms the above. The city lived under pressure
from the populace, and many artisans took part in the councils
held in August and September. It was decided to inquire into
the past administration of the city's finances, and a commission of auditors was appointed, containing one, two or several
members of each craft, a few citizens and merchants, and two
of the royal accountants—who were therefore in a very small
minority. The object was to punish past abuses, but also to
lighten fiscal burdens on the city. Meanwhile, the taxes were
reduced, the duty on wine being lowered from an eighth to a
sixteenth. A letter of remission which was granted to a courier
from the city throws light on the circumstances in which these
decisions were taken. We see this man mounting a bench and
crying out: "My Lords, may it please you to remove these
impositions, for a great throng is outside, awaiting the good
news!" An embassy (including two artisans) was sent to the
King, praying him not to come, or in any case not with armed
men. The council was busy trying to restore order, and to remove weapons (except swords and daggers). There being still
some question of the Jews, it was decided to expel those who
refused conversion and at the same time to separate the converts from the recalcitrant; but the last allusion to them dates
from 21 August.

Reaction followed little by little. After 9 October the councils
were composed as before the riots, the exceptional presence of
artisans being no longer mentioned. On 30 November, the
usual date, five new councillors were elected, and new members
of the Council of the Hundred appointed. It was agreed that the
former should swear to continue the examination of the accounts. On 13 December the commission of inquiry underwent

a significant change. The artisans were to succeed each other monthly, in groups of ten; but, of these ten, only four would in fact sit at one time, facing four citizens or merchants.

Repression had by now begun. On 6 December the first royal troops entered the city. On the 13th the gibbets were set up, and on the 14th eleven men were hanged in the principal squares of the city, the bodies remaining exposed for a week. On the 22nd ten more were hanged and two were quartered. Mascaro gives us the name of one of the latter, N'Armentera, a tailor, and he enumerates with a detail tinged with satisfaction the places where the fragments were to be exposed. One desire was clearly manifest: to inspire terror in the public. The King and Queen were able to make their solemn entry on 10 January 1392.

No less than eighty-two letters of remission, affecting ninety-two persons, have been preserved in the registers of the royal chancellery: these inform us of the sequel to the whole affair. The formula is practically repeated in each case. The crimes and faults of the beneficiary were remitted, even if he had taken part in the attack on the *Call*, in the attack on the Castillo Nuevo, in breaking into the Provost's gaol, in burning the Bailiff's archives, or in the massacre of the Jews—on condition, however, of satisfying the civil courts. The price for these pardons was usually fixed at a low figure, and these remissions evidently concern poor people, but the figure was sometimes higher. The same impression arises from a study of the beneficiaries' occupations. Seven were slaves, three were freed men; there were six sailors, two cobblers, two weavers, and a carpenter; but there were also three innkeepers, a notary and two silversmiths. A whole family—parents, two sons and three slaves—received a collective pardon. Some ten persons were strangers to Barcelona. A few collective remissions were granted to parishes near the city. In fact, there were many who managed to pass through the meshes of the net. Yet this insurrection cannot be regarded as a simply popular one.

We are fairly well informed too about the pogrom at Gerona, and we find the same ambiguity about it. Here the townsmen and the peasants of the countryside who had met for the

Festival of Saint Lawrence, assaulted the *Call* on 10 August; the victims were probably at least forty in number. Those who survived took refuge in the tower of the Gironella, and were under constant threat until near the end of September, so that agitation at Gerona was anti-Jewish to the end. But fiscal and social demands also quickly made their appearance. The poorer class demanded the abolition of the indirect taxes which were collected at the city gates; the *prud'hommes* of the crafts proposed to replace these by a levy based on an assessment of estates. The councillors belonging to the rebellious party were supported by the peasants, and in return lent them armed help. Eight of them in fact were suspended as accomplices in the attack on the castle of Cassà, ten miles south-east of Gerona. On 20 September the peasants again assembled outside the city, the gates being closed. They tried to attack the tower of the Gironella, but then dispersed; and this episode closed the period of agitation.

The final manifestations of violence may be very briefly mentioned. They had spread to the north of Catalonia, where Besalù, Camprodon and other places were scenes of brutality. On 13 August, a most violent pogrom took place at Lerida. Here again the Jews took refuge in the royal castle, though many were killed and the *Call* was devastated. Several of the King's officials who were protecting the Jews were wounded and the lord of the castle perished in a fire. Elsewhere precautions were taken in time to avoid worse things. The Jews of Perpignan sought shelter in the castle where some of them were converted under pressure from the clergy; though the authorities were unable to prevent thefts from the *Call*. Order was maintained at Saragossa and Huesca. Further west the wave of violence, coming no doubt from the south, reached Burgos and Logroño on 12 August. Agitation also spread through the regions of Palencia and Leon. Navarre and Portugal seem to have been exempt from trouble.

Such is the general picture which, in the present state of our knowledge, we can trace of the pogrom in Spain; but it is full enough to bring some of its features clearly to light, and for definite questions to be put for future research.

In the first place, the disturbances at Valencia offer a striking contrast with those in the towns and cities of Catalonia. At Valencia, a pseudo-religious emotion appears. Violence against the Jews comes from the most varied social strata and is exercised in a state of enthusiasm or excitement receptive to every rumour of miracles. At Barcelona and Gerona, anti-Jewish feeling springs rather from the common people, while the bourgeoisie tries to repress its violent manifestations. Here the underlying social problem very quickly comes to the fore. This concentrates mainly on the financial administration of the city, and on the reduction of taxes, especially indirect taxes. Opinion was less unfavourable to a direct tax levied in proportion to a person's income, this being considered less unjust.

The contrast between Valencia and the Catalonian cities doubtless reflects an unequal economic development or different social systems. Mademoiselle Claude Carrère has pointed to the large influx of immigrants into Barcelona; by furnishing abundant labour it resulted in a lowering of wages; and the trouble this produced, together with the presence of a very mixed population, is enough to explain the disturbances. It would be desirable to inquire into local causes of agitation in other places and compare them. It is likely that they will be found everywhere; but it was only in Catalonia, seemingly, that people's reaction went beyond the stage of blind anti-Jewish feeling and was consciously directed to the social question.

The chronology and diffusion of the disturbances would provide another subject for research. Between 6 June and 13 August the pogrom spread over the country in a little over two months. Agitation persisted in a few places until nearly the end of September. At the beginning of October order was everywhere restored, and repression followed, unhindered.

The contagion of anti-Jewish feeling was due to the circulation of news, as a few examples enable us to judge. At Xativa at dawn on 10 July people heard of the pogrom which had taken place the day before at Valencia, forty miles away. The mob began to growl, but the aldermen still managed to control it, or so they said; but at the end of the afternoon news of the pogrom at Alcira (ten miles distant) carried away the fragile barriers of the law, and the pillage and killing began. The letters dispatched by the King and the correspondence between cities then served the purpose of newspapers. Thus at Gerona, the pogrom at Valencia (9 July) was known both by a missive from the King who sent it on the 12th, and by a letter from the councillors of Barcelona, who had heard the news from a merchant. The King's letter was transcribed on the 20th, by order of the municipality and for the purpose of neighbouring communities. On 6 August, news that the Barcelona *Call* had been sacked reached Gerona in a letter from the councillors of Barcelona, and violence erupted on the 10th.

As regards the extent of the damage, the number of the dead was frequently recorded by contemporaries, but their estimates are far from agreeing, and some of them excite doubt. That 4000 died at Seville and more than 2000 at Cordova sounds unlikely. Other estimates sound more reasonable: from 100 to 250 at Valencia, 250 to 400 at Barcelona, 78 at Lerida. That was plenty. There were many converts, and efforts were made to separate them from the surviving Jews in order to prevent relapses. In any case, apart from the human and material losses, a kind of moral rupture had taken place. Continuity was broken, and it was impossible for the Jews to continue living on the same foundations as before. In spite of royal support, most of the *aljamas* never recovered their previous importance.

Lastly, it is the attitude of different classes to the events in question, that attracts our attention. The kings of Aragon adopted, at least in writing, the most definite stand against murder and forced conversions. Juan I wrote as follows to the consuls of Perpignan: "Neither civil law nor canon law permits that anyone should turn Christian under force; conversion should come in pure liberty"; otherwise converts would be living in a worse error than that under which they had previously laboured. Juan's weakness and indecision prevented these good intentions from being put much into practice. It was in Catalonia too that the more well-to-do classes clearly showed their desire to prevent and to combat violence; the instinct of the populace being definitely anti-Jewish. Unfortunately the people opposed to violence have not taken the trouble to explain their motives. These derived no doubt from respect for royal property (the Jews being, as already stated, possessions of the King), from a natural dislike of any breach of the peace, and from a human understanding with persons with whom they were connected by business relations. It is doubtful whether their feelings went much further or whether any ideal of toleration was awakened. Most people could not understand why the Jews were so obstinate in clinging to their errors: to the lower class, in any case, the indulgent attitude of the well-to-do seemed a sort of treason. So we see how the Jewish question actually served to bring out social conflicts.

*   *   *

In France after 1382 the repression produced an intimidating effect which seems to have lasted for a generation. Prior to the Cabochian Revolution of 1413, no disturbances reached any very serious level. Yet motives of discontent persisted, especially when problems of social or industrial structure increased them. Thus nothing better reveals the social causes of the events of 1378–82 in the past, and the future events of 1413–18 than the persistence of these latent difficulties.

In the north as in Languedoc, at Paris as at Laon, Amiens, Rouen, Caen, Orleans and Carcassonne, the inquiries vigorously conducted by the general commissioners, and still more the very heavy taxation, were enough to discourage the most recalcitrant of malcontents. Twenty-five years after the events of 1378–82, at Rouen in 1407, those who had not paid their share of the fine were still being prosecuted. The abolition of the Commune, like the suppression of the office of Merchants' Provost in Paris, maintained these two cities in which rebellion had twice threatened the monarchy, under the direct control of the King's officials. In Paris, to be called a *mallet* was long considered an insult. In the first years of the fifteenth century there was still talk of an *harelle* in Normandy, as we gather from a procedure recorded, though without proof, in the Exchequer of Normandy in 1403. The arrest of an inhabitant of Saint-Lô, which was judged arbitrary, led his fellow-townsmen to riot against the King's officials; there was "a great assembly bearing arms, in the manner of an *harelle* and conspiracy". The crisis at Louviers between 1407 and 1409 was more serious and more clearly of social origin. Being anxious to economize and at the same time increase production, the drapers had put in hand and started a disused fulling mill. This inevitably resulted in unemployment. Most of the fullers, finding themselves reduced to begging or looking for work elsewhere, rose in rebellion and threatened the use of physical force to prevent the drapers from sending their cloth to the mill. It was finally agreed that the mill "was breaking" the cloth, and the mill was closed: an ephemeral but revealing episode in the conflict between labour and automation.

Carcassonne presents an interesting case. Admirably situated at the passage between upper and lower Languedoc, the city had been defended since the end of the thirteenth century by particularly elaborate fortifications. On the summit of its hill the city was girded by encircling walls and military works which made it well-nigh impregnable. As the bulwark of royal power in Languedoc, it remained the "key to the whole province". To hold it was imperative for anyone who wished to assert his authority in Languedoc. Meanwhile, on the lower ground, an industrial town had grown up as one of the principal textile centres in southern France. The neighbourhood of the old stronghold and the bustling town was not peaceful for either. In 1355 the town, still defenceless, was destroyed by the Black Prince's army. When rebuilt the authorities provided it with walls. Now this town, perhaps with the complicity of the King's agents, had retained a municipal government which was extremely aristocratic, dominated, that is, by the wealthy merchants. In the whole of the Midi it was doubtless the place where the common people had obtained fewest concessions.

Probably for this reason, collection of the fine of 800,000 francs which had been imposed on Languedoc after the so-called *Tuchin* insurrection—and of which Carcassonne alone owed 35,000—was very slow and difficult, involving brawls, prosecutions and arrests. A decree of the King's Council in Languedoc, promulgated in May 1390, is significant of the tension then prevailing in the town. The Royal Attorney had accused the consuls, treasurers, assessors (*estimeurs*) and heads of crafts, who had been in office in the past forty years, of numerous misdeeds at the expense of the lower class (*le petit peuple*). They had neglected to render account of their administration, had diverted part of the public funds to their private use, had assessed the rich and the poor unjustly by levying on the latter a surplus of the taxation which weighed all the less heavily on the former: "By relieving the rich and oppressing the poor", we read, they had collected several subsidies in the form of a poll-tax or indirect taxation. In the end, and in return for a fine of 1500 gold francs, the King's agents acquitted the accused who "were not found to be as guilty as the King's Attorney had accused them of being". Can one be sure? In any case, after 1413, Carcassonne was to be one of the nerve-centres of agitation, and this is not too surprising.

We must return to Paris for the most dramatic of the revolutionary movements in the first two decades of the fifteenth century. Politics predominated here, because these movements were connected with the rivalry between Armagnacs and Burgundians. Party conflict however would have been less violent if it had not had social implications of two kinds. The first derived from the usual difficulties and miseries consequent on war—foreign war and civil war. The second were the outcome of social contentions, which we should keep in mind if we are to follow the sequence of events.

Bronislaw Geremek has recently pointed out the problems connected with the Parisian artisans. He has emphasized the great mobility of the labour force which corresponded with that of the Parisian population. The war had increased the influx of immigrants from the countryside, and the time had not yet come when lack of work in the city would cause them to flow back. The workmen who came in this way to offer their service often had no professional qualifications. Apart from this, any possibilities of being absorbed into the artisan class were limited, especially in periods of disturbance. That in these circumstances the labour-market in the Place de Grève was soon saturated, one can well understand. Paris therefore contained many unemployed and also a floating mass of unqualified workers who were not integrated into any of the crafts.

In the second place, human relationships were evolving inside the crafts themselves. The workshops had certainly continued to resemble family concerns; the master himself worked beside the journeymen (or "companions") and the apprentices. In times of trouble, the latter were sometimes seen hastening to assist the master. The meaning of the word "companions" (*compagnons*) which tends to be substituted for the word "workmen" (*valets*)—as in German *Geselle* replaces *Knecht*—is ambivalent. It expresses the relations between one man and another, deriving from work common to master and employee, and also common to the employees. The latter form of relationship was however acquiring a new importance in the fifteenth century, because it is to this period that we can trace back the formation of the unions of workmen (*compagnonnage*).

Other problems were appearing. A very great increase has been recorded in the number of artisans working for other men. Certain artisans who had attained the status of "master", for example as "small master-weavers", were obliged by economic and other difficulties to hire themselves out to other men. As to the wage-earners proper, it was the question of working-hours rather than of wages that brought them into conflict with their employers.

Great diversity prevailed among the crafts. Some, like those in the textile industry, included a greater number of subordinate workmen, occupied on tasks that were considered inferior, although as necessary as the others: thus there was a plebeian class of fullers. We should also remember the frequency and seriousness of indebtedness; debts to the master were often contracted, and their liquidation naturally affected any change of employment. In calm periods these legal or actual states of dependence, these economic or juridical inferiorities led simply to disputes, of which only the most important were brought before the *Parlement*; but in times of disturbance they greatly aggravated the political conflicts that were going on.

One class of men, the butchers, was fully disposed to exploit the ill-feeling. Their trade, or "craft", was homogeneous and active, rich and influential; but because, with few exceptions, its members had not yet managed to enter the upper bourgeoisie, along with the drapers, money-changers and goldsmiths for example, they were dissatisfied. This group therefore lived very much on its own resources; the families inter-married; the craft was as closed as any other, and the master-butchers succeeded each other from father to son. The number of butchers' shops was limited, but the *Grande Boucherie* at the Châtelet was by far the most important. As they were accustomed to go in all directions to buy beasts and as they killed these themselves, they were vigorous men whose familiarity with slaughter and blood had blunted their sensitivity; although the reproach of brutality brought against them was no doubt exaggerated in the records left by their adversaries. They had everywhere grown rich by speculating on meat, for which there was an increasing demand in the cities. They employed a great deal of labour of every class, flayers and others; and in Paris their confraternity, with its seat at Saint-Jacques de la Boucherie, enjoyed great prestige. In short, they were in a sense near to the manual trades, and shared, on a higher level, their desire to go up in society; and because in addition they were a powerful pressure group, they were naturally disposed to take the lead in popular risings. Allowing for certain differences, they may be said to have taken up the reins left by the drapers in the time of Etienne Marcel.

It will be interesting to acquaint ourselves with those whom we are to see most active in street troubles, namely the Saint-Yon, the Legoix, the Thibert and the Guérin families, old families in the trade, well housed, endowed with private incomes and enjoying respect in their parishes. Purveyors to the princes, they had become personally familiar to them. Guillaume de Saint-Yon was to leave his heirs 600 *livres* of annual income, a three-gabled house in Paris and three country estates, not counting the silver-ware, his wife's jewels and his whole business. Thomas Legoix was accounted a "handsome man and in his trade a good merchant". The most famous was the "flayer", Simon the Cutler, known as "Caboche", son of a tripe-dealer in the Parvis Notre Dame, the man who lent his name to the so-called revolution of 1413. If he displayed such initiative as to give the movement its popular character, he was in reality, like his colleague Capeluche, an instrument of others and himself of less intrinsic importance.

To understand the course of events and explain their social aspects, we must also take into account a very strong desire for reforms which had existed for nearly a century. The jurists in the sovereign courts as well as the members of the university were trying to get their aspirations put into practice. Ambitious men naturally wished to gain control of the movement; but one must try to discover whether, apart from the political and administrative aims of these intellectuals, their speculations involved any social intention.

It is, in truth, difficult to distinguish between political and social aspects which were so closely intermingled; but one characteristic feature of the time appeared at the outset. The Parisian people were sensitive to the smallest rumour and ready to follow anyone who would lead them in rioting. Parishes and confraternities constituted traditional groupings, within each of which people met, talked and got excited. And especially the separation of the groups into quarters, hundreds and tens commanded by a hierarchy of chiefs (*quarteniers*, *centeniers*, *dizainiers*), makes one think irresistibly of the famous Sections of 1793.

After 1405 difficulties had continued to accumulate. Charles VI being out of action through insanity, the rivalry between John the Fearless, the new Duke of Burgundy, and Louis d'Orléans the King's brother, came into the open. The murder of Louis d'Orléans in the rue Barbette on the evening of 23 November 1407 increased the tension. When civil war broke out (1411–12) street demonstrations became numerous, while the chains stretched across certain streets transformed the quarters beyond them into ghettos or centres of resistance.

Revolutions often begin with public assemblies. On this occasion, as the State was short of money, John the Fearless convoked the Estates of Languedoïl, among which he exerted influence through intermediaries. A fine speaker, ambitious and intriguing, this first-cousin of the King was the only prominent man with any political instinct. He knew how to attract and attach clients, while the vineyards of Burgundy enabled him to offer highly acceptable presents. The cellars of the principal butchers in Paris were furnished with a few casks of choice Burgundy. Caboche was thus gratified, as was Thomas Legoix. In 1411 when the latter was killed in an encounter with the Armagnacs, the Duke's presence at his funeral sealed an alliance between him and the butchers.

When the Estates met in January 1413 the university representatives spoke with the voice of 1356. The magniloquence of Benoît Gratien the theologian, and the passionate grievances of a Mendicant friar named Eustache de Pavilly, awoke echoes long slumbering. As in the days of Etienne Marcel, the Estates began by discrediting the King's councillors whom they accused of peculation, and by demanding their dismissal. But now, after yielding to the demand, the government reinstalled some of them, including Pierre des Essarts, the Provost of Paris, who was the most detested of all. He took the precaution of living in the Bastille. Then a rumour circulated that men were planning to assassinate Duke John. On 27 April the butchers led an armed demonstration to compel the Merchants' Provost (a post which had been re-established some few years back) to mobilize the militia of the quarter. The 28th proved a far more serious day. In the morning an armed mob of 3000 men surrounded the Bastille, where Pierre des Essarts refused to discuss surrender. John the Fearless explained to the assailants that they were incurring the charge of *lèse-majesté* by attacking a royal stronghold. The crowd which had increased in the meantime (the chronicles speak of from 20,000 to 25,000) moved off towards the Marais. But the most resolute, a small composite group (including the university notable Pierre Cauchon, one of the future judges of Jeanne d'Arc) surrounded the Dauphin Louis' residence, the Hôtel de

Guyenne in the rue Saint-Antoine. Jean de Troyes, a magistrate and doctor, demanded the surrender of the traitors living
with the Dauphin. The latter declared that he was not harbour-
ing any; but his chancellor had the unfortunate idea of saying
to the mob: "Say if you know of any, they will be punished as
they deserve." Whereupon they forced him to read aloud a list,
in which his own name came first. In face of the crowd's
audacity the Dauphin withdrew to his apartment; the mob
then invaded the mansion and arrested fifteen of its inmates.
Meanwhile John the Fearless's attitude had been uncertain
all that day. The Dauphin was not mistaken; an altercation
broke out between the two men. John next returned to the
Hôtel d'Artois and took supper with the prisoners, who were
then transferred to the Châtelet. The riot ended that night
with the Armagnacs being hunted through the streets; the
rest of the mob remaining camped in front of the Bastille. Next
day the Duke of Burgundy persuaded Pierre des Essarts to
surrender under promise of safety—but he was none the less
executed on 1 July.

These dramatic events were followed by a fête, a delegation
from Ghent having come to visit John the Fearless. The old
pact of friendship of 1358 and 1382 between Paris and Ghent
was renewed during a banquet in the Hôtel de Ville, in the course
of which the men of Paris and of Ghent exchanged hoods. Even
their colour was decided by fashion, since in the spring of 1413
everyone was wearing a white hood, if only for prudence sake,
so as not to be taken for an Armagnac, but the "Cabochian"
terror was now not far from exploding.

May witnessed a succession of almost daily demonstrations,
riots and arrests. The audacity of the armed bands led by the
butchers went on increasing. On the 9th and 10th they went
to the Dauphin's residence to instruct him in his duties. On the
18th, the King who had temporarily recovered sanity, repaired
to Notre-Dame to give thanks, amid public acclamation; but
on the 22nd he was told of what had happened during his
sickness. Meanwhile, the Hôtel Saint-Pol, serving as the King's
residence, was badly guarded and easily invaded by the mob,
which occupied its three courtyards; and a delegation de-

manded that the King should purge his court, meaning that he should weed out the unpopular ministers so as to effect a reform of the State. The mob refused to withdraw; and when the Duke of Burgundy, being alarmed by the presence of armed men, asked them to leave the palace, Jean de Troyes retorted by presenting a new list of suspects. These were members of the King's and Queen's entourage, Louis of Bavaria, the King's brother-in-law; an archbishop, and the staff of the Queen's residence, some fifteen ladies. John the Fearless had lost control of the insurrection, the leaders of which now threatened to come up and seize the suspects. In the end Louis of Bavaria offered himself as a hostage and the others followed. John the Fearless had the prisoners guarded by his own people; but he could no longer control the violence of the mob.

The people had hitherto acted as a striking force for the Burgundian party, but one might now well wonder whether all the riots were not going to develop into a genuine revolution which would transform the State. The commission to promote reforms, established in the early days of the troubles, was composed of experienced and intelligent men. Its work was a monument of logic and legal learning which deserves better than the degrading name of "Cabochian Ordinance". Its 259 articles took no less than four days (26–9 May) to be read out to the King. Earlier texts were here codified. Its very sub-titles (Demesne, Moneys, Aides, etc.) show that its object was essentially administrative. A certain desire is evident in it to relieve poor people of the complications and iniquities of the judicial system, of the excesses in taxation, of the violence of banditry, of abuses of seigneurial rights and notably of hunting-rights. But the object was above all to simplify administrative machinery, so that we are very far from a real political reform. The ordinance was not a constitution, and there was no question of controlling the government. It was a pity that the ordinance was not applied, but from the political point of view, it effected no change.

Can we regard this "Cabochian" agitation as a truly revolutionary movement? It is true that Caboche and his people tried to destroy things; yet we can hardly speak of more than riots. That the mass of the people desired changes is explained by the persistence of social problems. But what political inexperience there was, both in the leaders of the insurrection and among the men in power! John the Fearless inspired the agitation, but he did not wish to push it to the limit, and he was quickly outstripped and left powerless. He wanted to dominate the State, not to transform it. It is in vain to look for real revolutionaries.

Moreover, the arrests and executions which continued until the beginning of July ended by wearying people. The artisans were naturally worried by the cessation of work, while the violent elements were not interested in administrative reform. A king's advocate named Jean Jouvenel gathered round him a party for reconciliation and negotiated with the Armagnacs; during a deliberation that was being held in the Hôtel de Ville, Caboche being in a rage intervened with his men, and this finally discredited him in the eyes of the upper bourgeoisie. On 4 August the butchers were routed. While a huge crowd had assembled in response to Jouvenel's appeal, and while the Cabochians were counter-demonstrating, someone is said to have cried: "Peace! Peace! Let the man who doesn't want it move to the left! Let him who does desire it move right!" Practically the whole assembly took its stand on the right. At the same moment the Dauphin reached the Hôtel de Ville amid acclamation. This was a defeat for the Duke of Burgundy, who judged it prudent to leave Paris. A few days later the Armagnac reaction began, with as many victims as those killed by the insurgents. The Cabochian ordinance was cancelled, as it had not been presented or discussed in the *Parlement*.

Events in Paris had their counterpart in several provincial cities. In Languedoc, in 1411, the Burgundian party had obtained the dismissal of the unpopular Duke of Berry from his office as the King's Lieutenant. Great had been the joy, and equally short-lived, for in less than two years this uncle of Charles VI recovered his position. As in 1381, his return to power, accompanied by a demand for fresh subsidies, provoked rioting, especially at Limoux and in the town of Carcassonne— which we are not surprised at finding in the forefront.

According to the petition which was drawn up for the consuls after the events we are to relate, "some miserable common folk, of poor reputation and sorry condition" assembled, took up arms, hung chains across the streets and mounted guard on the walls. The movement proved irresistible, it was best to pretend to take part in it; and so, with the agreement of the royal officials—according to the petition—consuls and bourgeois went to keep watch with the commoners. Little by little they profited from the fact that the agitation was losing momentum to stop the assemblies, arrest several leaders, force others to fly and recover control of the town. They had now only to hand over the prisoners and implore the King's pity. It was granted without much trouble—if not without expense—but thirty-five persons were excluded from the amnesty, apart from the clerics who had taken part in the disturbance and were being held in the Bishop's prisons. Among the thirty-five there were agricultural workers (three labourers, two gardeners and a ploughman), textile workers (four fullers, a cropper and a dressmaker) and various artisans (two carpenters, a cutler and a belt-maker); but also three butchers and three "merchants", belonging apparently to the lower class and to groups connected with the middle "bourgeoisie". For some time therefore the agitation at Carcassonne was, in a sense literally, decapitated.

The Duke of Berry however died in 1416, and was not immediately replaced; but the Viscount of Lomagne, son of Bernard VII of Armagnac, managed to retain for his party the control of titular power in Languedoc, thanks to his position as Captain-General. The financial exigencies of the Armagnacs were more and more heavy, although growing discontent prevented the taxes from being collected. In these circumstances the manifestoes issued by the Duke of Burgundy, and his alliance with Queen Isabeau, produced a great effect. Ill will was increasing in Toulouse, and the *capitouls*, assuming the leadership of a rebellion which was scarcely resisted at all, refused to take account of Charles VI's letter conferring the Lieutenancy of the kingdom on his son Charles (January 1418)—Charles having become Dauphin owing to the death

of his two elder brothers. Toulouse even sent delegates to the
other cities of Languedoc and persuaded them to send an
embassy, representing all the cities, to Queen Isabeau. She
received the envoys at Troyes and readily agreed to all their
requests, which assured the victory of the Burgundian party in
the cities of the Midi.

Three days later the Burgundians recovered control of Paris.
They had entered the city by the Porte Saint-Germain, taking
the guard by surprise, and then profiting from the general
lassitude that had resulted from the Armagnac dictatorship.
Vengeance followed on a large scale, the Count of Armagnac
being the most notable victim. It was no longer Caboche,
grown "respectable" in the service of the Duke of Burgundy's
hôtel, who headed this new insurrection, but the executioner
Capeluche. The *Bourgeois de Paris*, in his journal, begins by
revealing transparently his satisfaction as a sincere Burgundian,
though in the end he is deeply moved by the scale of the
massacres which continued until August.

While the Burgundians were establishing their control over
Paris, a control that continued until 1436, the cunningly
varying policy of the Count of Foix and the Dauphin Charles's
cleverness were to turn Languedoc into the centre of national
resistance to the English. John I of Foix, a traditional foe of
the Armagnacs, naturally reaped the benefit of the Burgundian
victory. It was to him that the cities sent for protection against
the mercenary bands. His plan was to turn this influence to
practical account with the Dauphin and thus to impose himself
on both parties; and in fact, in August, Charles appointed him
his Lieutenant and Captain-General in Languedoc and
Guyenne. John I however was prudent enough not to assume
this title under December 1418, after concluding a curious
league with the Armagnacs, directed against the Burgundian
party.

The latter was then beginning to lose its ascendancy. After
assuming the responsibilities of power, it had also inherited
its unpopularity. It had been obliged to demand subsidies and
discipline the Estates. People wanted to reconcile their desire
to escape taxation, their need for protection and their loyalty

to the Crown; hence public opinion oscillated between the factions. On 9 January 1419 tumult broke out in the streets of Toulouse; but the partisans of Burgundy were still strong enough on 11 February to compel the people of Toulouse, who had begun to negotiate with the Count of Foix, to disavow their plans; whereupon the Count avenged himself by surrounding the city with his mercenaries. Yet the Burgundian influence continued to diminish. The *capitouls* were irritated by the control which the commissioners of Burgundy exercised; while the population was frightened by the prospect of a regular siege. In March, the Burgundians, headed by Bernard de Roaix, organized a popular rising to intimidate their adversaries, and had several of their houses set on fire. This was fruitless, for negotiations were still pursued with the Count of Foix and when, in April, an agreement was reached, a last attempt at insurrection fizzled out. Bernard de Roaix and several other leaders took flight, while the *capitouls* arrested large numbers of the defeated party. Finally, to save what little influence remained to them, the King and his entourage came in person to appoint John I Lieutenant and Governor in Languedoc, Auvergne and Guyenne.

Thus the Count of Foix' subtle manœuvring seemed to be crowned with success. But the Burgundians were too completely crushed for John I to be able to maintain the balance for long. He posed as an arbiter, giving out that he wished to unite the two parties. The murder of John the Fearless on the bridge at Montereau (10 September) finally threw the Burgundians on to the English side and clarified the situation. This last phase of the struggle was completed in March 1420 by the entry into Toulouse of the future Charles VII, who confirmed the Count of Foix in his Lieutenancy.

Here too, social factors had something to do with the political crisis. The lower class revealed itself as more prompt to get excited and less continually respectful of authority than the wealthy bourgeois; and this lower class found leaders among the malcontents, like the Roaix, a great family which had been deprived of any political power since 1380. But the social stability which was maintained in most of the cities of Languedoc enabled the Midi to become the principal base of the Dauphin's power, the region which provided his essential resources. Everything now became possible, beginning with the prodigious adventure inspired by Joan of Arc, which enabled Charles VII to reconquer his kingdom. The close combination of social and political factors appears here more clearly than ever.

Our information for the rest of the kingdom, though singularly incomplete, still contains records of a number of disturbances. From the beginning of the civil war in 1410 rebellions had broken out in the Parisian region. Insurgents, as usual, attacked the castles. The Count of Roussy was besieged by peasants in the Château de Pontarcy; the Archdeacon of Brie in the Tower of Andely. A few years later, in a reaction of self-defence like that of May 1358, the peasants took up arms (1417). Once armed, they behaved like those whom they pretended to be fighting. Turned brigands, they spread terror about their path. The monk of Saint-Denis speaks of this in his *Chronique*, when denouncing those who, "trampling underfoot all fear of God and man, think only of pillage, of putting everything pitilessly to fire and sword, under pretext of exacting vengeance for the injustice committed against them". Guy Fourquin observes that these "brigands" were working havoc in the very regions where the Jacquerie had raged in the preceding century. Was this a coincidence, or were the social and economic problems perennial?

"Frightening" disturbances recurred at Lyon almost every year; but generally when taxes were levied, as in 1420, 1424, 1430, and 1435. On the last occasion, the royal officials were put to flight by the insurrection. There was again trouble in 1436. In the course of a *rebeyne*, an assembly held at the Franciscans' elected "ten men to represent the people" and organize a refusal to pay the *gabelle*.

In the country districts of central France, and naturally in the poorest and those traditionally most prompt to rebel, agitations of a social kind had also broken out. Thus in December 1415 at Chamalières—at the gates of Clermont-Ferrand—Jean de Cholus, a knight "of weak head and possessed of little power", who had returned home after the battle of Azincourt, was forcibly obliged to agree to lead a band of "brigands" who were haunting the region. His only choice was between death and the burning of his castle, or the "alliance and company" of the brigands. On the other hand in Velay and Forez, which had once been Tuchin country, a "communist movement" prevailed during the first ten years of Charles VII's reign; though we know little about it. Popular preachers were dwelling on the primitive equality of all men and the original absence of social classes. Lords and idle clerics were no longer needed; one priest for a parish would be enough. On several occasions the King's men dispersed gatherings of armed peasants who were attacking the castles, even in the environs of Lyon. This kind of Jacquerie, with its marked resemblances with the Lollard and Hussite movements, was suppressed in 1431 with the help of Rodrigo de Villandrando's mercenaries.

*　　*　　*

The pogrom of 1391 was the sad conclusion of the rising anti-Jewish feeling characteristic of the fourteenth century. It appears to have been a deviation of the desire for social reform, and it was to lead much later to the expulsion of the Jews by the Catholic kings in 1492, and by the King of Portugal in 1496. The French crisis of 1413–18 was social to a certain extent, and we have insisted on that aspect of it; but it was mainly political, and it repeated the pattern of earlier crises, especially of that of 1356–7. We must now turn to more purely social disturbances, which were to give rise to a movement in the future.

In our account of the pogrom of 1391 we mentioned the share taken in it by the peasants, round Barcelona and Gerona. This must certainly be ascribed to changes that were taking place at their expense, to the whole problem of the *malos usos*.

Contrary to what one would be tempted to believe, the story of the peasant community was not one of progressive and uninterrupted liberation. In the Iberian Peninsula the condition of the peasants had generally deteriorated since the thirteenth century, that is, since the cessation of reconquest from the Moors had put an end to a certain dynamism in society. In Catalonia, particularly, the lords had succeeded in attaching to the land a very large number of their free peasants. They subjected them to a system of financial burdens in which basic obligations and manorial duties were combined with the *malos usos* proper. The latter were, briefly, as follows: some related to a tenant's inheritance, on which the lord took as his due a head of cattle or some other property, or collected it when the deceased left no direct heir. Others concerned a woman's marriage. She had to obtain against payment the lord's consent to her union; there was also a due on her dowry. The *jus primae noctis* (a right that the lord enjoyed to deflower the bride) was normally converted into a tax. Should the bride afterwards deceive her husband and thereby risk giving birth to bastards, presumed *ipso facto* to be free, the husband was further obliged to pay the lord an indemnity, the *cugutia*. If the peasant's house happened to be burned down, and the eminent rights of the proprietor suffered thereby, another tax, the *arsinia*, was due. To crown all was the *jus maletractandi*, that is, the lord's right to punish and imprison his tenant. All this was very much like serfdom, and jurists toiled over defining the exact difference. The peasant could indeed free himself from these burdens, but always and only by paying a high sum of money, which he had small hope of amassing. He was a *payese de remensa* ("peasant of redemption")—in short, a *remensa*.

The lords had patiently extended and completed this system. The troubles of the fourteenth century had no doubt, here and there, extracted concessions from them, necessary to insure the maintenance of agriculture. But before the end of the century they were trying to go back on them. In 1395 King Juan I himself counted the number of *remensa* households as between 15,000 and 20,000, that is, nearly a quarter of the total population. They were most numerous in Old Catalonia, in Ampurdan, on the plains of Gerona and Vich and the mountains separating them, and in the environs of Barcelona.

These disabilities the Catalan peasants did not suffer passively. Manifestations of local resistance became numerous in the fourteenth century, and one wishes that the research so far effected had enabled us to picture them. According to Jaime Vicens Vives, the principal historian of these matters, the generation of 1380 was "the first revolutionary *remensa* generation". One can understand the peasants taking part in the agitation of 1391. Saint Vincent Ferrier, when preaching in the country districts of Catalonia in 1409, found the population troubled and even exasperated. In 1413 the representative assembly, the *Corts*, forbade the *remensas* to set up crosses as signs for a rally, or to threaten to kill the lords. This kind of interdict was repeated in 1432, a sign of persisting agitation. Above all, the peasants were holding assemblies and forming unions, although forbidden to do so; they were thus able to discuss means of buying their freedom and exerting pressure on the lords.

They had at least the satisfaction of being morally supported by one section of the jurists, although the other group backed the lords. Liberty, according to the former, derives from natural and positive law, confirmed by Roman law. The preambles of the various charters of freedom reflected this view: "All men desire liberty, which is granted to each man by natural law" (1335). The *malos usos* are "contrary to divine as well as to human law" (1402). An outstanding figure of the time was a fifteenth-century jurist, Tomas Mieres, who was also an administrator of the royal estates. He did not hesitate to assert the *remensas'* right not to recognize laws contrary to divine law; and he proclaimed the King's obligation to intervene every time that a lord was oppressing his men and to liberate the oppressed.

The monarchy and central government were in fact constantly favourable to the peasant community. Dynasties of royal officials, like the Jaime Ferrer family, transmitted from father to son the ideal of freeing the *remensas*. The sovereigns' motives have been regarded as suspect. To exploit the "rich vein" (as Sanpere i Miquel calls it) consisting of the sums offered by the *remensas* in return for the King's support; and to

weaken the seigneurial classes—nobles, clerics and bourgeois—
very jealous of their autonomy in respect of the central government: these may also have been motives, and all may have
played their part, but they no doubt only reinforced a sincere
dislike of abuses which implicated the dignity of man. In the
view of Juan I and of Martin "the Humane" (king from 1396
to 1410) the relations between lords and peasants had developed
in an abnormal direction, and this was an execrable "novelty".
To this attitude the peasants responded with one of great
confidence in the monarchy. On the other hand they felt
nothing but distrust of the *Corts*, the representative assembly,
which in fact represented the interests of the lords and landowners only too well. As to the Church, one must recognize that
its teaching was also influenced by the latter. Bishops and abbots
went as far as threatening their tenants with excommunication.

The epilogue to these events belongs to a later period. When
Juan II was proclaimed a public enemy by the Catalonian
insurrection of 1462, a war between the lords and their
peasants was added to, and interfered with, the war which they
were waging against their former King. This went on for ten
years. Finally Juan II, having gradually isolated Barcelona,
forced the city to surrender in 1472. It remained for the heir
to the throne, Ferdinand the Catholic, to arbitrate by the
judgement of Guadalupe, in 1486, in a sense favourable on the
whole to the peasant community. The castles were indeed
restored to their owners, the lords were compensated, crimes
committed during the period of violence were punished with
heavy fines; but the peasants held prisoner were freed, the
malos usos were suppressed, and the personal freedom of the
peasant was guaranteed.

By comparison with the dramatic events in Catalonia, the
episode we are now to relate may appear a slight one; though it
has a certain originality in its causes as in its development.
Marcel Delafosse has analysed the problems of work among
the wine-growers of the Auxerre district. The social milieu
was complex. Most of the viticulturists owned a few vines, but
the majority were working for other people. Abbeys, noblemen

and bourgeois owned the vineyards, the fruits of which were organized commercially to supply Paris and the north, and brought in substantial profits. Certain of these proprietors let their vineyards on a short-term basis—from two years to nine— to men who kept two-thirds of the produce for themselves. Many employed workers who were paid by the day or the piece of work. The average daily wage, starting from 8 *deniers tournois*[1] towards 1345, had gone up to 20 *deniers* after the Plague, had been stabilized towards the end of the fourteenth century, and for several decades, had been about 30 to 35 *deniers*, without prejudice to marginal benefits, such as meals. To appreciate the real value of these wages one should be able to compare them with commodity prices. Towards 1390 people were complaining of the cost of food, but the conflict between employers and workers was less on the ground of wages than of the working-hours. The facts are known to us through an order which the bailiff of Sens published in the Auxerre district in April 1393 and which was followed in July by a judgement of the *Parlement*.

The trouble started with a complaint by the employers. In spite of high wages which, they said, enabled the vineyard-workers to become "fattened by their wealth to the point of a superfluity of enjoyment", these workers did not perform their work conscientiously. They "delay a long time over each meal, and between dinner and the snack (*goûter*) they sleep at leisure so as to be . . . fresher and stronger to work for themselves and tend their own vines". The main point at issue was the hour for stopping work. This was marked by the cathedral bells, but the vine-dressers had little by little brought the hour forward from vespers to nones, that is, to three in the afternoon. On 1 April the bailiff, taking the employers' point of view, ordered that work should be pursued from sunrise to sunset. The workers of Sens and of the villages round Auxerre complied with the order, but those of Auxerre itself, being more united and

---

[1] The *denier tournois* was a penny (*denarius*) minted at Tours. There were twelve in a *sou*, 240 in a *livre* (pound). The £ s d, in our former currency, perpetuate the original Latin words. The *livre* later became synonymous with the *franc*. (Translator.)

capably advised, did not agree. Details of the struggle are revealed in documents which reflect the employers' opinion.

The first form of protest was to leave the vineyards still earlier than usual, and to relapse even after being fined or imprisoned by order of the Provost. In words humorous though rather hasty, the employers declared that the vine-dressers were "obstinate as Pharaoh". Action in common was the second aspect of the resistance. The men kept in touch by shouting to each other to stop work simultaneously. This was forbidden, though in vain, because they then went on strike by simply doing nothing.

"When the bell struck nones, they hooted and uttered loud cries, so that they could be heard all over the parish, and this by agreement and evil conspiracy among them, in order that, at this cry, all should depart and leave their work. And because the said cry was forbidden by law, certain of them set the law at defiance by shouting 'Wolf!' They intimated to each other by the said cry that, since they dare not abandon their work, no one should do work that was worth anything."

The third phase consisted of spreading the revolt among the vine-dressers of neighbouring villages and in holding tumultous meetings, first in the vineyards in the course of the working day, then at Auxerre in the Bishop's house, and lastly in getting the royal officers officially to recognize the legality of their concerted action. They thus secured the right of being summoned to meet by a sergeant of the King, on the order of the Bailiff's Lieutenant, in order to appoint attorneys who would defend their interests.

The affair was now acquiring new dimensions. The vine-dressers were to have councillors during the period of complex legal procedure, and they manœuvred so well that the case was brought before the *Parlement*. And now a man of initiative appears upon the scene: they "sent one of their number, a vine-dresser named Fansy", says the document, "at whose instigation everything was done on their behalf, in respect of our lord the King, or his sovereign court of *Parlement*, and they obtained an agreement that the King's Attorney and

Thomas Geneste (the Notary Royal) . . . should be summoned to appear . . . and the Church dignitaries of Auxerre, several noblemen and the bourgeois" should also appear.

Not content with action at law, the vine-dressers exerted pressure on the population. The King's Attorney had reasons for fearing "a kind of commotion among people". The vine-dressers left the city "so that the patrimonies (that is, the lands) could lie fallow". The cost of labour, grown scarce as a consequence, went up. The employers accused the wage-earners of doing all this "in order to injure the other inhabitants of Auxerre and to put them in a state of need". The vine-dressers also tried to extend the movement outside their own trade; they were reproached with using threats to recruit "a great number of small workmen outside Auxerre, men who have no home or dwelling in Auxerre, to constrain them, contrary to their wishes, to support their cause". The conflict gradually became aggravated. Vine-dressers uprooted the plants in the Bailiff's Lieutenant's vineyard, they "spied on the Attorney at night, in his house", they threatened the bourgeois who then asked for the "King's guard" to protect them. They themselves were "hunted through the vineyards by mounted men with drawn swords". Some were imprisoned and fined. And then a new grievance arose, full of disquieting memories: the vine-dressers were suspected of "conducting and promoting a kind of Jacquerie and Mailleterie".

The conflict, which was discussed in the *Parlement*, was moving from the social plane to the psychological and moral. Employers invoked respect for contracts, argued that a diversity of wages corresponded to a diversity of tasks and that, for the general good, everyone should be satisfied with a "wage suitable to the nature of his trade". The vine-dressers' arguments sound curiously modern, as invoking the dignity of the person: "The soil of Auxerre is very tough and hard. . . . Although they are poor folk, yet they are men, and one should not demand of them such pain and toil as one would of an ox or horse. . . . They are free persons and one cannot, in reason, constrain a free person to work against his will, for that would be against the nature of liberty."

One must suppose that in 1393 there existed in the *Parlement* advocates well-versed enough, whether in traditional Christian doctrine, or in the naturalistic trend, or in humanistic principles of the dignity of man, to formulate in rational terms the aspirations of simple vine-dressers of Auxerre, confused as these may have been in their minds. The details of the compromise by which *Parlement* settled the dispute are unimportant. There were neither victors nor vanquished. It is believed that the ruling was observed for forty years, which would be remarkable. There was no more question of a maximum wage, and the hour for stopping work was settled by compromise. For the moment the vine-dressers rejoiced, because they had won agreement for stopping at three o'clock in the afternoon. "Several of them came", we read, "at the hour of nones, blowing trumpets as before and by way of mocking the other dwellers in Auxerre, their adversaries".

We have lingered over this episode, a very original one owing to the collective pressure which was exercised, and which throws light on the social and mental habits of a region half rural and half urban. Was the case unique? We think not; a few facts gleaned at hazard encourage us in this view.

K. A. Kaser, an historian of the Empire, has systematically differentiated political conflicts from social. Among the former he classes all the fourteenth-century conflicts and a number of the fifteenth-century disputes. As we have already noted, the struggle between patricians and craftsmen for access to urban councils was in the first place political, even if certain social consequences of it were discounted. But the crafts as a whole were at peace with each other, even if some of them were definitely richer. Here is an example from Magdeburg: the five "great corporations" of drapers, mercers, furriers, bootmakers and tanners, and linen-dealers, which had absorbed the patrician class after 1330, were opposed by the five "common corporations", which were less well-to-do and less esteemed. In 1402 members of three of the latter rose in rebellion: farriers, fishermen and butchers pillaged the episcopal Mint, tried to take over the seats of the wealthy corporations and asked for the arrest of the members of the council, although these had been craftsmen. Here the conflict was largely due to hatred of the poor for the rich, and such conflicts were to increase in number.

The general view we have discussed is not unfounded, provided we do not press it too systematically. From the fourteenth century onwards the relatively poor crafts with large memberships were the spear-head of revolt. At Frankfurt in 1358, at Augsburg in 1368, at Cologne after 1370, the weavers were the most prompt to take action. But they were satisfied with playing the part of a striking force, and made little difficulty about returning to order. At Augsburg the insurrection had been led by Hans Weiss, a weaver; but when it was a question of appointing one of the two mayors from among the crafts, as envisaged by a sworn agreement, a salt-merchant named Hans Weissbrunner, was successful. To exercise power was monopolizing; a poor artisan, tied down to his workshop, could not think of it. The general impoverishment, however, was leading the poor to extend less and less confidence to the well-to-do artisans and merchants. At the opening of the fifteenth century the number of city-dwellers without property and excluded from the right of bourgeoisie (i.e. from having political powers) amounted to half the population at Rostock and even more at Stralsund. The pressure they exercised was felt more and more, even if the conflicts involved had not changed in character.

Other struggles were also acquiring an increasing importance, namely those which, within each trade-craft, were bringing workmen into conflict with masters. As we have seen, the changes which successive attacks of plague had hastened had more definitely separated these two classes. The masters sought to limit the number of their competitors, to reserve places for their sons and sons-in-law and more or less completely to block the access of workmen to the mastership. The latter, for their part, demanded an increase in wages and various guarantees in connection with their work. Many of these workers or "companions", anxiously seeking an employment centre, moved from city to city, at least during the early years of their careers; and the contacts between them which were multiplied in this way, were developing a class consciousness.

So the relatively family atmosphere which obtained inside the trade-crafts was disappearing little by little. Regulations were framed so as to maintain the patriarchal system: thus at Strasbourg in 1387 the master bootmakers required the companions to live and take their meals with them. In Silesia in 1361 it was agreed that the companion tailor should accompany his master to the public baths and that the master should see to his cleanliness. It is true that signs by which these workmen might recognize one another such as a hat or other article of clothing, were forbidden, and that was disquieting.

The workmen or "companions" were seeking more and more to form separate associations, often of an apparently religious nature. The Church encouraged the movement, as on occasion did the patricians who saw in these workmen possible allies against the crafts. As early as 1321 an association of companion coopers is recorded for Lübeck, Hamburg, Wismar, Rostock and Stralsund. In 1331 the heads of the companion weavers of Berlin received rights of jurisdiction. And the movement went on growing. In 1404 forty-eight companion furriers from various regions, even as far afield as Bohemia and Tyrol, founded a confraternity at Strasbourg which soon went beyond its officially religious objects.

The movements of workmen, the bonds that were being formed between companions of different cities, led the masters in their turn to organize on the inter-urban level. Thus the master bakers of the cities in the middle Rhine valley and that of the Main—Mainz, Worms, Speyer and Frankfurt—formed a single group in 1352, and the master smiths of the same cities followed their example in 1383. All the workmen dependent on the various crafts in the same cities retorted in 1421 by founding a general association. Similar alliances were made in Alsace, and about the middle of the fourteenth century the master cutlers grouped themselves in four great confraternities centred upon Augsburg, Bâle, Heidelberg and Munich.

The adversaries thus came to face each other in conflicts which often acquired considerable importance. In 1329 the companion curriers of Breslau decided to go on strike for a year to obtain higher wages, and their employers retorted with a lock-out. This precocious conflict still remained local, but not for very long. In upper Alsace about the year 1400 companion bootmakers were frequently at odds with the masters, and the bailiff of Ensisheim issued an order forbidding the former to take any unilateral action. Dissatisfied with their wages, they none the less went on strike in 1407, and tried to widen the conflict by two alliances, one with their fellow bootmakers on both banks of the Rhine, in Baden and in Alsace, with whom they had planned a general assembly at Rouffach, and another with the companions in the other crafts, tailors, saddlers and metal-workers. The authorities feared that the companions might triumph over the masters (*herren über ir meister*) and succeeded in preventing the meeting at Rouffach, and also another which it had been planned to hold at Haguenau in 1408. The confraternities were suspected of being hotbeds of agitation. Following the above episodes, an official assembly held at Selestat and presided over by the Imperial Bailiff prohibited all confraternities of workmen, from Hauerstein in the south to Mainz in the north. These were vain precautions, because they did not touch the heart of the problem. Agitation continued to be lively and to give rise to other conflicts, in 1421 and above all in 1436. In view of a general movement on this date of the companions in all the crafts who were preparing to form a common organization, the municipal authorities of all the Rhenish cities, from Basle to Mainz, decided at the invitation of Strasbourg, to hold a general meeting at Breisach to draw up a Statute of Companions. The workmen on their side boycotted sometimes a master who was considered particularly hard, sometimes even a city where wages were too low. Thus the furriers put Selestat on the index in 1463.

The problem evidently was how to find a jurisdiction able to settle conflicts otherwise than by force. It was often the tribunal of the trade corporation itself, though this was dominated by the masters and its sentences might be challenged. Exceptional examples of joint commissions can be cited, as at Strasbourg in 1363 when an *ameister* selected five masters and five companions to settle the conflict which had arisen in their craft. He himself presided over the arbitration and reserved the right eventually to decide between them. Often, too, the sentence was pronounced by the city council, and was generally favourable to the masters; but at Colmar in 1450, the masters having lowered the wages of the companion linen weavers, the council obliged them to restore the traditional rates of pay. The conflicts being new in kind and widespread prevented any general principles from being laid down.

*   *   *

The Europe which documentary records have led us to envisage hitherto has been especially the western portion and a part only of central Europe, that is the portion of the "European peninsula" most penetrated by the sea and most deeply affected by the economic and social revival. We must now turn our eyes eastward, where Bohemia will appear as the theatre of a movement both vast and novel. Here western influences awoke echoes of unparalleled magnitude. As will be the case in the twentieth century an eastern country plays a part of first-rate importance in the history of revolutions. The parallel has not escaped the notice of historians who have strongly emphasized it in the last thirty years. "Hussitism", writes J. Macek, "was the first medieval movement in Europe to awaken powerful revolutionary echoes among the lower classes of the country-districts and the cities."

The importance of the Hussite War, and its significance in respect of European history as a whole, have been stressed since the publication of F. Palacky's researches. In France Ernest Denis' *Huss et la guerre des Hussites* (1878) remains a classic. Writers insisted mainly, however, on the religious and national aspects of the movement as a sanguinary prelude to the Reformation and an upheaval of Czech nationalism against the Germans in the very heart of a Europe more and more nationalistic. One soon observes the limits of this interpretation. Some of the most vigorous thinkers in the Hussite movement like Nicolas of Dresden, were German, while the cities of Bohemia took up a position as regards Hussitism very independently of their racial character, or at least of that of their governing classes. On the other hand the social aspects of Hussite preaching very quickly became evident, and make it impossible to treat of these religious questions in isolation. Marxist historians have been studying these social questions for about thirty years, and if certain of them have done so in a slightly scholastic fashion and with an inadequate sense of nuances, others, like Josef Macek, have guarded themselves against a too absolute social determinism.

This is why we shall avoid treating here of the Hussite revolution as a simple phenomenon of the class-war. We believe it to have had some connection with the social evolution of the time, and yet members of the most varied classes—nobility, middle class, artisans and "poor folk" of town and country—rubbed shoulders in the Hussite camp. It was within the camp that their interests clashed more than once. We do not intend to reduce the movement of ideas which then flourished so actively to a conflict between classes, but rather to evoke the specifically social aspects of the crisis, and situate them in their historical context.

This crisis had been preceded in the fourteenth century by some of the most brilliant pages in Czech history. The reign of Charles IV of Luxembourg (1346–78) is justly famous by reason of his efforts to strengthen the material foundation of his power and to endow Bohemia with a large measure of religious autonomy by erecting the bishopric of Prague into a metropolitan see (1344) and by founding the university (1348). This policy would have been fruitless if the Czech silvermines, particularly those of Kutna Hora, had not provided abundant ore for the royal mints: the *groschen* of Prague was one of the strongest currencies in Europe. This production of silver served to finance notable public works, of which the monuments of Prague still give us a partial idea, and to pay for expensive imports of textiles and luxury objects, the cost of which was not balanced by the export of wheat, timbers, wax and furs.

But this kind of progress had another side to it. It strengthened the German merchants in the cities, it enriched the

Church, and raised the cost of living, which was particularly felt by the humbler classes. It perhaps also involved an increasing exploitation of the peasants, on whom the forced labour exacted for wheat-growing, or the payments consequent on the development of papal taxation, weighed more heavily. Furthermore, after 1378, under Wenceslas IV, the economic decline was marked by notable devaluations, which especially affected the smaller denominations, such as *kreuzer* and *heller*, and therefore the humblest strata of the population. Aided by the accounts of Saint-Guy's cathedral, Frantisek Graus has studied the poor town-dwellers of Prague during the pre-Hussite period; and he has also used the deeds of sale of unredeemed pledges, sales effected under the direction of the municipal intendant. It was a question of a great variety of objects which thousands of people in Prague had had to put in pawn in order to borrow the money needed for their subsistence and for the payment of taxes, and which they had been unable to redeem. The impression left by these documents is one of great poverty. The offers of employment in the building yards such as that of the cathedral were inadequate for the numbers of workers coming in from the countryside. Graus estimates that these poor folk who had no property and depended solely on their wages represented about 40 per cent of the population and that their numbers were rather tending to increase owing to the depression which affected the artisan class. Now according to the standards of the age, Prague was a great city, with a population of perhaps 35,000. None of the other cities of Bohemia, some forty, with from 2,000 to 5,000 inhabitants each, could be compared with it; which did not prevent their experiencing similar difficulties.

Throughout the fourteenth century these circumstances gave rise to a few social disturbances, of no major importance. In 1339 a peasant agitation broke out in southern Bohemia where the tenants refused to pay their dues and rose in insurrection. The lord, Oldrich de Hradec, the principal authority in that region, had to use military force against them. The survivors then called to witness the example of the "poor of Lyon", and were consequently summoned to appear before the inquisition, an episode that interests us as a witness to the penetration into Bohemia of Vaudois doctrines. In the cities a few disturbances among the artisans marked the second half of the century. At Prague a linen manufacturer was put to death in 1366, and seventeen of his accomplices were banished "by reason of a confraternity and association which they had created among themselves"; fourteen artisans were exiled in 1377 on account of a plot against the magistrates; at Brno in 1378 representatives of the artisans complained to the council about the high cost of living and asked that eight masters of the crafts should take part in the most important decisions; while at Ceske Budejovice, the weavers agitated in 1379, the artisans in 1384, the companion bakers in 1401. These episodes can be connected with the disturbances we have described all over western and central Europe and are quite secondary manifestations of them. If the Hussite revolution was to break out, it was necessary for the economic depression to increase, and above all, for the moral and intellectual atmosphere to become revolutionary.

Nothing, however, was more normal than the beginnings of this great movement. Charles IV, King and Emperor, having obtained a favourable bull from the Pope, founded the university of Prague in 1348. The new *Stadium generale* would train the administrators whom the King needed; it would teach them Roman law and strengthen monarchical power. By distributing diplomas valid everywhere, particularly in the Empire, and by opening the way to numerous benefices, it would respond to the hopes of the best kind of people, who would no longer be obliged to study far from home; it would offer good positions for the rich, and the possibility of social promotion for the humblest. The masters were mainly foreigners at the outset, Germans, Silesians and Poles; and for several decades they followed the current of predominantly nominalist doctrines conducted by the University of Paris.

Czech students, however, also had occasion to encounter the realist doctrines which were taught above all in England. When they came to complete their studies in Paris, they enrolled in the English "Nation", and had English or Scotsmen as patrons. Examples of such students were Voytech Rankuv who spent twenty years in Paris, even became Regent and Rector, then returned to Prague, was a canon and high official of the cathedral, and became a helpful friend to the reformers; and Mathias Janov, who studied for ten years on the banks of the Seine, and in Prague received the flattering title of "Parisian Master".

The debate about universals is less foreign to our purpose than may appear. To be a realist was to attach very little importance to the "accidents" which claimed the attention of the nominalists—that is, to titles, social positions and rites—and to insist rather on the real substance of persons and things. The nominalists held that a man's authority was guaranteed by his title, or function; the realists thought that authority, to be real, should be founded on the state of grace, or on being predestined to salvation. But who could know the true basis of authority, except God? By rejecting judgements pronounced by a man who was considered unjust, by denying the efficacy of sacraments conferred by an unworthy priest, the realist was in danger of ending in anarchy.

It was by these university channels that Wyclif's influence came into Bohemia. It has been shown above that Wyclif's ideas were foreign to the Peasants' Revolt of 1381, although his adversaries afterwards forged an accusation of collusion, in order to discredit his disciples. If, on the other hand, Wyclif's influence on John Huss and the Czech reformers is undeniable, it cannot be considered absolute. His doctrines were disseminated over an area prepared in advance by his own reflections, and the Hussites differed with the English master on several important points. Wyclif's ideas, however, could be adapted in a genuinely revolutionary direction, particularly the doctrine of the *dominium ex gratia:* "Grace is not foreign to lordship, but is its true foundation." Should a pope, an emperor, a sovereign behave like a sinner, the individual is permitted to challenge the reality of his power.

Wyclif's theses provoked lively debates at the University of Prague, and the line of cleavage, apart from exceptions more numerous than appears at first glance, was national. The

Czechs were enthusiasts for Wyclif and his moral exigencies, the Germans remained faithful to nominalism. The very constitution of the university was soon in question. After 1348 other universities had been founded in Germany itself, while at Prague Czech masters and students were playing a part of increasing importance. The organization of the university, however, still gave the preponderance to the Germans, who were divided between three "nations", the Bavarian, the Saxon and the "Polish"; whereas the Czechs were grouped in the Bohemian nation. In 1409 King Wenceslas who wished to secure the university's support for his religious policy and who knew that the Germans would not follow him in his attitude of neutrality between the rival Popes, issued the "Decree of Kutna Hora": henceforth the Czechs were to have three votes, the Germans one. This decision led to the departure of a thousand German masters and students, while the university acquired a national character which it had not hitherto possessed. It now became the supreme authority in the nation.

At the same time there was developing a very remarkable movement in preaching. Charles IV had built many churches in Prague, had bestowed rich endowments on them, with numerous relics. All this was of a kind to promote a mainly external and ritualistic cult. The multitude of clergy shared widely in the vices of a society corrupted, save among the poorest elements, by material well-being: examples of simony, concubinage, non-residence and negligence in the conduct of services, were very numerous. The efforts at reform inaugurated by Archbishop Ernest of Pardubice were accompanied by the preaching of sermons, which, however, could not be purely moral. Conrad Waldhauser, an Austrian installed by the Emperor, denounced the exploitation of funeral services. Mathias of Janov, scion of a family of lower nobility, saw the source of all evils in the cupidity of the clergy. He protested his obedience to the Roman Catholic Church, but deplored its thirst for power and wealth, especially marked since the time of Innocent III; and he described the Pope of Avignon as Antichrist, which was conceivable in a period of Great Schism, but revealed a disaffection as regards the visible Church. He and Voytech Rankuv took part with several burghers and knights in founding the chapel of Bethlehem (1391), which was to be a centre of preaching in Czech. In 1402 John Huss became preacher there.

The bearing of these sermons was mainly moral. There was no question of overthrowing the social order. Jakoubek of Stribro wrote: "Let all and each, united, *the rich and the poor*, work for the holy Christian union, one with the other and with Christ, in the Gospel of Christ and its obedience, so that, with God's help, they may dwell together in harmony." Simplicity of life, severity in morals and devotion to the Eucharist constituted the ideal. Inevitably, everyone could apply it to the present situation, could observe the abuses of which the powerful were guilty and question their authority. The success of this preaching is certainly explained by the echoes it aroused in that direction. "It is not against adversaries of flesh and blood that we have to fight, with a material sword, but against principalities, against the rulers of this world of darkness who have been introduced into the Church, against the spirits of Evil in high places in the Church"—so also wrote Jakoubek, paraphrasing St Paul (Ephesians 6:12). When in 1412 Jean XXIII caused indulgences to be preached in Prague, to collect the funds necessary for the war against the King of Naples, protests were violent, not only in the university but also in the streets. Three young laymen, disciples of Huss, were executed, after which the people took possession of the bodies and carried them in solemn procession to the chapel of Bethlehem.

Banished from Prague soon after this, John Huss preached in the south and then in the north-west of Bohemia. He had large and attentive audiences of peasants. Himself of humble origin, having been born in a small village near the Bavarian frontier, he seems now to have adopted a very radical attitude and to have protested against certain seigneurial pretensions to inherit property from a peasant tenant who had died childless. And yet he was sheltered in castles and supported to the end by many noblemen.

We shall not dwell here on the unfolding of those events of which the origin has just been outlined. November 1414 saw the meeting of the Council of Constance which was to put an end to the Great Schism, extirpate heresy and reform the Church. Summoned before the council and abandoned by the Emperor Sigismund, John Huss was condemned and burned at the stake (6 July 1415), a fate shared a few months later by his friend Jerome of Prague. These condemnations provoked intense emotion in Bohemia, where the nobles formed a league, directed by a triumvirate, and drew up a national programme, in which utraquism became an essential factor. Utraquism means communion in both kinds, up to then reserved generally for priests. The Hussites did not confine themselves to demand it as possible, they regarded it as the only communion which could be reconciled with the usage of the primitive Church. Had not Christ declared: "Except ye eat the flesh of the Son of man, and drink his blood, ye have no life in you" (John 6:53). The chalice was therefore a necessity. Utraquism provided a convenient platform and a clear line of demarcation between Hussites and Catholics. By putting laymen on the same level as priests, it exalted man's dignity rather than his position or function. It aroused fanatical enthusiasm. The small town of Litomerice in northern Bohemia still contains a house with a roof formed like a chalice. There was a Hussite bourgeoisie and a Hussite nobility.

The reformers denied the Church's right to possess property, and very many secularizations took place to the advantage of the nobles, who have been accused of being led astray by this prospect of greater wealth. As a matter of fact, in the midst of the confusion, a number of Catholic lords and barons also took possession of Church properties. But secularization especially offered the Hussite nobles the advantage of strengthening their power over "their" clergy. In any event, nobles and burghers represented a moderating, even reactionary, element in the heart of Hussitism, an element always prepared for reconciliation with the Pope, and, after the death of Wenceslas IV (1419), with Sigismund. Their existence precludes our regarding the Hussite conflict as a mere episode of the class war, but they do not otherwise concern our purpose, and we should wish to turn rather to popular tendencies, to Prague radicalism, Taborism and Picardism.

Prague was the scene of a very lively conflict between the Hussite clergy and the Catholic, while, as we have seen, social conditions in the city also raised serious problems. Radicalism here found its most vigorous exponent in John of Zeliv, who was supported by the humbler classes: these were predominant in the "New City". This John was a Premonstratensian from Zeliv, in south-eastern Bohemia, but he had left his monastery to preach in Prague. In 1418 he was the preacher and perhaps the vicar, of the parochial church of St Stephen. Expelled by the Catholic reaction of 1419, he took refuge in the monastery of the "Mother of God of the Snows," one of the three churches which the royal decree had allotted to the Hussites. He actually came out in the spring of 1419, when the Hussite leaders in Prague were hesitating whether to resist Wenceslas IV and were keeping silent; but from this time on, his fiery eloquence and ascendancy over the crowd made him the most authoritative speaker in Prague.

There was in his sermons a social emphasis, of a degree as yet unknown. He constantly attacked the masters in the university and the prelates, corrupted, or so he said, by their rich patrimonies and by "despoiling the poor". His teaching was reflected in a then popular song:

"Had the masters been really wise, they would have counselled God to arrange things thus: that the poor should never eat nor drink, that they should go naked, that they should sleep neither by day nor night, but work constantly for the lords, and constantly pay them dues. The lords, counselled by the priests, would become harder still and would command that still more should be paid them. When they can no longer obtain payments, they turn the poor man's body into a beast of burden and subject him to forced labour, which was never instituted by God nor by any valid authority. Such is the torment of the poor in all countries and especially of the Czechs, thanks to the arrogant clergy."

Many of the poor folk in Prague cultivated small field or garden plots outside the city, and cannot have been insensitive to such statements.

The idea that deprivation confers on the poor a certain perspicacity is also to be found in John of Zeliv. When speaking of Jesus's eating with publicans and sinners, he cried: "The masters did not understand why he sat at table with sinners, but the villains did not fail to appreciate it."

While attacking the Catholics, John of Zeliv also denounced the conservative Hussites; and also the lords, burghers and municipal magistrates. He seems at the outset to have reposed some hope in the King, and approached him through the intermediary of a small nobleman, a radical, named Nicolas of Hus. Nicolas asked the King for freedom to communicate in both kinds, for children as well as adults. Wenceslas's only reply was to dismiss Nicolas from his court. John of Zeliv came little by little to extol the use of violence. In July 1419 he commented on Ezekiel's prophecy (6:3) "Behold, I, even I, will bring a sword upon you, and I will destroy your high places", and applied to Prague the lamentations of Jeremiah over Jerusalem.

One of his procedures was to organize processions which, on feast days, marched singing through the streets. On Sunday, 30 July, he headed a procession of this kind. The King had just installed in the New City some new councillors who were anti-Hussites. The Catholic reaction was in full swing; parochial schools had been restored to Roman priests, processions forbidden and utraquists arrested. The demonstrators were expecting resistance and had come armed with swords and staves. They marched first to the church of St Stephen, where they forcibly celebrated a utraquist service. They then repaired to the city hall of the New City, where the councillors were holding an extraordinary meeting. The latter, being summoned to liberate utraquist prisoners, thought it wise to negotiate; but the discussion quickly degenerated, the building was invaded—perhaps under the direction of John Ziska, who was later to become famous—thirteen councillors and burghers were thrown out of the windows, and those who were not dead were finished off by the mob. A permanent guard was then established under the command of four Captains-General. Elections, held under pressure from the radicals, designated new councillors, and Peter Kus, a butcher, was promoted burgomaster. The King had to give way, but he died a few days later.

John of Zeliv then became a sort of dictator. His power rested on the support of the New City, with the help of which he exerted pressure on the Old City, which was more bourgeois and hostile. On 2 July 1421 he united the two communities, the councillors thereafter forming a single body. However, he was not really a social reformer, he provoked no "democratic" revolution. Most of his partisans were poor folk who could neither vote nor occupy public office. Under the pressure of necessity, John of Zeliv could bring his crowd into the streets, force the councillors to retire and have new ones elected. Once the mob had dispersed, these new councillors proved sensitive to the demands of a reality which had not changed; so they were not, for his purpose, reliable. One of the councillors who had been elected on 2 July 1421 refused to accept the office conferred on him in conditions which he deemed irregular. John of Zeliv never could, nor really wished to, overcome this obstacle.

Politics in Prague were, despite his efforts, very unstable. There were moments when radicalism appeared triumphant, particularly when contingents of Taborites encamped in the capital. On 3 April 1420 a general assembly had proclaimed the four articles which were the basis of union among all the Hussites; and yet, none except the third, which envisaged the secularization of Church properties, had any social bearing. At other times power seemed to escape John of Zeliv's hands, while Prague sought a rapprochement with Rome and tried to set a Polish prince on the throne of Bohemia. On the very morrow of his victory in July 1421, he was subjected to a severe counter-attack by his enemies, and the situation remained uncertain for several months, with frequent changes of fortune. Finally, on 9 March 1422, John of Zeliv and nine of his followers were summoned to the city hall, arrested by surprise and beheaded. This act provoked a riot, but the arrival on 17 May of the Polish prince, Sigismund Korybut, marked a final victory for the conservatives. Thus Prague never moved definitely towards the Hussite revolution, and the effective wing of the party was formed rather by the Taborites.

The Taborite movement had begun a little before the first defenestration[1] of Prague. Its origin was due to the anti-Hussite policy pursued all over Bohemia by Wenceslas IV. In all regions where the King's agents or the nobles faithful to his cause were able to prevail, utraquist priests were driven from the churches which they had taken over, and had to celebrate service in precarious conditions. Resistance to the reaction gathered great force in southern Bohemia in the environs of Usti and Pisek, the very region which had been a notable centre of heresy in 1339 and which had welcomed John Huss when exiled from Prague. Celebration of the utraquist service took the form of mass assemblies of the faithful of the whole region, directed by priests like Vancek and Hromadka. A hill near the castle of Bechyne was given the name of Mount Tabor, the Galilean mountain on which, according to tradition, the transfiguration had taken place (Matthew 17:1–5); after which, though at what moment is not clear, Jesus had instructed the eleven disciples to meet him after the resurrection on a certain mountain in Galilee (Matthew 28:16).

The first meeting of the Taborites took place in 1419, at Easter, a festival on which even the lukewarm received the communion; but a particularly numerous assembly was held on 22 July, eight days before the defenestration. The spirit of communistic fraternity which reigned in these "congregations" was recognized even by enemies of the Taborites. "They called each other brother and sister, and the rich shared with the poor the food they had prepared for themselves" (Lawrence of Brezova). "They shared [food] among themselves, even eggs and crusts of bread" (anonymous verses). "They wanted to live in the manner of the primitive Church; they all called

---

[1] Not to be confused with the more celebrated "defenestration of Prague" (May 1618) which marked the revolt of the Protestant Czechs against the Emperor, Ferdinand, and also the beginning of the Thirty Years War. (Translator.)

each other brother; and what one lacked was provided by another" (Aeneas Sylvius Piccolomini).

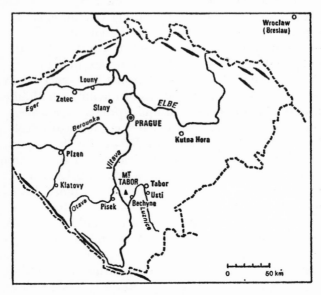

Fig. 9 Bohemia in the Fifteenth Century

The movement soon acquired a permanent character. Meanwhile the King's attempt to exterminate the Hussites in the provinces grew steadily more violent. Many of them were brought to Kutna Hora and thrown into the mines, one of which was called Tabor in derision. They could scarcely count on the support of Prague which was then seeking to come to terms with Sigismund; and it was in these conditions of a struggle for survival, of solitude and despair, that the Adventist doctrine began to spread. At the beginning of 1420, wrote Lawrence of Brezova, "certain Taborite priests announced to the people a second coming of Christ. All bad men, all the enemies of truth, would perish and be exterminated, while the good would be saved in the five cities." Then, just as Lot in the days of old departed from Sodom, so now many men and women took refuge in these five cities, which were

Plzen, Zatec, Louny, Slany and Klatovy. "Many simple folk ... sold their goods, even at a low figure, and from all parts of Bohemia and Moravia, with their wives and children, hastened to these priests at whose feet they laid their money." The world was bad, it was decidedly impossible to remove the evil and so to reform the Church; God alone could put an end to these abominations. Such were the apocalyptic visions that sustained the hope of his second coming.

In this negative attitude, this incurable pessimism regarding the world, a certain Vaudois feeling will be noted, although the Vaudois were essentially pacifists. Now while they awaited the coming of Christ, serious questions were arising. Ought the assemblies of the faithful to organize, to establish a central authority, and defend themselves against foreseeable attacks? A serious debate occupied the winter of 1419–20. Jakoubek of Stribro, one of the principal Hussite doctors, wrote from Prague to deny that one could foresee the exact date when the terrible events announced by the prophecy would take place—between 10 and 14 February, a *Taborite* priest had declared; but these days had passed without anything happening. So Jakoubek added: "Urge the people not to leave their dwellings but to remain and do salutary penitence; then, whatever happens, all will be well for them." He conceded, however: "I dare not blame simple folk for meeting, under the spur of necessity, with a view to their salvation. . . ." But he did not go as far as granting them the right of self-defence. Not that he denied the possibility of legitimate wars, but these should be waged "by the higher secular powers, to whom, as stated in the Epistle to the Romans [ch. 13], the sword is given for the punishment of the wicked. Let the people take care not to usurp that sword!" Respect for traditional authority prevailed, then, in Jakoubek. On the other hand, Peter Chelcicky was animated by absolute pacifism. This radical layman, who was to be a centre of great moral influence, ascribed the deviation of Hussite teaching in the direction of militant Taborism to the subtle machinations of Satan.

While this debate was going on, the Taborite communities were beginning to organize, though not without conflicts. At

Plzen the community directed by the priest Wenceslas Koranda and the military leader John Zizka, destroyed churches and monasteries; before long, however, this group was besieged by the Catholics. The community of Pisek had to flee; it occupied Usti for some time, and then, as the town was difficult to defend, gained the abandoned fortress of Hradiste, which was named Tabor. The group from Plzen joined it there. The population was organized in four political and military divisions. While actively pursuing the work of fortifying the place, they formed contingents which operated outside, attracted numerous peasants and brought the whole region under control. In this agglomeration of improvised shanties, the strictest communism prevailed. "Everything must be in common for all men; no one must possess anything in private, otherwise he is guilty of mortal sin." The roughness of this Taborism was largely due to the precarious conditions of life, but also bore the marks of Valdeism. There were no more chalices or priestly vestments, no more feast days, except Sundays, no more fasting, no more oral confession or prayers for the dead. Unshaven priests consecrated the bread and wine anywhere. Baptism was by immersion in rivers, confessions were made in public. No longer was there a question of reforming the Church, as in Prague, but of strictly and exclusively imitating the primitive Church.

A current of Chiliast[1] doctrine soon appeared among the Taborites. Certain priests, Martin Huska in particular, announced that Christ's second coming, foretold by the Adventists and still not manifest, had really taken place, but in secret. The time had come to massacre all those who did not belong to the Taborite community, which alone represented the Church of God—in fact "to purify and sanctify one's hands in blood". Once this destruction was achieved—and it had to be the work of the faithful, assisted by Christ—God would appear in glory and the elect, risen from the dead, would join him: "And they said that that would soon take place, in a few

---

[1] Chiliasm (from Greek *chiliasmos*, from *chilioi* = a thousand) was so called because its adherents believed that God would shortly inaugurate a golden age of 1000 years.

years' time, so that many of them would, in their life-time, behold the resurrection of the saints, and among them master John Huss." John Pribram, an adversary, wrote these lines, but he does not seem to have misrepresented their message.

Then would begin a golden age, for a thousand years, said some of them. God in person would exercise authority. There would therefore be no more kings or princes or prelates. The Chiliast priests indicated that "henceforth you will pay no more rents to your lords, nor be subject to them, but you will freely possess their villages, their ponds, and meadows and forests, and all their domains". The New Age would fulfill and "evacuate" the New Testament, as the latter had fulfilled and "evacuated" the Old. Everything that derived from man's sin, everything that recalled his redemption by Christ, would vanish. There would be no more hunger, or thirst, or suffering; no more church or prayers. To baptize children would be useless. Holy Communion would be replaced by a new kind of sacred banquet.

Chiliasm stands out as very novel by virtue of the active part in the advent of the New Age which it ascribed to the faithful: it was by them that God would destroy the present world, which was irremediably bad. It was equally novel by the kind of earthly happiness it promised: contemporaries were keenly aware of this. Peter Chelcicky indignantly records a conversation he had with Martin Huska. "But Martin was not humble", he writes, "nor in the least ready to suffer for Christ. . . . He declared to us his belief that there would be a new kingdom of the saints on earth, and that the good would suffer no more. He said: 'If Christians should have always to suffer in this way, I should not want to be a servant of God.' That is what he said!" And Jakoubek concluded: "We do not regard as true the news which certain people announce, namely that a good era is coming, in which there will be no wicked persons, in which men will not suffer, but be filled with ineffable joy. For all this will come to pass in heaven; but what will happen here below is uncertain."

Did this doctrine take shape little by little? Or was it present from the outset, inherent in the class-consciousness which animated so many Taborites, and did it come to the forefront as a result of circumstances? Historians argue the point, without the documents enabling them to arrive at a very clear solution. In any event, the growth of ideas foreign to Hussitism and to Valdeism raises the question of their origin. They are most often related to an event of 1418. Among the many foreign heretics attracted to Bohemia by the toleration born of an era of confusion, forty "Picards" who said they had been expelled by their prelates, arrived in Prague and were well received. Did this company come from Picardy, or was the name a deformation of "Beghards"? In any case they quickly disappeared, though not without making Czech disciples, one of whom was Martin Huska. Thus Chiliasm was presumably connected with the prophecies of Joachim de Flore regarding the Third Age, but also with the ideas of certain Beghards, "the Brothers of the Free Spirit", whose existence has been recorded at Brussels in 1411. The Brothers of the Free Spirit professed that man, if he grew up in a period of absolute poverty and humility, could attain here below a perfection which would bring him the same beatitude as in heaven, and render him incapable of sinning; henceforth he would no longer owe obedience to any human authority, nor reverence for human manifestations of the cult. Chiliasm was, in some small measure, the collective realization of this state of perfect innocence which was promised to the individual by the Brothers of the Free Spirit.

There was therefore a fundamental opposition between strict Taborism and Picardism or Chiliasm, and this appears clearly in their respective attitudes towards the Eucharist. Hussites and Taborites were passionately attached to it, as appears clearly from their insistence on utraquism. For the Picards, the communion, which commemorates the sufferings of Christ, was connected with sin; it would be transcended in the New Age, and there was no ground for displaying much respect for it. This problem was to excite the most violent debates and conflicts. Meanwhile, however, the material changes that were taking place were already causing a rift between Taborites and Chiliasts.

In fact, in proportion as Taborite society continued to exist, it organized itself after traditional norms, and went beyond the enthusiastic communism of its beginnings. The priests told the peasants that they would no longer have to pay dues to their lords, all "exploiters" having disappeared. Yet, on the customary day of St Gall (16 October 1420) they themselves collected the usual dues from the peasants, including those who adhered to their faith. They are even said to have exacted a supplementary tax, called *holdy*; it was necessary after all to raise a regular revenue for the community; which no doubt soon had a financial administration. In the cities private property reappeared, strict communism was abandoned. At Pisek councillors appropriated the property seized from non-Taborite bourgeois. The evolution was doubtless slower at Tabor, a simple encampment at the outset; but commerce and handicrafts developed, and the usual division of labour between town and country appeared. The common funds, increased by personal gifts, were probably destined for the clergy. In September 1420 a Taborite bishop was elected, Nicolas of Pelhrimov, a Bachelor of Arts of Prague; his duty was no doubt to divide the money among the priests and to maintain among them a certain degree of orthodoxy.

In these circumstances, a break with the Chiliasts was inevitable. It was hastened by the mutual effort of the Taborites and the people of Prague to discover a *modus vivendi* beyond the grounds of dispute. In Prague the radicals were bombarded with accusations of Picardism, charges which they denied. In the discussions that followed, Martin Huska was reduced to silence, while Nicolas of Pelhrimov and John Zizka strove to maintain contact. At the end of January 1421 Martin Huska was arrested and held in prison for some time. Then from two to three hundred Picards were expelled from Tabor. They settled near at hand round the fortress of Pribenice, and here their ideas were pushed to extremes. They denied the real presence in the Eucharist. Esteeming themselves above sin, they celebrated "love-feasts", practised ritual nudity and extolled sexual emancipation. In the account we have of the activities of these Adamites—which was their final name—

and of the debauches to which their ideas gave rise, it is hard to distinguish the exact truth. John Zizka led several expeditions against them, and a certain number were killed; the survivors, headed by the priest Peter Kanis, were burnt at the stake. Martin Huska, who does not seem to have belonged to this group, fled with a companion towards Moravia; but they were arrested and handed over to the Hussite Archbishop of Prague. Though subjected to torture, they refused to denounce their accomplices or to repent, and on 21 August 1421 they perished at the stake.

It is not our intention here to describe the Hussite War. Five crusades launched against Hussitism by the papacy, between 1421 and 1431, were repulsed in succession by the Czechs, and the latter pushed several counter attacks into the German lands. Under the command of John Zizka and, after his death, of Procopius the Great, the Taborites were in the forefront of armed resistance. Their people's armies, full of religious enthusiasm, well disciplined and provided with the famous "war-vehicles" which protected the soldiers on the offensive and on the defensive, were the military expression of this egalitarian society. They triumphed regularly enough over the feudal cavalry which opposed them. In spite of all, however, weariness of a war with no end in sight began to spread. The defeat and death of Procopius on the battle-field of Lipany in 1434 strengthened the peace party; and peace was finally signed in 1436 after the Compactats. The Taborites were defeated, although they continued to resist orthodox Hussitism until 1452.

It remains only to say a few words about this experiment in the new kind of society represented by Taborism. It is true that the initial phase of communism did not last long, that social classes reorganized themselves in a traditional way and that the economic foundation of society was not modified. The peasants continued to pay dues and their condition perhaps even deteriorated. The cities retained their constitutions and magistrates. Yet a new spirit imparted to this society original features of which it is important to take note.

The Taborite community aimed at reviving the primitive

Church, the Church that existed in the days when Christ was on earth. In practice this was realized in the form of a city-state: a self-governing city which recognized no overlord, which was supported by the nobles and peasants of the surrounding country, and governed them. The priests of Tabor several times asserted the principle of popular sovereignty: to this sovereignty it appertains, when the legitimate powers are in default, to wage war and punish criminals. Lay jurisdiction, to which even the priests were subject, was exercised in the name of the community of the faithful. This principle, as we have seen, was one of those on which the Taborites were opposed to the men of Prague. Of course, the community found its most immediate expression in the armies, which impress one by their popular and revolutionary character.

Within the community the priests played a leading part. Procopius the Great, who became the supreme commander of the armies after Zizka's death, is the most striking example, though evidently exceptional. On a more modest level, they set out the law in their sermons, denounced sinners and saw to it that they were punished by the civil magistrates. But, "if by God's permission the secular powers show themselves to be incapable or incorrigible, then any priest moved by God's spirit may duly arrange peace between laymen and re-establish harmony, so that the poor may not suffer from these conflicts" (Nicolas of Pelhrimov). In the last resort, the priests, interpreters of the scriptures, were the chiefs of the people.

This society, subject to collective watchwords, insisted a great deal on the spiritual development of the individual. Boys and girls, even of humble birth, received a careful education, according to the standards of the time and in the spirit of the Taborites. They took part in discussions and acquired a fairly deep knowledge of holy scripture. Aeneas Sylvius Piccolomini, the future Pope Pius II, made a stay among them and recognized that "among the Taborites one scarcely finds a woman who cannot display familiarity with the Old and the New Testament". The rigid, puritan discipline which reigned in this community so strictly subject to a collective spirit, was voluntary. One must not, of course, idealize this society or forget the failings, weaknesses and abuses of every kind which grew more frequent as time passed. All the same it was, in a certain measure, a new kind of society.

[Chapter Six]
Outline of a Conclusion

DURING A PERIOD of about a century and a half we have, so to speak, unrolled "the film of events", striving not to weary the reader by repetitions, but to describe the characteristic and original features of each episode in the narrative. A chronological treatment has been adopted, not only to bring some clarity into the whole but because it seemed to us to correspond with the inner nature of the social evolution. As early as the thirteenth century very diverse and widespread signs of discontent appeared to culminate towards 1280–5, unless this is an optical illusion. In the first half of the fourteenth century we have witnessed the "democratic revolution" in a number of cities, what was really a certain success on the part of the middle groups at the expense of the "great"; and also, in the most advanced regions, the entry of the peasants on to the stage. Meanwhile famines and plagues lent a still more dramatic character to the struggle, while the Black Death introduced into this agitated period an element of synchronism which appears in the course of the "revolutionary years" from 1378 to 1382. Then, while struggles which had become traditional were repeated or growing systematic, labour conflicts were acquiring a more "modern" appearance; and the Hussite crisis introduced very novel features. Treatment on the above lines seems to us to furnish a reasonable basis for further investigation.

No region appears to have been exempt from agitation, as would very probably be proved by an analysis of the various disturbances more complete than ours. We have said little about the Iberian Peninsula, apart from Catalonia; but the insurrection of 1383 in Portugal, which brought the Avis dynasty to the throne, was not unconnected with the advent of a mercantile middle class, of *nouveaux riches*, in Lisbon and Oporto. Symptoms of trouble were present elsewhere; but in the last resort anti-semitism served as an outlet for the discontent. Other regions which we have had to sacrifice are southern Italy, the Balkans and eastern Europe, where the social and economic development no doubt presented distinct features. Yugoslav historical research has, however, recently brought to light the riotings in Split and Dubrovnik. There were others in Salonika and Adrianople. All this is enough to enable us to regard the phenomenon we are trying to analyse as broadly European.

There of course existed areas more sensitive to social conflict. It is now more than a century since L. Vanderkindere described Flanders as the "paradise of social struggles". This industrial region, along with the neighbouring principalities, was in the forefront of these conflicts; often the first to rebel and the last to be subdued. It can be said that here insurrections achieved enduring results. Northern and central Italy were the other great industrial regions, and Florence, owing to the complex questions which arose there, engrossed our attention for some time. The areas of great peasant agitation were apparently those in which agriculture had developed most intensively (Flanders and England), the grain-growing districts injured by the slump in the price of wheat (England, the Parisian basin and Bohemia), or those where, owing to the action of the lords, the condition of the peasants was deteriorating (England again, Bohemia and Catalonia). The England of 1381 and Hussite Bohemia are notable for the national amplitude of the movement.

There were everywhere great mercantile cities in which social peace seems to have been the reward of prosperity and which were hardly, or not at all, disturbed. Venice would no

doubt be one of them, as would Bordeaux, and Toulouse to some
extent, or Nuremberg. The present state of research permits
us as yet to indicate only these few features in the geography
of social agitation.

It is fitting now that we attempt an analysis of the materials we
have accumulated. What were the main causes of these disturbances? What essential features can be distinguished in
them? What results did all the movements lead up to? Let us
for a few moments consider these questions, without pretending
to exhaust them, but with the object rather of providing
directions for further research.

The problem raised by the causes of social agitation has
given rise to a fundamental debate between historians, Marxists
and non-Marxists in the main. For the latter, the troubles
were principally the result of the recession. The economic
expansion of the twelfth and thirteenth centuries led to an
over-population which the technical possibilities of agricultural
production were inadequate to cope with. Hence the famines
which increased in number at the beginning of the fourteenth
century; hence, even more, the frightful effects on an under-
nourished population of the epidemics of plague. They involved
western and central Europe in a recession which was to last for
at least a century. The demographic factor was then, in the
eyes of these historians, the essential variable. And the disturbances resulted from the misfortunes of the age, they were
accidental in nature.

This is not at all the Marxist point of view. The relations
between various kinds of production were, such historians hold,
organized in such a way within feudal society that they led to a
veritable "class war", which became manifest before the
recession. The recession was above all the result of an aggravation of this war; and so its course appears to be mainly social.
It was connected with the "crisis of feudalism", which was
to be solved by the steady passage from feudalism to capitalism.

There is no question here of completely settling this dispute,
which indeed goes far beyond the scope of the present work.
But it shows clearly that the popular revolutions of the

fourteenth and fifteenth centuries do not present simply the interest of successive events and they do not form merely a collection of colourful episodes, of which one feature or another suggests more or less piquant comparisons with what we have witnessed since those years. By carefully scrutinizing the causes and the chronology of these disturbances, it should be possible to draw from them some answer to the general question we have asked. Were the social troubles unhappy accidents associated with the recession, or the phases of a "class war" inexorably brought on by feudalism, as a cloud brings on a storm?

At the conclusion of our narrative, the answer is scarcely in doubt, but it must comprise many nuances and take account of the complexity of the situations. *Esprit de système* is a dangerous temptation for historians.

We have recorded a few rare forerunners of the social troubles properly so-called, as far back as the second half of the twelfth century. They pile up in the thirteenth century, "so readily quoted as a symbol of political or intellectual stability, of moderation and prosperity", says Robert Fossier, a good observer of rural evolution. We noted, at the beginning of this book, that at the end of the thirteenth century and before the appearance of any serious sign of recession, economic expansion itself raised grave social problems. Now social relationships which brought capital and labour into opposition appeared in the most highly developed regions, those which, by the import of raw materials and the export of manufactured articles, entered the circuit of big-scale commerce. A growing inequality resulted from the economic expansion itself: on one side, those who had been able to take advantage of the new techniques and who had received the cumulative profits; on the other, the majority, now destined to new forms of dependence. One can speak of a real process of social fission, in the country as in the towns. Indebtedness had no doubt increased considerably, although its extent cannot be measured. People contracted debts for current expenses, and all who could had recourse to borrowing, from the gentleman who was a spend-thrift or a victim of war, to the peasant on the poverty-line—

men who still had some kind of property to pledge. But there were also debts for production, often contracted in the form of annuities and the proceeds of which were invested in various kinds of equipment.

It was then that contingent causes intervened and that the demographic factor acquired a bearing which it seems difficult to ignore. If we take account of the state of its agricultural techniques, were western and central Europe over populated at the end of the thirteenth century? Certain Marxist historians have rebelled against this view, wishing to explain the troubles exclusively by the vices of social organization. However, all the research hitherto effected reveals a state of extreme tension. Certain zones were more thickly populated than they were to be in the nineteenth century, when the possibilities of an adequate food supply were to be far greater. Then the very small extent of most of the farms, further diminished by a splitting up of the lots, was unfavourable to an efficient exploitation. This did not prevent the defects of "feudalism" from complicating the problem, or the working of the manorial system from being such that it prevented the peasant from devoting himself entirely to the farming of his tenure—thus reducing the possibilities of production which were already inadequate—or the poor farmer or the one with a larger tenure from being obliged to limit his own consumption of bread, whether he had to deprive himself in order to sell enough of his harvest on the market, or whether he could not buy enough grain for his physiological needs. Each of the two explanations technical and social—seems to us to contain a part of the truth. Rather than excluding each other, they may be taken in combination.

In these circumstances, the multiplication of dearths and famines at the beginning of the fourteenth century appears as a consequence of this tension. The scourge affected the towns at least as much as the countryside; in the towns it raised problems of food supply, which inevitably had social aspects. The death-rate which seems to have already been heavy among the poorer classes at the end of the thirteenth century, was accentuated. In northern Europe the famine of 1315–17 in particular mowed down many lives.

It was then that a phenomenon occurred which historical research has recently brought to light: the stagnation or even decline of prices for cereal crops, whereas hitherto the price had risen steadily along with economic expansion. This circumstance has been noted in England. Apart from abrupt rises in times of dearth, a slow decline took place after 1320. R. H. Hilton has calculated that if one takes 100 as the average index for the decade 1300–10, this figure fell to 90 for 1330–50. G. Fourquin has revealed a probably similar situation in the Parisian region. During the period 1330–42, the curve of cereal prices showed more violent fluctuations than before, but especially did it fall to a lower level: which was a surprising phenomenon in an age of demographic tension. Two explanations appear possible: either the dearths brought about a reversal of the demographic tendency,[1] or else over-production was mainly due to an under-consumption of social origin. The poor would have liked to eat more cereal food, but either they could not buy enough, or else they themselves had to sell too much, and the market became unbalanced. However that may be, this fall in cereal prices directly affected the regions of intense agricultural production, and this helps to explain that increase of peasant discontent which we have recorded.

After this, new causes for a recession were added to the old: in some regions war, or political and military anarchy; everywhere epidemics of plague which caused the maximum of evil in an environment prepared for them by dearth. Impoverishment there certainly was. To many people the burden of debt became intolerable. Depopulation brought about a crisis in the supply of labour, which was immediately reflected by various statutes of labourers, and in the long term by the evolution of the statutes regulating the crafts, which itself led to further social tensions.

There were therefore rebellions due to misery; short spells of fury, particularly in times of dearth; or brigandage which prevailed in the poorest regions, the Tuchins furnishing a good example. But the best organized insurrections took place in

[1] That is, a decrease in the population after a period of increase. (Translator.)

districts formerly prosperous but now touched by the recession, and the richest peasants formed good officers for a revolution. This was doubtless the case with the insurrection in maritime Flanders. The Jacquerie, it has been observed, broke out on the wheat-growing plains of the Ile-de-France. And it is in this sense, if we take account of social prejudice, that we should interpret Froissart's reflection about the England of 1381: "Owing to the great ease and abundance of good in which the lower class was living, this rebellion broke out."

Two questions then arise, which we are not yet in a position to answer. If the crisis in the labour force was really marked, if it brought about wage increases which legislators did not manage to stop, was not the fourteenth century, especially in certain sectors of the urban artisan class, the golden age of the workers? This has been said, and the assertion perhaps rests on some foundation, in certain precise cases. But was the rise in wages anything but a temporary phenomenon? If we consider the situation in France, and over the whole century after the Black Death, it seems on the contrary that wage rates were remarkably stable. On the other hand, the very frequent efforts, within the sphere of "corporative" regulations, to slow down or even prevent the access of companions to the status of master, closed many prospects of social ambition and developed dangerous tensions among the artisans.

A second question is to ask whether the recession aggravated or attenuated the inequalities resulting from the expansion, which have been observed at the end of the thirteenth century and the beginning of the fourteenth. This question, which is fundamental, has scarcely been touched; because the state of documentation on the subject does not facilitate a reply. The few records available hitherto appear rather contradictory, so it seems better at the moment not to attempt a general answer.

The causes of social agitation appear to have sprung both from the structure of society and from contingencies. The changes that took place in the thirteenth century had already created fissures in society and conflicts of interests. When the depression came some of these were perhaps attenuated; but most of them came to the fore, and others were added.

To be more precise, the struggle took place round three in-stitutions, of very unequal size, but which have been examined in the light of facts: the seigneurial or manorial system, the urban community and the state.

The seigneurial system—and we are thinking here of country districts—was evidently an object of dispute. "In the his-torian's eyes", wrote Marc Bloch, "the agrarian revolt appears as inseparable from the seigneurial regime as, for example, strikes from large-scale capitalist enterprise." The subsistence of a small minority, the lords and their families, whose business was to command and to make war, was assured by the work of the greater number, toiling on the land, from which people did not yet know how to produce the best yield. All the heavier then was the payment of dues which, in the framework of the manorial system, operated to the advantage of the lords over the peasants. In the poorest districts the squire lived hardly less miserably than the rustics, but he managed to do so only by putting on them all the pressure he could. In the wealthiest regions, the sale of surplus agricultural products brought gain to everyone, but it led the lords to stretch the scope of the manorial system in order to net the maximum profit. In any case, men's interests were opposed.

Was the seigneurial system, then, out of date, a means of exploitation without corresponding benefit? Could it at this time have been suppressed with advantage? Few of the rebels seem to have thought so, apart from outbursts of anger. The "Jacques" have not told us what they were thinking, but Jean de Venette, a son of peasants, ascribes their discontent to the fact that "the nobles, far from protecting them, were oppressing them as heavily as was the enemy". Now here appears a justi-fication of the system: it had to bring to the peasant the pro-tection of his customary rights in daily life, and the armed protection of the lord in case of conflict. This was of course the theoretical justification. In fact the abuses committed by certain lords, those who were unjust, extravagant or oppressive, were not the only factors involved. Seigneural authority, which rested on the personal bonds between man and man and drawn closer in the course of generations, was often severely impaired for various reasons. Too often the lord was absent, his time completely absorbed by administrative or military duties, or by sojourns at the Royal Court, or else he lived in isolation from the peasant community, delegating the management of his domain to stewards or judges frequently harder men than he. In certain regions which changed hands as the country was conquered or reconquered, deaths, flights and confiscations maintained a state of instability in the system, as observed for example in the region round Bordeaux. Now all the above applies mainly to the lay domains, and it may then be asked whether conditions were better in the ecclesiastical lordships. It is not certain that they were.

One of the historians who has most strongly insisted on the importance and seriousness of the social change in the country districts (Picardy in this instance), Robert Fossier, has tried to picture what the peasants' point of view could have been:

"The maintenance of a really active manor in the hands of the lord, even at the cost of their pennies, seems to them a guarantee of security, and even the first condition of their own success. Without a lord, how could they conceive of the proper application of local usages, of the rotation of crops, of the building of mills, and the organization of exchanges useful to everyone? Without the master's presence, there would ensue the disorder which the countryman, far more than the city-dweller, is in dread of; or else the hand of the Church, of which only the clerics thought it lighter than the hand of the nobleman."

These reflections appear reasonable and seem to be verified by experience in various places.

A close study of the situation in Flanders at the time of the 1323 insurrection would lead to a similar conclusion, although one should note shades of difference between the country inland where the lords had retained a firm hold, and the Polders on the coast where the land which had been won from the sea was divided among many small free farmers. The development of the farming lease among the latter had enabled a small number of big farmers, like some of those at Pitten, to be able to own some forty "measures" of land, that is, about forty-five hectares, together with farm implements and a whole herd of cattle. Rather than on the institutions, it was on the conduct of all the rich men, the new and the old, in addition to the great abbeys, whose administrators (the *Keuriers* or *Poirteurs*) were exploiting them, that the insurgents laid the blame. They rebelled against abuses committed by the Count of Flanders's agents but, once these had been expelled, they appointed new ones, chosen from among them, within the traditional framework. Furthermore, the rebels counted on the greatest noble landowner of the most feudalized region in the country, Robert de Cassel, uncle of Count Louis de Nevers. The blame, then, was laid to the door of the rich, and there was no thought of new social structures.

Both in England until the eve of 1380, and in Catalonia, what we observe is the peasants' opposition to a hardening of the seigneurial system, and their attachment to old-time custom, which perhaps appeared more idyllic than it really had been. Certainly, our sources leave the impression that in 1381 the English labourers went much further. It was the very existence of the gentleman, his usefulness, and the predominance of private property that were at issue, in the words which Froissart, more clearly than any other chronicler, ascribes to John Ball. But even if these audacious and revolutionary views were really expressed, were they anything but a stimulant to revolt? In any case, only a part of them appears among the articles presented to the King, whether at Mile End or at Smithfield. The most radical request concerned the secularization of Church properties, which were to be shared among the "commons" or the parishioners. For the rest, the abolition of serfdom, the repeal of the Statute of Labourers, the concession to the peasants of the rights of free use of the woodlands (except in the royal demesnes), did not bring into question the existence of lay lordships. It is true that the lords opposed the progressive disappearance of serfdom and tended to limit the use of the woodlands, reduced in extent by the movement to clear more land for tillage, by the peasants. Now, the poor peasants in particular absolutely needed this, to complete their meagre resources. To sum up, it was a question of preventing

the seigneurial system from growing harder. The secularization
of Church property evidently went further. In a whole sector
of rural life, it meant the disappearance of the lords, the growth
of a class of small peasant proprietors, and perhaps the extension of the collective property of the "commons". We must not
however forget that this measure was demanded, in the first
place, for religious reasons—the purification of the Church.
More definitely, but with less realism, did the Taborites demand the abolition of the seigneurial regime. The putting of
all goods in common, the denunciation of all private property,
the freedom to make use of all property, and the suppression of
seigneurial dues—these constituted the kind of life prescribed
for the young Taborite communities, and they were intended as
the programme for a kind of paradise, of which the advent was
impatiently awaited. But the initial enthusiasm, as we have
seen, did not last long. Private property began to develop among
the Taborites, and the burden of seigneurial dues once more
fell on the peasants. Later on, when the Taborites were
vanquished, the Czech nobility hardened, following the general
evolution in central and eastern Europe.

Thus, the system of rural lordship was subject to many
challenges, and the judicial archives, if many (as in England)
had remained for us, would reveal many other episodes, more
obscure than the great rebellions, but also more continuous.
On the whole, however, it was the abuses, the distortions and
the asperities of the seigneurial system that were combated.
Traditional seigneury or "lordship" offered the peasant the
protection of its old customs and armed force. What he demanded, rather, was its maintenance, not only against individual excesses but against the general evolution which was
weakening the system in one way and hardening it in another.
The peasants' ideal thus presents a certain "reactionary"
aspect, and this enables us better to understand the deep
causes of the agitation.

The urban communities had grown up in the heart of this
rural world. They had in a large measure freed themselves
from strictly seigneurial burdens. When they had not succeeded

in doing so—and this was especially true of ecclesiastical urban lordships—the old-time conflicts were renewed on the occasion of general waves of disturbance. This happened in England in 1381, where the rebellions at St Albans and Bury St Edmunds, among others, were of this kind. Elsewhere, lords tried to find among the middle and lower class of people allies against these proud urban "aristocracies" which had originally led the battle for civic liberties. But if these struggles were prolonged into the fourteenth and fifteenth centuries, they do not directly concern us here.

On the whole, then, the lord had been deprived of power. Who now would exercise it, and how would it be shared among the elements of the urban population? This was an important problem. If power, undivided and uncontrolled, belonged to a more or less large coterie, the latter would find it easy to indulge in many abuses, conceal irregularities, and spend money to serve its private interests. The financial side of the problem was fundamental: the control of expenditure and, still more, the amount to be raised by taxation. In a general way, the rich preferred indirect taxes levied in proportion to what the taxpayer bought, rather than to his real needs and, even more, than to his means. The burgess, a hundred times richer than another man, would still not consume a hundred times more, and the tax would not affect him in proportion to his means. It would be possible to come a little nearer to this ideal by recourse to direct taxes: the poor rebelled on many occasions to obtain this system. But it was still necessary to arrive at a regular assessment of the tax by means of honest, verified and frequently revised declarations of income or property.

Other aspects of the question should be considered. Urban bye-laws (as we should call them), imposed by the magistrates, covered many essential matters. They took the place of town-planning, decided how the markets should be policed, and might also concern wage rates and prices, conditions of employment and work, etc. The town magistrates administered these regulations and much evidently depended on the way they settled cases. At all times the provisioning of a town presented difficulties, at least for certain commodities, such as timber, grain and salt. In periods of dearth, municipal policy might be more or less favourable to the poor; might or might not establish maximum prices; might or might not search houses and granaries to build up food stocks, display more or less zeal in bringing in supplies from outside and disposing of them at more or less high prices (at a loss, in general). If in addition one takes account of the exercise of unpaid jurisdiction it will be seen that the most varied sectors of private life itself did not escape the scope of these civic regulations; they affected contracts of marriage, purchases, sales, hirings, apprenticeships, etc.

When the cities had won a comfortable amount of autonomy, owing to the default or weakness of the State—as in Italy and Germany—"high politics" were at stake. The city might declare war or make peace, seek this or that ally, take part in a league or assembly, and the decision always involved more or less of expense. The political and financial aspects were closely intermingled.

It was therefore very important for the most modest elements of the population to share in municipal power, so rich in possibilities, and to exercise some supervision. One must not underestimate the bearing of the struggles which took place in so many cities from the thirteenth to the fifteenth century, though one could not describe them as really revolutionary. They could not aim at the overthrow of society, or the abolition of private property within the city bounds (although that was the object for a short time in the Taborite cities). The real urban revolution was emancipation from the lord. That was achieved, on the whole, but now new forms of dependence, this time on the State, were looming up.

The invasion of society by the State, this was in fact one of the causes of social conflicts. The State had asserted itself in France, in England and in the Iberian lands before the fourteenth century, and this was obviously a result of the general evolution of societies. The Great Interregnum had marked the definite failure of the Empire, but its functions were taken over by principalities, such as the papal states, the kingdom of Naples and the kingdom of Bohemia, or by the cities which established *contadi*[1] subject to their government, or formed leagues. That the city's power was too limited in scope to deal with certain questions is what appears clearly from the evolution of the Empire. In the fifteenth century great numbers of coalitions were formed between the masters as between the workmen of various cities, so that conflicts concerning labour were more and more acquiring a regional character. It is evident that super-municipal institutions were lacking. The situation here was like the negative of a photograph, of which those countries endowed with a vigorous State furnish the positive. In what sense could the development of the State give rise to, or facilitate, social disturbances?

There was first of all a negative aspect. To develop the authority of the State amounted in a certain measure to dispossessing traditional authorities of their power. The seigneurial world was deeply shaken by the repercussions of this movement. Because they entered the administrative or military service of the State, many lords more and more often absented themselves from their castles and cut themselves off from the peasant community. An increasing number of cases escaped from the jurisdiction of the manorial courts. This weakening of the powers of seigneury might serve as a stimulus to peasant agitation; but with the disappearance of these powers, the traditional protection which they, and the customs of which they were guardians, offered to rural life, disappeared also. We have already noted this. With respect to the cities, the State rather substituted itself for the governing bodies in so far as their incapacity or the abuses they committed made it necessary.

In Flanders the conflict between Ghent and the Count about the year 1380 was to some extent that of a city in competition with the State. No doubt the social problem, which caused the *poorters* to be opposed to the artisans, led the former into alliance with the prince. But the pretext for the struggle and its out-

[1] That is, a more or less extensive territory surrounding the city, as in Tuscany and northern Italy. (Translator.)

break, apropos of the Lys canal, reveal a competition between the interests of the city and those of the whole county, for which a direct connection between Bruges and the country further inland was quite as useful. Generally at stake in this conflict was the pretension of Ghent to absorb the greater part of the county into the jurisdiction of its own castellany. Finally, Philip van Artevelde, endowed with the title of *ruwaert* (or governor), acted as the head of a government and played a diplomatic game with the English court, in competition with the policy of Louis de Male. The whole energy of Philip the Good, Duke of Burgundy, would be needed in 1453 to break the independence of Ghent.

Meanwhile, the growth of the royal administration inevitably increased the burden of the State's finances. More frequently and with a wider scope, taxation weighed upon the prince's subjects. To appreciate this fact fully, one must bear in mind the centuries' old eclipse of the State which, everywhere if unequally according to the various regions, had prevailed during the preceding centuries. The role of the State had been so diminished, its demands had so often corresponded with the cupidity of the rulers, that a kind of moral reprobation attached to the raising of taxes. To encourage a collective refusal to pay, to burn the lists of taxpayers, were a few of the meritorious acts which the lives of the saints ascribe to the bishops of the Merovingian age. After that a new image had arisen, that of the good sovereign who in normal times lived on "his own", that is, on the ordinary revenues of the royal demesne. Now just as the feudal lord might seek the financial aid of his dependents in cases which old-established "custom" defined and limited, so it was admitted that the prince might ask his subjects for a subsidy, but always in exceptional circumstances, to carry on a just war for example, and after negotiating with those who would be paying. Various needs made these appeals more and more frequent, but it took several centuries for the principle of a regular, annual tax to be accepted; and it cannot be regarded as really established, and then not every-where, until the fifteenth century. Meanwhile, the prince had been obliged to have recourse to subterfuges, like those currency

changes which, because they modified the relations between
creditors, credit-annuitants and proprietors on one side and,
on the other, debtors, debit-annuitants and tenants, were
themselves a source of social tensions.

The modes of taxation which were sought raised as many
problems. Numerous were the experiments tried, mainly with
a view to efficacy. We must not forget that one of the most
violent revolutionary crises of this epoch, the Peasants' Revolt
of 1381, was directly occasioned by a form of imposition, the
poll-tax, the injustice of which we have analysed better than
contemporaries could do, and which in the end was abandoned.
That was an extreme example, but discussions proceeded
everywhere as to the best means of taxation. In the cities,
royal subsidies were superimposed on the municipal taxes, and
aggravated the financial problems which we mentioned a
little earlier. It has been possible to make a detailed analysis
of the public accounts of Toulouse for the fiscal year 1404–5;
now the money raised for the King represented 90 per cent of
the expenditure, and the strictly urban needs of the place were
deliberately sacrificed. When a State did not superimpose
itself on the cities, the latter were obliged, more or less, to
assume the functions and expenditure of the State.

To raise money, but for what purpose? The financial
problem soon merged into the political. According to the
country involved, the grant of subsidies was more or less
accompanied by the discussions related to the prince's policy.
To develop this idea would, in a certain measure, be to study
the origins of Parliamentary government in Europe. In any
case, the control of royal policy was what most escaped the
"middle" and "lower" strata of the population. Beside the
prelates and nobles, only the bourgeois class appeared in the
assemblies of the Estates. There were short periods when the
bourgeois opposition made use of popular movements as a
striking-force, but, as can be seen in the case of Etienne
Marcel, those coincidences were only momentary.

In a few extreme instances, popular leaders might think of
exerting a durable influence on the sovereign. The problem
certainly arose in England in 1381. When the promises of Mile

End and Smithfield were once extracted from Richard II, what was there to guarantee that they would be carried out? Thomas Walsingham puts the following words in the mouth of Jack Straw at the moment when he was to be executed:

"At the time when we assembled on Black Heath, when we called upon the King, our plan was to deliver to sudden death all the knights, esquires and other nobles who had come with him, and then to exhibit the King from place to place, enthroned in our midst, so that having seen him, everyone, and especially the common people, would be encouraged to rally to us and our party, since the King himself would have appeared as the instigator of our insurrection. . . . Then we should have executed the lords who might have given counsel against us or resisted us. . . . In the last place we should have killed the King. . . . No one then being greater, nor stronger, nor wiser than we, we should have made laws at our will, by which laws the people would have been ruled. And we should have created kings, Wat Tyler in Kent, and others in the other counties. . . ."

The fantastic nature of these words show that it is advisable to admire Walsingham's imagination more than his accuracy. But it emphasizes how insoluble no doubt was the problem that faced Tyler and the leaders of the insurrection. The text reflects a reaction against monarchical centralization, and may have some foundation in fact.

The problem of the State also arose in Bohemia. As we have seen, the Hussite Revolution originated in a movement for religious reform encouraged by King Charles IV. But his successors, Wenceslas IV and then the Emperor Sigismund, were soon revealed as incapable of appeasing the emotions which had been excited and of taking the situation in hand. What could the reformers expect of a sovereign who was weak or ill-disposed, or both together? It was on this matter that they differed fundamentally with Wyclif. Whereas Wyclif counted on the State to purify the Church, Huss placed his hope in "a national Church, organized according to the democratic principle of the free election of priests and bishops, realizing in the Church the fundamental sovereignty of the people" (Bartos). The men of Prague persisted in electing a king, although they did not count on leaving him much power. The Taborites would not hear of a king; neither they nor the Picards admitted any sovereign other than Christ. In the blessed world of their dreams, the State would be left to perish.

The Hussite episode strongly emphasizes the fragility of these states that were being reborn. It was their crises that unleashed the revolutionary tempests: one thinks of the French monarchy on the morrow of Poitiers or at the time of Azincourt. In 1381 the English crown was weakened by the extreme youth of Richard II and by the progressive loss of territories in France, but these were temporary phases. The governing bodies were to regain the upper hand, the march towards absolute monarchy was to begin anew.

The limitation that was finally to be imposed on them, control by an elected representative assembly, could hardly suit the popular leaders. The assembly represented almost exclusively the "great" or the "middle" classes of people— nobles, clerics and bourgeois. In several cases, such bodies revealed themselves as more jealous than the sovereigns themselves of their interest as proprietors. In England Parliament reinforced the legislation controlling the labourers, which had been sketched out by Edward III and his councillors. In Catalonia the *Corts*, acting contrary to the King, supported the lords against the *remensas*. Parliamentary monarchy might be a political solution, it could not be a social one.

To these circumstances, which provoked so much protest, must of course be added the Church. It was the target of the rebels, first and above all as proprietor and lord. Bishops and abbots were particularly vigilant and combative lords, because they considered themselves accountable for the patrimony which they had received and which they had to transmit intact. Some of the most violent and often repeated struggles took place in the ecclesiastical seigneuries, both rural and urban. More generally, the possession by the Church of landed estates was regarded by many thinkers as a source of considerable evil, of a moral kind, for the Church itself. The secularization of Church properties was no doubt sought for in Flanders; it was expressly asked for in England; it was achieved in Bohemia. This last was indeed a revolutionary change, one which the future, still more or less distant, was to take up and carry out.

The organization of the Church was also an object of serious challenge. We can leave aside in this work the problem of the papacy, which the Great Schism, coming after the residence at Avignon, raised in all its gravity. The "revolutionaries" aimed particularly at the higher clergy, those most affected by luxury. Bishops sometimes appeared too numerous, and the English labourers demanded that there should be no more than one in the whole kingdom. On the other hand the Hussite Church retained bishops, and even the Taborites elected one. Only the Chiliasts were absolutely averse from them. Benedictine monasticism was also exposed to attack, because the abbeys were often big landed proprietors and because religious feeling had partly turned away from the Benedictine ideal. The question of the Church's authority was raised several times, but nowhere so clearly as in Bohemia, where a democratic election of priests and bishops was demanded more than once.

In what measure was the dogma of the Church called in question by these revolutionary movements? This question raises the whole problem of the relations between orthodox faith and revolutionary ideas. Heresy and revolution—the two notions have been considered as equivalent. Heresy is a rupture with the beliefs commonly shared in a society, it is a social rupture as well as a doctrinal. That heretics were numerous among social agitators is certain. There was, first, a current of Vaudois thought which rejected a part of the institutions on which the social order was founded. There was a series of tendencies more or less grafted on to the predictions of Joachim de Flore, relative to the coming of a Third Age and the reign of the Spirit: Beghards, Brothers of the Free Spirit, and so on. And there were Wyclif and the Lollards, the revolutionary implications of whose teaching we have examined. If they did not, at least directly, influence John Ball and the labourers, their after-effect in Bohemia is a certainty.

Even so, one may ask whether these heresies could provide a basis for a revolutionary ideology. In this matter, their failure is evident. The pacifist nature of the Vaudois was opposed to it, and we have seen what arguments the Taborites had to pursue with such an end in view. Many of these heretics advocated the practice of poverty; but this could be no basis for revolutionary action, which on the contrary aimed at the suppression of poverty. Most of those who awaited the coming of an Age of the Spirit confined themselves to a passive attitude; they put their confidence in God to promote the new age, by means in some sort mechanical. On this point the Chiliasts seem to have been really original, since they abandoned the notion of transcendence, and ascribed an active role to the faithful: to exterminate everyone who did not adhere to the true faith—which, all the same, was a tall order!

Contemporaries sometimes identified heresy with revolution, but wrongly so, and from interested motives. We have seen this in the matter of Wyclif and the English labourers. One is struck, on the contrary, by the absence of any heresy in numerous revolutionary movements which limited themselves to anti-clericalism; like the parishioners of Blacy-en-Champagne who, according to a letter of remission of the time of the Jacquerie, "thought that the priests of country villages were favourable to the nobles and obeyed them, and who for that reason held these priests as traitors and accused them of selling the (Church) bells to the said nobles".

In any case, what heresies took up, distorted or applied without heed to contingencies, were elements taken from the Gospels and from the very teaching of the Church: the impossibility for the rich to be saved without abandoning their riches, and hence the condemnation of private property; imitation of the apostolic life, of the primitive Church, long proposed as a model simply for monks and canons, but now extended to the laity; and application of the principle of holding all things in common. Glorification of the poor has never been so intense as on the eve of the practical decline of this theme; the theme of the "dangerous classes" competed with it, as we shall see. On the political plane, the *minuti* of Florence did not hesitate in August 1378 to call themselves the *popolo di Dio*. An attentive study of Langland's *Piers the Plowman* and of its pictorial commentaries reveals the idea of a new relationship between Christ and the poor—no longer a connection of similarity, but an identification in nature, consisting less in the sublimation of the poor than in the humanizing of Christ, incarnate in the person of the poor man. From this connection Langland did not doubtless wish to draw any revolutionary conclusions; he even declared himself opposed to innovations contrary to public order. Nevertheless the ambiguity of his extolling of the poor has led commentators on to risky paths. It was serious enough, towards 1380, to liken *Piers the Plowman* to Christ, justicer of the rich, and to make him a sort of new Messiah. John Ball might regard himself as the herald of this Saviour of the Apocalyptic times, the worker chosen by God: "John Ball salutes you", he said in presenting himself as the Announcer of the Apocalypse, "John Ball makes known to you that he has rung the bell."

Iconography is still more explicit. One theme of wall-painting has been called "The Christ of the Craftsmen"; another, "Piers the Plowman as Christ." Around the person of this suffering Christ, the artist has substituted the peasants' and artisans' tools for the familiar instruments of the Passion. At Stadham, Christ is represented standing in a farm-cart, while the peasants' tools, arranged round his head, are added to the halo of the crucified. At Ampney St Mary, the symbolism is still more explicit: the "glory" of Christ the Saviour, customary in medieval iconography, is composed entirely of working-tools: the mallet, wheel, hammer, knife, comb, axe and roll of rope have supplanted the traditional halo. An allegory, perhaps; yet in a confused and uneasy atmosphere, was not this picture, presented by the most popular of arts to the eyes of the humble, charged with psychological suggestions of the gravest import?

There is in fact no real revolution without a mysticism; and where could the men of the fourteenth and fifteenth centuries have found one, save in the only book from which, through words and images, the humble received the message of the "good news announced to the poor"? This was a mysticism; orthodox, somewhat deformed and tinged with heresy, it was still founded on the Gospels. But it was not an "ideology of revolution". Using the words in their strict sense, and setting aside the Chiliasts, there as yet existed none.

We should like to add another factor. That, in the end, a certain more or less conscious sense of human dignity inspired the revolutionaries and that, along with such mean motives as rancour, jealousy and cupidity, one should ascribe something to this feeling, is what certain episodes tend to show: the episode of the Burgundian vine-growers, the protests of the Catalan jurists, the idealism of the Taborites; or that singular story which R. H. Hilton discovered among English archives. In 1293 in Worcestershire a free tenant of the Earl of Gloucester, Adam le Yep, was constrained by poverty to accept a servile tenure, which turned him into a villain. He had often sworn to kill himself rather than accept such a lot; and in fact he drowned himself in the Severn.

*   *   *

Having studied the causes of these agitations we are led next to analyse their modes—the ways in which they broke out. By this means we believe it possible at least to discern the degree of a collective consciousness of their community of interests, to which at the end of the Middle Ages large groups of men had attained. Was it consciousness of such and such a common problem, class-consciousness, *esprit de corps* or corporative sense, or simply the contagion of a quasi-physical reaction to a situation identical for everyone? Rebellion could be, according to the case, spontaneous or stirred up. If spontaneous, it is a manifestation of anger against a man, a group of men or a situation, and its outburst results simultaneously from a collective predisposition to emotion and from a concrete incident. Such is very often the case with peasant commotions, at least at the beginning; for example, the initial incidents of the Jacquerie, the attack on some castle or other. Such, in the city, is an altercation and assembly of a crowd which lead to sedition, as in Paris the altercation between a greengrocer and a tax-collector at the beginning of the insurrection of the Maillotins.

If instigated, rebellion—while remaining a violent reaction and, for most of its participants, of primary character—has been conceived and prepared, and its hour chosen, by one or several men. This kind of a directed rebellion appears most often on the economic level and in the most advanced cities. Was not this the case with Bruges and Ypres in 1279 and 1280, with Paris in 1358, with Florence in 1378, with Ghent in 1379? In a general way the urban agitations of the craftsmen against the patricians seem to belong to this category. One of the clearest criteria for the type of disturbance involved is to discover whether it was concerted: at what moment in the rebellion, and how, did the rebels act together? The insurrection of maritime Flanders in 1323, the Jacquerie, and the Peasants' Revolt in England became co-ordinated movements only after the peasants had formed assemblages and the first acts of violence had been committed. In the cities, in many instances, plans were concerted before the action was taken. This was naturally due to men's mutual proximity, geographical in the town, or professional in the daily performance of work. The individualism and isolation of the peasants lent themselves less to such proximity.

Immediately connected with the manner in which outbreaks took place, is the question of how they were propagated. To begin with, one must of course remember the importance of news, true or false, or simply distorted. A study of the events enables us to note examples that have been faithfully transmitted by chronicles and other documents. The use of the word "fright" (*peur*) apropos of peasant commotions enables one to imagine how contagion was spread by rumours passing from mouth to mouth with amazing speed and by the call of the Tocsin, set in motion by someone or other. People assemble in crowds. The chronicles describe this phenomenon by which, as by a snowball, the bands of French Jacques and English peasants found their numbers swollen. They also tell how mere onlookers joined these bands. Letters of remission were granted to simple idlers who in 1382 joined the Maillotins in Paris, out of curiosity. One meets with similar happenings in Florence in 1378, at the time of the manifestations against the Signoria from the quarters of Santa Croce, of the Santo Spirito and of Santa Maria Novella. Many other examples could be cited. From them all an essential fact emerges: It is the unlawful assembly, or mob, leading its participants to some collective act, an attack on a country manor or the house of a wealthy citizen, the assault in 1378 on the Palazzo della Signoria in Florence, on the Count of Flanders's castle in Ghent in 1379, the siege of the Bastille in 1413 or of the residences of the King or the Dauphin.

Violent action was generally preceded by a mass-assembly at which passions became inflamed. The importance of popular eloquence and the significance of the places of assembly become factors at this point. The *"grand'places"* of the cities of northern France, the "piazze della Signoria" of the Italian cities; the market-places, like the Friday market in Ghent, and Smithfield in London; the cemeteries surrounding churches, like the Aître Saint-Eloi, and especially the famous graveyard of the Innocents in Paris, not forgetting the Place de Grève; in such places popular speakers, who enjoyed an immense vogue in the fourteenth century, had every chance to indulge in regular feats of oratory, remarkable for the length and energy, if not for the tartness, of their speeches. The importance of lay eloquence was one of the novelties of these times of revolution. All the orators had not learned the art of rhetoric in the schools, like Jean des Mares, the advocate who essayed the role of a Cato at the time of the Maillotins, or Jean de Troyes, the physician who tried (by anticipation) to play the part of Mirabeau in 1413. In Flanders the heroes of Bruges, Coninc and Zanekin, and, at Ghent, the Arteveldes and Francis Ackermann were to inflame the mob, as much as a Salvestro dei Medici or a Michele di Lando in Florence. For princes also, the mania for speechifying became a means of government as well as a vehicle for propaganda. The Dauphin Charles had indeed to practise the art in 1358, and not without success since he managed to counterbalance the ambitious oratory of

Charles the Bad. Richard II tried it in 1381, the Dauphin
Louis failed no doubt to do as much against the demagogy of
John the Fearless in 1413. All these lay orators however were
probably inferior in *savoir-faire* and in influence to the ecclesi-
astics. The latter had learned how to argue, to distinguish, to
prove, to refute and finally to convince, at least on the surface.
Fourteenth- and fifteenth- century crowds had a liking for long
discourses and patiently endured the interminable harangues
which were a kind of permanent spectacle for the public.
According to the *Bourgeois de Paris*, Friar Richard spoke for
hours together at the graveyard of the Innocents. Authentic
preachers like Bernardino da Siena or Vincent Ferrier met with
equal favour, as did the Mendicant Friars whose contacts with
the people inspired language as revolutionary on the social
plane as it was ardent on that of charity. Learned again and
amazingly spirited were the copious and flowery sermons of
the Carmelite, Eustache de Pavilly, in 1413; though there were
fewer flourishes and more acidity in the discourses of most of
the popular preachers, especially after 1378. To discredit the
men of Bruges the Minorite Brothers indulged in a riot of
language on the battle-field to encourage the men of Ghent,
"the people of God". In fact the multitude's sensitivity to the
spoken word can only be compared to its present-day re-
ceptivity to the effects of mass-media. The first attempts at
mass-propaganda date from the second half of the fourteenth
century, and it is only with the Wars of Religion that we find it
again, on a large scale.

The story of the anti-Jewish pogrom of 1391 enabled us to
follow with a good deal of precision the geographical advance
of rioting, the speed of its progress, and the manner. We are
therefore led to ask whether a revolution in one country influenced another. Certain writers have thought so. Froissart
does not hesitate to assert that the rebellion of 1379–82 was
international in character:

"Now, see the great folly. If they had achieved their intention,
they would have destroyed all the nobles in England; and after
that, in other nations, all the small fry would have rebelled,

and followed the example of them of Ghent and of Flanders, who rebelled against their lord. And in that same year the Parisians did the same, and contrived to fashion iron mallets, of which they made more than 20,000. . . ."

Certain contemporaries, without going so far as to suppose that these agitations were co-ordinated, have at least sometimes noted analogies and resemblances, for example between the Maillotins and the Ciompi. Other writers sound a different note. Walsingham, so severe on the English rebels, describes the events in Flanders and Paris in a manner hostile to the King of France, who was the principal enemy of the rebels, and favourable rather to the rioters. The Flemish rebellion shone like a beacon in the course of these years. It was certainly known in England. The example of Flanders may well have encouraged the risings in Paris and in Rouen: Charles VI let events take their course until the day of Roosebeke. On the other hand, the crushing of the Flemish militia gave the signal for repression.

The Hussite crisis provides another field for reflection. While deriving from causes peculiar to Bohemia, the movement still underwent outside influences. Those which came from England, more intellectual than social, are obvious, even if it seems advisable to reduce their exact importance. Traces of Valdeism have subsequently been detected in the Taborite doctrines. Bohemia after the rebellion became a place of refuge, and the Picards may perhaps have brought there the teaching of the Beghards of the Free Spirit. In 1420 Gilles Meursault, a citizen of Tournai, came to Prague; and on his return home he conducted active Hussite propaganda; moreover the people of Prague sent messages all over Christendom to justify their proceedings. Czech expeditions into Germany inspired there a bitter revolutionary attitude. We have already mentioned the case of Bamberg which, when besieged by the Hussites in 1430, revolted against the rich burghers and the convents; five years later, another insurrection drove out the Bishop and the clergy. We may suppose, too, that the disturbances which broke out at Breslau in 1418 were influenced by Czech agitation; the craftsmen rebelled against the council, several magistrates were killed, others took refuge in flight and the leaders of the lower orders entered the new council. But this was abolished by the Emperor Sigismund, and the tribunal he set up condemned forty-six people to death; of these sentences twenty-six were executed. Hence the Crusaders who invaded Bohemia on several occasions, lacked the feeling that they were contributing to solve a purely Czech problem, or a purely religious one, but at least some of them felt that they were trying to extinguish a fire which threatened to spread to large parts of Europe.

It does not seem that we can say more, and there can be no question of an "invisible conductor". News circulated, but slowly, and was unintentionally distorted on the way. One recalls the episode of the Abbot of Chester's serfs, whom the revolutionary contagion led to rebel at the end of July 1381, whereas the main body of the insurrection had been crushed since 15 June.

Another question which arose in a different way is that of the relations between rural and urban movements. Sometimes it was a mere tactical alliance, due in fact to a misunderstanding, as was the case for Etienne Marcel and the Jacquerie. The understanding was deeper and more complete with the insurrection of maritime Flanders (taking account of the local rivalry between Bruges, an accomplice of the rebels, and Ghent, a rampart of public order), or with the Peasants' Revolt in England. In Catalonia, the lower orders in the cities had an understanding with the peasant *remensas* in 1391; while during the crisis of 1462–72 the peasants were opposed to the cities which were dominated by the bourgeoisie. The difficulty arises from the fact that by comparison with the cities the countryside was one revolution late, so to speak. The seigneury still appeared powerful in the country, even if it had had to make concessions. The cities, on the contrary, had already partly freed themselves from their lords. A coincidence in the objects sought might however lead to a more or less solid and lasting alliance between the poor folk of town and country. At all events, the problem of relations between peasants and artisans, even bourgeois, was fundamental, and was to become more and more so as it evolved. The revolutionaries of modern time have taken good account of this.

So a "revolutionary contagion" did exist, and did play a certain part. But we must exclude any real co-ordination between rebels. What strikes one, on the contrary, is the incoherency of the risings, and the absence of any understanding between those who provoked them. The cases of synchronism we have noted proceeded rather from deep-seated causes operating almost simultaneously in various countries or regions.

These rebels were running their heads against a powerful obstacle—the State, with the strength of its organization, but also the incomparable prestige that surrounded the sovereign.[1] On many occasions we have been impressed by the reverence which the revolutionary leaders and their followers displayed for his person, as witness Berenguer Oller protesting his loyalty and then letting himself be entrapped by Pedro III; and also, however much the details of the episode may be discussed, Richard II holding in respect the mob which had been stupefied by the murder of Wat Tyler. The rebels' anxiety to assert that they were acting in the true interests of the monarch, to take shelter under his name, is no less remarkable. Such was the main difficulty: to conciliate in their favour, in a lasting way, a power which they had temporarily influenced. In the fourteenth and fifteenth centuries no one overcame this difficulty, and indeed the task seemed impossible. One must of course take into account the cities and regions where no sovereign existed, or else where he was too far distant to be encountered in person, such as a part of Italy and of the Empire. In Bohemia the Taborites might suppose that they had rendered useless the monarchical form of government; but their programme was wrapped in so many illusions that one may wonder if this attempt of theirs, at least in this form, had any chance of taking root.

We advisedly set apart labour conflicts properly so-called—

---

[1] "There's such divinity doth hedge a king..." (*Hamlet*, IV, V).

those which concerned wage-earners. No surprise will be occasioned that we have recorded some among the vine-growers, a class of peasant-worker in which wage-earning was the most advanced. But the main feature of these conflicts is to be found among the artisans. The growing separation between masters and companions accounts for them, pending the time when large-scale industry was to give them another dimension.

If, finally, among so many movements, we had to name those which most truly deserve the name of "popular revolutions", we should cite the Ciompi in Florence, the peasants in England and the Taborites in Bohemia—not forgetting one or two episodes in Flemish history. In two instances at least it was a question of peasants, no matter for surprise in a world of which the civilization was still predominantly rural.

*   *   *

Of the revolutionary leaders we have no knowledge save from sources hostile to them, and we shall doubtless never be able to portray them save in a form coloured by our own tendencies. Certain of them were genuine "sons of the people": in the cities, probably the Catalan Berenguer Oller, and certainly the Bruges weaver, Pierre de Coninc, the Florentine carder Michele di Lando, and Geoffrey Litster, the dyer, of Felmingham in Norfolk; in the country districts, the Fleming Jacques Peyte, Guillaume Carle, the leader of the Jacques, Wat Tyler in England, and Fansy the Burgundian vine-grower. Many other names might be cited. The lower clergy, combining a popular attitude of mind with some rudiments of instruction, provided eloquent spokesmen, as was natural: of such, John Ball remains the best example no doubt. Czech priests assumed very varied parts, whether as preachers, like John of Zeliv, or as military chiefs, like Procopius the Great. Other leaders came from different social groups. Jacques, and then Philip van Artevelde, Etienne Marcel and Salvestro dei Medici embodied the "sacred union" between the upper bourgeoisie and the people, united temporarily on the same side of opposition.

Later on, the corporation of butchers, very comfortably off but victims of a tenacious social prejudice, provided leaders, of whom Caboche is only one example among others of whom the texts give us a glimpse. Certain leaders belonged to families that were going downhill, and rancour may explain their attitude: such was probably the case with Heinrich Pater-nostermaker at Lübeck, and Bernard de Roaix at Toulouse.

One can, after all, understand that for certain well-determined reasons the bourgeoisie should have made common cause with the "people", or have led the latter to make common cause with it. That members of the lower nobility should have taken a hand in peasant disturbances is more paradoxical. In the Flanders of 1323–8 the case of Guillaume de Deken, lord of Sijsele, has been recorded. England in 1381, above all, pro-vided many examples. Bertram Wilmington raised a rebel band at Wye in Kent; in Norfolk Sir Roger Bacon made himself Litster's lieutenant, willingly; it appears, led the band which seized Yarmouth, and tore the town's charter in two. In Norfolk as in Suffolk, many other gentlemen played less eminent, and yet very active parts. Historians have been lost in conjecture as to their motives. Some of these nobles may have been forced, against their will, to follow the movement; but others, so to speak, "added" to it. Powell believed it was from idealism. Oman ascribed their motives to a taste for agitation and to cupidity: he dwells on their extortion of lands and purchase of manors at a low price. . . . Such interpretations put us on guard against too simple a presentation of the events.

The situation was comparable in southern France, where several esquires received letters of remission for their com-plicity with the Tuchins, whom they afterwards stated that they had been compelled to follow. In Bohemia two lords are mentioned as Taborites: Brenek of Ryzmburk and Valkoun of Adlar; since they went as far as they did, there can be little doubt about their idealism. In any case, most of these leaders, whether or not they were men of the people, came to a tragic end.

One striking contrast must be noted, the destiny of Pierre de Coninc. Knighted, along with his two sons, before the battle of Courtrai, he afterwards possessed a seal and a banner repre-

sented on a fine wooden chest which is preserved at New
College, Oxford: on this chest, seven episodes in the events of
1302 are pictured in carvings. He was given, free of rent, in
the rue Haute at Bruges, a fine house which had been confiscated from a Leliaert, as well as a pension of 1,000 livres a year,
which made him a rich man. However, though accomplishing
various missions, he exercised no official function in the government of Bruges. He was not really harassed at the time of the
Peace of Athis (1305); but the situation was more serious for
him in 1321-2. Riots against the Count of Flanders having
broken out in Bruges, he sided with the Count and was obliged
to slip away for a time. He played no part in the insurrection
of maritime Flanders in 1323-8, though his son John was the
leader of the weavers. He died peacefully in 1332, and the city
granted his widow an allowance for the funeral expenses.

Our documents generally recognize in these leaders a gift for
effective oratory which assured them of a certain hold over
their followers, although more than this was obviously needed.
They had to impose their authority, take decisions regardless
of individuals when necessary, and make men obey them.
"Do you know how to act the haughty and the cruel leader?"
a Fleming asked Philip van Artevelde when he was appointed
Captain-General of Ghent. All this supposed strength of
character, reinforced by faith in a mission. Unlike Cola di
Rienzo, all these leaders did not believe themselves to be
divinely appointed; but all possessed a sort of vocation, which
was not mere ambition.

Only a very few of them displayed any political sense, apart
from a real talent for organization. A genuine revolutionary
leader works to accomplish, if not a formal programme, at
least definite changes in the existing state of things. He has
ideas, he is thoughtful enough to take the data of an initial
situation, limited though it be, as the starting-point for a wider
and more general policy. Pierre de Coninc and especially the
two Arteveldes extended their enterprise at Bruges and Ghent
to the whole of Flanders; they made it a social and national
cause. Wat Tyler raised the problem of villainage and of the
agricultural wage-earners for all the peasants in England.

Etienne Marcel did not perhaps mean to limit his actions solely to Paris; he presented Paris as champion of the liberties of all the French cities, in connection with Flanders. And what are we to say of the vast changes advocated by the Taborites?

Contemporary chroniclers do not necessarily deny the existence in these leaders of lofty motives or of courage. William Grindcobbe, leader of the movement at St Albans in 1381, affords a fine example of this. Thomas Walsingham, to whom we owe a knowledge of Grindcobbe, reproaches him with having played this part, whereas he "had many obligations to the monastery, because he had been educated, fed and maintained there and because he was a relative of several monks". He nevertheless extolls his courage when defeated. After being arrested, and then freed simply that he might explain the Abbot's conditions to the villains, he exclaimed: "Fellow citizens, you, who for a short time past, have been freed from long oppression by a particle of liberty, stand fast as long as it is possible to stand, and fear not lest I be punished. If I die for the cause of this liberty, I shall think myself fortunate to have been able to end my life in such martyrdom. Act then as you ought to have acted if I had been beheaded yesterday at Hertford." The peasants followed his advice and refused to give in; he himself returned to prison and was hanged. One scents literary influences in this passage, straight from ancient history,[1] but one is struck all the same by Walsingham's applying them to a man of whom he elsewhere asserts that "his heart was already hardened in evil".

Should we not make distinctions among the thousands of men who took part in riots and rebellions, as we do for their leaders? They were extremely varied and changing. It was precisely the co-operation among men very unequal in fortune, culture and organization, that made these movements so strong. Well-off peasants often rubbed shoulders with the penurious, distinguished bourgeois and artisans with the mass of ordinary workers. One must remember that pauperism

[1] Such as the story of Marcus Atilius Regulus returning to Carthage, after advising the Roman senate to refuse the terms proposed. The parallel is very close. (Translator.)

was increasing, the "dangerous classes" appearing and that, towards the end of the fourteenth century the category of the poor was being infected by the latter. As an inevitable result of this, social attitudes were markedly modified as regards these classes, which were improperly identified. For many people the poor man became a suspect being, a delinquent today, a rebel tomorrow, and potentially a criminal. In face of the poor and the vagabond, there spread an attitude of recoil and, later, of hostility. Let us consider the matter more closely.

The poor, defined in the limited sense of the economically weak, are those who are involuntarily undergoing a precarious existence which may—beyond a threshold variable in time and place—become indigence and absolute destitution. They are those who have no personal means of raising themselves, save by the help of others, whether sought or granted by compassion. As long as the number of the poor did not exceed a coefficient, difficult to assess, in relation to the whole social group, it raised no problems. In the same way, as long as the poor, even living on the margin of this group, did not leave it, as long as they remained known, a minimum level of subsistence for them was accepted as a natural charge on the community. The monastery, the parish, the confraternity, the "table of the poor", had their "clients", accustomed to receiving a regular distribution of food and clothing. But things seem to have changed with the growth of the urban populations inflated, in time of war, by refugees from the surrounding country; and also with the economic difficulties productive of unemployment especially in industrialized cities, and with the evolution of prices and wage-rates. This picture corresponded with the situation of the wage-earners in the once prosperous agricultural districts in which there arose the Flemish insurrection of 1323, the Jacquerie, the English revolt of 1381 and the Czech revolution. The same situation arose among the unqualified "hands" or labourers of a great city like Paris; and among the crafts and minor Arts of Flanders and Italy. The word *Ciompi* well expresses the existence of a medieval preproletariat. What was serious was that, from the mid-fourteenth century there developed a floating population both in town and country; people who, not content with inactivity and individual vagabondage, were beginning to form regular bands. To describe, disparagingly of course, all these people with their disquieting appearance, among whom real poverty was more or less confused with do-nothing destitution, a completely new vocabulary appeared. Certainly, all the mendicants assisted by traditional Christian charity, were not so condemned. It remains no less true that the ordinances concerning the "idle or able-bodied poor", the tramps, vagabonds, good-for-nothings, etc., were enacted in order to forbid vagabondage and repress crime. Even the notion of "confining the poor" was already in germ in the language of forerunners of the police-control of the poor in our modern age.

We cannot always exactly describe the organization of these bands of vagabonds or simple indigents, few aspects of the question having been so neglected by our sources. The parish must have been the centre most often used, particularly in country places. It was after Sunday Mass that John Ball used to harangue the peasants. And this too seems to have been the structure on which was founded the army of labourers whom Wat Tyler exerted himself in disciplining, or the "great society" which Litster led to the conquest of Norfolk. But we must be satisfied with guesses. Old-time divisions of the English people, like the hundred, may equally have served the purpose.

Nor, in certain cities, should we exclude the use of the parish, though here many other possibilities offered themselves. A town was often divided into quarters, hundreds, fifties, even tens—a division more or less military in character since the urban militia and the service of the watch were its normal outcome. These insitututions are very little known and deserve careful and systematic study.

There were also the crafts, of which the banners were more than once raised above the crowds in an urban insurrection, particularly in Germany and Italy. Finally, certain texts lead us to suppose that people were officially organized on the basis of their fortunes in several cities of southern France. At Foix the rich, the "middle" group and the poor, appointed, in presence of a notary, their respective representatives who, between themselves and with the consuls and the seigneurial agent, negotiated compromises.

Various means were adopted to ensure the cohesion of these groups. Sometimes the leaders exacted an oath of loyalty, a system expressly indicated apropos of Berenguer Oller at Barcelona. Among rallying signs, hoods of a certain colour are mentioned; in some circumstances it could be very dangerous not to wear them. The English labourers in 1381 had a password, recorded by the anonymous chronicler of St Mary of York in his savoury mixture of French and English: "*Et lesdits communs avaient entre eux une wache-worde en Englische:* 'With whome heldes you?' *et la réponse fut:* 'With kinge Richarde and the true commons.' *Et ceux qui ne savaient ni ne voulaient répondre étaient décollés et mis à mort.*"

We learn that songs and poems were current among the rebels. Judicial archives have preserved a few traces of them as also they record the tenor of an English poem composed in Yorkshire in 1392, and read in public at Beverly, Hull and other places in the county. Fragments of a popular literature, "involved" as we should say, must have existed, though they were usually oral or have been forgotten. All the same, we possess some fragments, still in England, whether because archives have been preserved there better than elsewhere, or because in England such literature was particularly abundant. There remain two ballads belonging to the cycle of Robin Hood, the good yeoman, righter of wrongs, of which the popular success is well known. *The Tale of Gamelyn,* dating perhaps from about 1380, relates the story of a self-appointed justicer who attacked monks and clerics. Summoned before a tribunal, he has the judge, the sheriff and the jury all hanged; he none the less wins the King's favour and makes a fine marriage.[1] A curious reflection of the dreams of the humble!

*   *   *

[1] It is a romance in verse. Gamelyn is actually the son of a knight, who, after his father's death, is defrauded by his elder brother of his share of the estate. He runs wild and, assisted by the "spencer" Adam, joins the outlaws, before committing the notable deeds mentioned. The story seems to have been the main source of *As You Like It*. (Translator.)

We may now ask what were people's attitudes to these rebels, or at least those which are revealed in our texts and other documents? The jurists, as we have seen, took up divergent positions. Philippe de Beaumanoir appeared extremely severe as regards conflicts connected with labour, and advised the authorities firmly to repress coalitions and strikes; but, on the other hand, he expressed very pessimistic opinions on the rich, whose tendency to oppress the poor he regarded as natural. He therefore recommended lords to keep an eye on the "good towns" under their authority "so that the rich, if they do wrong, may fear severe punishment and that the poor may earn their bread in peace". The love of order, understandable in a jurist, is thus associated with traditional Christian doctrine supported by passages from the Gospels which are so hard on the rich. Mieres goes further; he does not hesitate to threaten the "established order" in the name of the basic demands of human dignity. Of course there also existed a number of jurists who simply sided with the powerful.

Gerald R. Owst has noted, in the sermons delivered in fourteenth-century England, or at least in those which have been preserved in writing, pitiless denunciations of the vices of the powerful and the rich. The nobles are proud and extravagant—"the tournament of the rich is the torment of the poor"—the clerics selfish and greedy, the jurists pay little heed to justice, the merchants are slaves to worldly riches. There is no end to the number of writers who merely reflect this teaching. John Ball's famous words ("When Adam dalf" etc.) were in fact only a commonplace, repeated again and again to inspire more modesty in the great. But the lower orders received their lessons too: artisans and peasants were mean and idle. This teaching was in fact moral; it called upon men, whatever their station in life, to struggle against the vices peculiar to their social class. It discouraged them from seeking to rise in the hierarchy, which could be achieved only by great pride and avarice. Death would carry all men away. This theme of equality in the face of death has been abundantly illustrated, we know, in the *Danses Macabres*. Beyond the grave everyone would receive his just reward. There was therefore no question of advocating a social upheaval; and that is why such sermons were thundered out, without censure or censorship, after as before the insurrection of 1381.

A similar tone can be heard among French writers. Alain Chartier's *Quadriloge invectif* (1422) presents a churchman, a knight and a peasant arguing with each other and with "France" who tries to reconcile them. "The people complain of us", says the knight. "The common folk murmur against the noble. . . . They have our castle [to protect them] and now they cry out against us." And he concludes with a moral corresponding to the ethics of the time: "Since adversity is common to the whole kingdom, everyone must endure that portion of it which God sends him."

No less suggestive is a reading of the *Terç del Crestia*, composed by Francesc Eiximenis, a Catalan moralist of the fifteenth century. He too has no illusions when he denounces the oppression of the peasants by their lords. "They who have lordship are called oppressors of others, and their oppression is cruel. They care not for the principal end for which God ordained lordship in this world, which is the preservation of charity in public affairs; but all their wishes tend to weigh up money and riches, and to get from their subjects everything which they can, on whatever pretext or title whatsoever, good or bad." In vain would the lords seek to excuse themselves on the ground of their poverty and the obligation of maintaining their rank. Why do they not attack the causes of this poverty, their excessive spending, the bad management of their estates, and the thefts committed by their subordinates? God grants lordship only in so far as it serves the cause of peace and the public weal; it cannot be invoked to support actions contrary to these.

That the reality did not conform to the ideal, Eiximenis was, then, aware. And yet rebellion seems to him monstrous: "David was speaking of this rustic malice when he said: *Quare fremuerunt gentes et populi meditati sunt inania?* [1] That is to say, why do coarse rustic fellows rebel, why do they let themselves be moved maliciously by thoughts, mad and insensate?"

[1] "Why do the heathen rage, and the people imagine a vain thing?" Psalms 2:2. (Translator.)

The Doctor of Theology replies: "O Lord, it is because they are brutish and rustic, insensate and deprived of reason, like brute beasts, and very malicious. Thus from their brutishness it comes that they do not listen to reason, and from their not listening to reason comes all the evil. They think that everyone wants to deceive them, and in their hearts is born a terrible malice, with which they want to cover and defend themselves. . . ."

Revolutionary on the moral plane, conservative on the social —such appears to have been the official teaching of the Church. Thinkers may have insisted more strongly on one principle or the other, according to their temperament or the *milieu* to which they belonged. The episcopate, being recruited from the aristocracy, would find it hard to approve of disturbances. The Mendicant Friars, on the other hand, asserted, more than once, that the vices of the powerful might explain, if not excuse them. The writings of laymen reflect these attitudes, so that we can now explain the apparent contradiction in Froissart's text, as cited above: a keen awareness of social inequalities, but a rough condemnation of rebellion.

Could it be otherwise? It was impossible at that time for the mind to conceive of social problems in terms of social structures. Poverty and misery were simply the sum of human afflictions. One tried to relieve sickness, one sometimes even cured it; but what means could one have thought of, to abolish it? The perennial nature of poverty seemed self-evident, following Christ's words: "The poor ye have always with you." It was only in the eighteenth century that the idea took root that society can be an object of study and analysis, and therefore could be transformed. Up to that time it had appeared as something willed by God, and bound up with original sin. To rebel against the organization of society was, strictly speaking, inconceivable.

These were theoretical, and often bookish, attitudes. But what of individual attitudes, tested by experience? A good example is that of an English bishop, a contemporary of the Peasants' Revolt, Thomas Brinton. A Minorite Friar before becoming Bishop of Rochester, he had retained, in spite of his honours, the simplicity of the mendicant. Better still, before the insurrection broke out, he had, in the sermons which have been preserved to us, preached the virtues of poverty and the exercise of charity and justice with a vigour comparable with the language of the popular preachers. Now came the events of 1381. Brinton, at Rochester, was living in the heart of the insurgent region. A hundred yards or so from his house, the King's representative fell a victim to the rebels. It was still more impressive for him to hear of the death of Sudbury, his metropolitan. What effect had this on his mind? The topic of social charity disappeared almost entirely from his sermons. Appointed as one of Wyclif's judges, he also sat on the commission entrusted with suppressing the rebellion. And yet his life and mental attitudes do not appear fundamentally to have changed. To accuse him of ambition would seem unjust and contradicted, in any case, by the rest of his life, which was short. It appears that, like many of his contemporaries, he had thought that a general revolution was coming. He disapproved both of rebellion and of heresy.

*   *   *

This leads us to speak of the repression, and the way it was carried out.

At the time nearly all the rebellions appear to have taken place in something like freedom. Nothing is more surprising than the ease with which the Parisian rioters gained access to the King or the Dauphin. One recalls too the critical situation in which Richard II found himself, almost defenceless for a few days; or, on a lesser scale, the apparently easy initial success of so many urban or rural disturbances. The absence of a permanent force for the maintenance of public order, a force at all efficient, is a general phenomenon in the Europe of the fourteenth and early fifteenth centuries. The reaction might come from some person in authority, like Walworth the Lord Mayor of London or Bishop Henry Despencer, at the time of the Peasants' Revolt—or from an agent of the King. But to suppress the great Flemish insurrections, no less was needed than the intervention of the suzerain's army, that of the King of France, on three occasions: at Courtrai, at Cassel and at Roosebeke—although the first of these battles was not a royal victory. On the other hand, the reaction might be delayed until weariness, a disgust for bloodshed, or a realization of economic difficulties, overcame the crowds which had formerly rioted. That such crowds are wavering and changeable is a matter of common experience.

The roughness of the repression corresponded with the ease first encountered by the rebels. Case after case could be examined. Hangings, spectacular beheadings of the persons most deeply involved, even drawing and quartering, make up a dismal story. Sanctions were founded often enough on the principle of collective responsibility; penalties, whether physical or pecuniary, affected in an arbitrary fashion a whole group— or some elements of a group—which was presumed guilty, if not of the deeds, at least of not having prevented them. Everything took place as if government wished to intimidate even more than to punish. A guarantee of regular justice was rarely granted to those condemned at the outset. There were executions on the spot on several occasions, as in 1285 at Barcelona; the setting up of special tribunals which pronounced judgement expeditiously; the ordinary course of justice, with regular procedure, much less often. The experience of Barcelona in 1334 is of great interest. Here the King's agent did not trouble himself with legal niceties; but, because a sense of legality was rather well developed in Catalonia and still more because the municipality was always jealous of its autonomy in respect of royal power and feared that a dangerous precedent might have been created, the sovereign officially blamed his employee. The case remains exceptional.

The property of those condemned was confiscated. In Italian cities the Signoria seems to have had recourse to capital punishment less often; but Florence was not sparing of banishments[1] and confiscations. In kingdoms where rebellion represented an outrage on the sacred character of the monarch

---

[1] Dante was only the most illustrious of these victims. (Translator.)

or emperor, punishment was often collective. Onerous fines
and administrative sanctions were aimed at discouraging any
further attempts. We know how much it cost the Flemish
cities as well as Rouen and Paris. Suspension of administrative
privileges placed these cities under the direct government of
the crown.

After urgent measures had been taken the procedures of
inquiry enabled the authorities to strike in all directions. These
inquiries have furnished the historian with clear documents:
judgements, lists of names, reasons adduced and motives. This
is how we know the names of the victims of repression at Arras
and Douai at the end of the thirteenth century, and the heads
of accusation brought against them; how too we dispose of the
lists of the dead and the despoiled at the time of the insurrection
in maritime Flanders. We also know the geographical extent
of the repression in England and France after 1381–2. The first
two cases are examples of inquiries on the communal level;
the last two depended: that of France, on the normal procedure of appeal to the *Parlement de Paris*; that of England, on
the jurisdiction of royal commissioners and investigators,
invested with full powers. The fourteenth century witnessed a
kind of progress in judicial procedure, parallel to the aggravation of the perils which threatened the public peace.

At last came an amnesty, after more or less long delays. In
Florence certain leaders, like Michele di Lando, never returned
to their native city. In France the royal clemency was extended
through letters of pardon or remission, so precious for historians.
These did not at all approve of deeds previously condemned.
They insisted on the generosity of the prince, who in return
called for the loyalty and fidelity of the beneficiary. Remissions
were often as collective as condemnations had been, notably
in the matter of fines, as at Rouen and at Paris. As regards
institutions, cities sometimes had to wait for years before the
commissions for repression were abolished and the privileges
of which the rebellious cities had been deprived were restored
to them. Rouen never recovered, in their original state, the
liberties which she had enjoyed before 1382. Paris recovered the
office of the Provost of the Merchants only thirty years after

the affair of the Maillotins. The new Arts created in Florence by the minor crafts and by the Ciompi were never re-established after 1379.

Chroniclers often spend some time in explaining to us where the bodies were exposed, or the fragments, and what fragments. We should not interpret this as a sort of refined sadism. It was a question of impressing public opinion strongly and enduringly. This terror took the place of what later would be a police force numerous and impressively paraded. Its aim was to awaken among the lower orders a sort of conditioned reflex, of fear and prudence. It was no doubt efficacious, for some time. Repression was to serve its apprenticeship, little by little, as was revolution for that matter.

*   *   *

There remains a final question: what results did these agitations and insurrections achieve, at the time and in the long term? A general reply can arise only from an analysis of individual cases; we may at least try to evoke a few, and also the discussions they have given rise to.

In most of the cities of upper Germany, the urban revolution introduced into the councils a more or less notable number of representatives of the crafts. This can be described as a sort of "democratic revolution" comparable to the one which took place in Flanders at the beginning of the fourteenth century. Philippe Dollinger has examined the consequences of this advent of a regime dominated by the crafts:

"With this [regime], it was a new state of mind, with profound consequences, that became rooted in the medieval city. Whereas the patrician class was characterized by egoism, but also by boldness in enterprise and a spirit of competition, the ideal of the crafts was an equal sharing out of work and profits between the masters of the corporation—hence a constant desire for regulations, for control of production and of exchanges. Fritz Rörig has taken a severe view of this limited outlook. In a brilliant parallel he has compared Nuremberg, the patrician city, enjoying great prosperity in the fifteenth century owing to its economic liberalism and the initiative of its merchants, with Freiburg-im-Breisgau sunk in decadence at the end of the Middle Ages, with the corporations bullying foreigners, hampering commerce and imposing a disastrous autarchy. There is some exaggeration in this contrast. The Hanseatic cities were also decadent in spite of patrician regimes. But it is beyond question that it was under the aegis of the patricians that the cities experienced a marvellous economic expansion in the thirteenth century, while under the aegis of the crafts they were doomed to stagnation."

With this we may compare the melancholy observation of Hans van Werveke, a Flemish historian: "By a tragic coincidence, the crafts came into power to assure a better sharing out of material wealth only at the moment when the great source of prosperity was beginning to dry up."

We may inquire, moreover, whether this regime of the crafts really constituted a democratic change. Erich Maschke, a German historian, has devoted a minute and penetrating article to the question. He starts from this somewhat external observation: the active policy pursued by the cities from the mid-thirteenth century onwards excited popular discontent by the expenses it involved and prepared for the accession to power of representatives of the crafts. Now this changed nothing in the cities' line of conduct. How can that have come about?

Maschke has no difficulty in showing that the crafts were not composed only of artisans (*Handwerker*). The richest and most respected included business men, wine- and salt-merchants, mercers, minters, furriers and brewers; though it was no doubt the weavers, fullers and carpenters who furnished what may be called the shock-troops. If the revolution succeeded, it was the former who reaped the benefits. In so far as the manual crafts secured seats in the councils, it was the most well-to-do members who occupied them. It was not by merely exercising their official craft that they had rounded off their pile, but by taking part in some related trade—leather for the tanners, cloth for the weavers, etc., or by investing their capital in companies. We must not imagine that an even approximate equality reigned in these crafts between the small employers; here, as in Italy and southern France (countries cited because they kept registers of assessments which clearly reveal the position), differences were strongly marked. These merchants and enriched artisans asked for nothing better than to mix with the patricians. At Strasbourg, their daughters regilded more than one coat-of-arms. At Constance in 1429 disturbances were calmed by the promise that close relations should be established between the crafts and the patrician club of the Cat (*Katze*); at Ratisbon until 1444 the former were trying to gain entrance into the club of the Ass (*Esel*). Besides, even if membership of the councils was slightly changed, the patricians who had more free time and were more experienced, continued to occupy posts of responsibility: those of mayors, judges, chief accountants, army-commanders and diplomats.

If we turn now to the south of France, one case will engage our attention. Castres was certainly a very modest centre, a town numbering at most nearly 10,000 inhabitants on the eve of the Black Death, but it combines conditions exceptionally favourable for analysis. Towards the middle of the fourteenth century, it adopted a system of equal representation for the rich, the "middle" group (*mediocres* or *comus*), and the poor (*minores*, *menutz* or *paubres*). Each category held one position of consul and six of councillors. From the same period date registers of assessments which enable us to balance the names, and to know if, for example, it was really poor men who represented the poor and defended their interests.

Taken as a whole, the personal fortunes of those elected corresponded with the group of which they were the representatives. The average fortune of the "rich" men elected was about 3,250 *livres*, as against 875 for the *communs* and 390 for the *paubres*. Apart from this, the six greatest fortunes in the place belonged to the first category. Once this has been said, it would be someone very clever who could establish a limit between the various groups. Assessed at between 300 and 1,000 *livres*, in the uttermost disorder, we find seven "rich",

fifteen "middle" group and twelve "poor". Certain facts cannot
fail to intrigue us quite as much. Among the representatives of
the rich in 1374 figures a *nichil* (a citizen not assessed because
too poor), who was said to be overwhelmed with debts, and
whose assessment in 1380 was to be at a mere 68 *livres*;
while the Paga family, assessed all together at between 3,000
and 4,000 *livres*, furnished consuls and councillors both for
the rich and the poor! Personal and family relations must have
played a great part in all this. We should beware, in any event,
of any extreme interpretation. The system at Castres cannot be
regarded as a mere comedy, but neither should we take it very
seriously.

Moreover, other results of changes must be taken into
consideration. The preference for direct taxation, the registers
of assessments, of which some at least represented an effort
towards social justice—all this is not negligible. We should not
forget, either, that the *remensas* finally succeeded, in Catalonia.

So much for the revolutions which were successful, at least
in part. But what of those that failed? The question has been
raised apropos of the Peasants' Revolt in England in 1381, and
answers to it have varied a great deal. Historians have observed, first of all, that the poll-tax was the immediate cause
of the rebellion and that it was never levied again. But what
were the long-term consequences? The older historians, like
Thorold Rogers and Stubbs, formed fairly optimistic conclusions. After the events in question, judges were as a whole
more favourable to the serfs, and the lords more prudent. To
sum up: the rebellion, although repressed, hastened the disappearance of villainage. In 1906 Oman roughly dissipated
these illusions. He showed that in numerous instances the lords
had judged their tenants more severely after 1381, and besides,
that disturbances had continued to take place in country
districts as in towns. It was the gradual evolution of the
economy that was to bring about the disappearance of manorial
demesnes, hence of forced labour and villainage. The revolt of
1381 had nothing to do with it. Present-day historians would
be perhaps less peremptory. By exacerbating class-hatred, the
insurrection rendered impossible the legal amelioration of the

manorial system. It marks the beginning of the social revolution in England, as Richard II's deposition was to mark the beginning of the Whig revolution.[1]

It is certain that the more modest, precise and limited were the objectives of the humble, the better the chances they had of being achieved—but the less did they unsettle the social fabric. In a general way, however, and taking the long-term view, we may ask about the prolongation of these popular revolutions. Later centuries have realized many of the objects of their leaders, even beyond what they could imagine. The seigneurial system has disappeared, Church properties have generally been secularized, city government has often become everyone's business, unions and strikes have been officially admitted; while collective property, if not of consumer goods, at least of the machinery of production, has been realized in a certain number of countries. But centuries have been needed for all this, and the general evolution of civilization.

We should beware of comparisons which might be too approximate. Can one speak of "classes" in the Middle Ages without risking an anachronism? Class-consciousness has not appeared to us as evident in those days. Yet the dialogue between the poor and the well-to-do remains, *mutatis mutandis*, comparable from age to age. The fortunes of the word *Jacquerie* are a sign of it. The repetition of the same moves in the war of the German peasants in the sixteenth century, then during the Wars of Religion in France, and during the *fureurs paysannes* of the seventeenth century, bears witness to the persistence of the same problems and the same angers. The dream of an egalitarian sharing out of property could not but be upheld by the humanistic respect for the individual, a feeling born at the end of the Middle Ages. From the little groups of "Apostolics" to the Vaudois, Hussite and, later, the Protestant communities, the analogy is certain, if the actual connection is not always evident. It has been from the nineteenth century onwards, especially, that things have been changing.

[1] A. Steel, *Richard II* Cambridge, 1941.

In an opposite direction, the misery of which the disturbances have often been a manifestation has inspired a movement
of compassion and charity which, in France for example, was
to issue in the rational organization of general hospitals.
Charitable societies have renewed their traditions and diversi-
fied their forms according to their objects. From the fourteenth
century onwards they aimed at assisting foundlings and lonely
women. They regulated mendicancy and no doubt tried to
suppress vagabondage. The establishment of homes or work-
houses for the destitute has aimed at removing from them the
temptation to violence but also at providing work for them,
and by force when needed. It would no doubt be insulting to
men to ascribe private foundations and municipal policies of
assistance simply to the defence of class-interests. But some
time will be needed for the problem to be raised in terms of
justice.

Such, at first sight, are the conclusions which it seems possible
to suggest, at the end of this study. They pretend neither to be
complete nor definitive. May they inspire the curious to
pursue studies which have been too long neglected, may they
furnish a comparative basis for such research! After all, the
origins of the revolutionary movement in our old Europe
ought not to leave in a state of indifference even those who are
thinking about the present or the future.

Index

Index

Index